P9-CME-069

# PRAISE FOR *PERSONAL PRODUCTIVITY SECRETS*

*Personal Productivity Secrets* offers unique insights not only into how technology has dramatically changed people's lives but also into ways people can harness it most productively. The book is written for a broad audience in a highly accessible and engaging way. It nicely illustrates the ways that technology is seductive and how to effectively adopt it without the common pitfalls that lead to inefficiency. *Personal Productivity Secrets* is, at the same time, informative, provocative, and pragmatic, and the perspective on productivity as achieving one's significant results is an essential reminder. Most importantly, the book offers practical suggestions that anyone can use—and everybody should use—to manage their lives successfully.

John F. Dovidio

Professor of Psychology, Yale University

Drowning in emails, to-dos, and meetings? Maura's methods will help bring clarity and focus back to your work.

Doug Smith

Vice President, Global Partner Strategy & Operations, VMWare, Inc.

Learning Maura's system is the single most important thing I've done for my career. Being truly organized and in control has far greater implications than any expertise and magnifies the effectiveness of every skill.

Mason Arnold

Cookie Monster, Greenling.com

Maura's passion, zeal, and expert advice on how to work from a more productive and empowered place is inspiring! If you're looking for a comprehensive, highly accessible, fun guide to reclaiming your time and learning how to better manage your attention, *Personal Productivity Secrets* is for you. This book is a gem!

Renee Trudeau

Coach, speaker and author of *The Mother's Guide to Self-Renewal: How to Reclaim, Re-Balance and Rejuvenate Your Life,* www.ReneeTrudeau.com

This book will totally change your perspective on just how much you can really accomplish if you implement Maura's ideas and strategies. It's amazing how much more productive, organized, and sane I have become after learning these powerful secrets.

Steve Harper

Entrepreneur, speaker, and author of *The Ripple Effect: Maximizing the Power of Relationships in Your Life and Business*

Maura's system and her passion for personal productivity have had a huge positive effect on my personal and business success.

Bill Harrison

CEO and Founder, Epicom Corporation

Maura Thomas has distilled the complexities of being more productive and organized into an approach any of us can succeed with. Her writing is clear and engaging. Her ideas are simple enough for anyone to implement and use, whether you're technologically sophisticated or not. I'm impressed with how easy it is to follow her method and simplify my life while being more productive.

Steven "Doc" List

National Agile Evangelist and Agile Coach, Neudesic LLC

Learning the Empowered Productivity™ System has been one of the best investments I've ever made in my business. My employees love Maura's system because it allows them to be more productive, better organized, and less stressed. I'd recommend this book to anyone except my competitors.

Cuatro Groos

Principal, CuatroBenefits

After learning Maura's system, our company saw an immediate impact to our overall efficiency and our company culture. Having a productive team that can communicate well with each other while staying focused on productivity is a key component to our success and growth.

Kevin O'Brien

CEO and Co-Founder, Petrelocation.com

This book provides a foundation for the modern leadership skills required to succeed in today's distraction-rich economy. Businesses can produce measurable financial results by simply applying even just a few principles of the approach outlined here.

Christopher Justice

CEO, Sparksight, Inc.

# Personal Productivity
# SECRETS

# Personal Productivity
# SECRETS

**DO WHAT YOU NEVER THOUGHT POSSIBLE WITH YOUR TIME AND ATTENTION...AND REGAIN CONTROL OF YOUR LIFE**

Maura Nevel Thomas

WILEY

John Wiley & Sons, Inc.

**EXECUTIVE EDITOR:** Carol Long
**PROJECT EDITOR:** Charlotte Khugen
**TECHNICAL EDITOR:** Bryan Schatz
**PRODUCTION EDITOR:** Kathleen Wisor
**COPY EDITOR:** Luann Rouff
**EDITORIAL MANAGER:** Mary Beth Wakefield
**FREELANCER EDITORIAL MANAGER:** Rosemarie Graham
**ASSOCIATE DIRECTOR OF MARKETING:** David Mayhew
**MARKETING MANAGER:** Ashley Zurcher
**BUSINESS MANAGER:** Amy Knies
**PRODUCTION MANAGER:** Tim Tate
**VICE PRESIDENT AND EXECUTIVE GROUP PUBLISHER:** Richard Swadley
**VICE PRESIDENT AND EXECUTIVE PUBLISHER:** Neil Edde
**ASSOCIATE PUBLISHER:** Jim Minatel
**PROJECT COORDINATOR, COVER:** Katie Crocker
**COMPOSITOR:** Craig Woods, Happenstance Type-O-Rama
**PROOFREADER:** Louise Watson, Word One
**INDEXER:** Johnna VanHoose Dinse
**COVER DESIGNER:** Ryan Sneed
**COVER IMAGE:** © Chad Baker / Lifesize / Getty Images

**Personal Productivity Secrets**

Published by
John Wiley & Sons, Inc.
10475 Crosspoint Boulevard
Indianapolis, IN 46256
www.wiley.com

Copyright © 2012 by Maura Nevel Thomas

Published by John Wiley & Sons, Inc., Indianapolis, Indiana

Published simultaneously in Canada

ISBN: 978-1-118-17967-3
ISBN: 978-1-118-22733-6 (ebk)
ISBN: 978-1-118-24024-3 (ebk)
ISBN: 978-1-118-26493-5 (ebk)

Manufactured in the United States of America

10 9 8 7 6 5 4 3 2

No part of this publication may be reproduced, stored in a retrieval system or transmitted in any form or by any means, electronic, mechanical, photocopying, recording, scanning or otherwise, except as permitted under Sections 107 or 108 of the 1976 United States Copyright Act, without either the prior written permission of the Publisher, or authorization through payment of the appropriate per-copy fee to the Copyright Clearance Center, 222 Rosewood Drive, Danvers, MA 01923, (978) 750-8400, fax (978) 646-8600. Requests to the Publisher for permission should be addressed to the Permissions Department, John Wiley & Sons, Inc., 111 River Street, Hoboken, NJ 07030, (201) 748-6011, fax (201) 748-6008, or online at http://www.wiley.com/go/permissions.

**Limit of Liability/Disclaimer of Warranty:** The publisher and the author make no representations or warranties with respect to the accuracy or completeness of the contents of this work and specifically disclaim all warranties, including without limitation warranties of fitness for a particular purpose. No warranty may be created or extended by sales or promotional materials. The advice and strategies contained herein may not be suitable for every situation. This work is sold with the understanding that the publisher is not engaged in rendering legal, accounting, or other professional services. If professional assistance is required, the services of a competent professional person should be sought. Neither the publisher nor the author shall be liable for damages arising herefrom. The fact that an organization or Web site is referred to in this work as a citation and/or a potential source of further information does not mean that the author or the publisher endorses the information the organization or website may provide or recommendations it may make. Further, readers should be aware that Internet websites listed in this work may have changed or disappeared between when this work was written and when it is read.

For general information on our other products and services please contact our Customer Care Department within the United States at (877) 762-2974, outside the United States at (317) 572-3993 or fax (317) 572-4002.

Wiley publishes in a variety of print and electronic formats and by print-on-demand. Some material included with standard print versions of this book may not be included in e-books or in print-on-demand. If this book refers to media such as a CD or DVD that is not included in the version you purchased, you may download this material at http://booksupport.wiley.com. For more information about Wiley products, visit www.wiley.com.

**Library of Congress Control Number:** 2012934968

**Trademarks:** Wiley and the Wiley logo are trademarks or registered trademarks of John Wiley & Sons, Inc. and/or its affiliates, in the United States and other countries, and may not be used without written permission. All other trademarks are the property of their respective owners. John Wiley & Sons, Inc. is not associated with any product or vendor mentioned in this book.

This book is dedicated to my mom, who instilled in me a love of reading and an appreciation for proper grammar, both of which make my writing so much easier than it might otherwise be. Without these gifts, this book—and in fact, my entire business—may not have been possible. Thanks, Mom. I love you.

It is also dedicated to my amazing and inspiring husband, Shawn. You have no idea how much strength I draw from you. You are my rock, and the love of my life, and I am grateful for you every minute of every day.

—Maura Thomas

# About the Author

**Maura Thomas** has spent her entire professional career of almost 20 years in the productivity training industry. This expertise led her to found RegainYourTime.com in 2003, a productivity training company that offers keynotes and seminars for business groups, conferences, and events, as well as training and consulting for corporations of all sizes, both nationally and internationally.

Throughout this time she developed and refined the Empowered Productivity™ System, a process for defending your attention and achieving significant results. Because of her success with the System, Wiley Publishing approached Maura to literally "write the book" on personal productivity.

Maura has a strong social media presence, publishes a widely read blog on productivity issues, and has been featured in local and national media outlets. She earned an M.B.A. from the University of Massachusetts, and throughout her career she has worked with clients in a variety of industries, from solopreneurs to Fortune 500 companies and every size in between.

Maura is very active in the local community in her home base of Austin, Texas, and she holds leadership positions in a variety of different community organizations and nonprofits. She was selected from almost 7,000 applicants for The Climate Project; and in 2007 and 2010, she was personally trained by former vice president and Nobel laureate Al Gore and his team of leading climate scientists to help educate interested people about climate change. Social responsibility is very important to Maura, and RegainYourTime.com offers pro bono training to local nonprofits and donates to charity a percentage of all training and speaking fees.

Maura will proudly admit that she's from Boston, but she does love living in Austin with her husband, Shawn, their three-legged dog, Elliot, and cross-eyed cat, Sassy.

# About the Technical Editor

**Bryan Schatz** is a freelance journalist and editor based in the Mile High City. When he isn't working, he's either exploring the nearby Rockies or seeking out live music.

# Acknowledgments

I've been lucky to work with smart and seasoned business professionals, trainers, and instructional designers throughout my career, and every one of them has helped me to create, refine, and explain what I know about productivity improvement.

Although I didn't know it at the time, the singular experience that shaped my career was my tenure at Time/Design, Inc., formerly the U.S.-licensed distributor of Time/system International. Time/system has, in my opinion, the world's best paper-based planner. Time/Design, during its U.S. ownership, developed training on how to use this superior planner, and my tenure there gave me the best education I could imagine on the foundational principles necessary for peak personal productivity.

There were two specific people also working with Time/Design from whom I learned quite a bit. The first is David Allen, before he wrote *Getting Things Done*. When I was at Time/Design in the early 1990s, David was employed there also, and then he became a consultant. As I understand it, he helped to create the curriculum for the Time/Design training and was also one of the instructors. It seems that he used what he helped to develop at Time/Design as the foundation of his GTD process.

The second person from whom I learned a great deal is Dr. Valerie Young, who took over curriculum development when David Allen left. I had the pleasure of working more closely with Valerie, and I was somewhat involved at various levels in revising and refining the methodology and curriculum over the years. Working with Valerie at Time/Design considerably helped me to internalize sound productivity principles, and the rest of my tenure at Time/Design gave me the opportunity to learn about competing ideas and principles from other experts and companies, such as the Franklin Planner and Stephen Covey—both before they merged and after—DayTimer, DayRunner, and a handful of others.

This experience was my background for examining and selecting the specific components of peak personal productivity, assembling and explaining them in the way that I have found works best for my clients, adopting them to ever-changing technology, and continually refining the process that I teach today. I'm very grateful to have had the opportunity.

Since I started my business in Austin in 2003, so many people and circumstances have combined to bring me to this point. Austin, Texas, is absolutely the best place in the world to start a business. The small business community, especially the network and resources provided by the Bootstrap Austin Network, have been invaluable to me, and I appreciate every single member.

My "Austin family," the Bixbys, and the other friends in our close circle here in Austin helped to give me roots when I was feeling homesick for my family and friends in Boston. You know who you are. Thank you!

There are some friends in particular who have been my biggest champions, given me advice, and helped me to navigate the challenges of entrepreneurship. Steve, I don't think I would know half the people I know today if it weren't for our friendship. Thank you for your constant encouragement and support. Steven, Lisa G, Brian, Lisa BB, and Tim, your advice, suggestions, and support have made all the difference. Thank you!

I'd also like to thank my "Medford friends," whom I usually refer to as "the Burget Ave. crew," even though most of them did not live exactly on Burget Ave. There is no bigger blessing than having friends who have known you throughout your entire life. I would be a different person today without you all, and I'm not sure it would be pretty. One of these days, there will be a book about us! Thank you for everything. I love you!

Lastly, I had no idea how much time, effort, and details go into writing a book, and I'm so grateful that for my first one I got to work with one of the premier publishing houses in the world. Thank you to Mary James of Wiley, for finding me and taking a chance on me. Thanks to Phil, Liz, and Uncle Jack for their invaluable advice navigating the process and to Jenny, for "working your magic" and being a fan of my work from the beginning, and especially for meeting the tight deadlines and working on the weekends for me. Thanks so much to my "informal" editors, Mom and Bob. Your input, especially at the beginning when I was floundering, really helped me to find my footing. Thanks to Bryan, for jumping in even when no one could really tell you what to expect, and to the rest of my great team at Wiley, especially my editors, Luann Rouff and Charlotte Kughen. Thank you to Charlotte for talking me back from the ledge all the times when I was sure everything was going horribly wrong. Everyone at Wiley, and in fact the entire team behind this book, has been a pleasure to work with, and I consider myself lucky to have had the opportunity.

# Contents at a Glance

# Contents

# Read This First

**It's 6:30 a.m.** and Ava Bradley's alarm went off 30 minutes ago, but she fell back to sleep. Now she's going to be late getting her 12-year-old daughter, Emma, up and out the door for school. It also means that she missed the workout she scheduled in her calendar. "Maybe," she thinks, "I can get in a yoga class after work." Ava is a successful insurance agent, in the business for 15 years, with a small office of her own. She has another agent in her office, younger and less experienced, and a part-time office manager.

Ava's husband, Ben, is a partner in a small law firm, and he's arriving back home from his run. The Bradleys live just outside of downtown Seattle. As Ben enters the bedroom, Ava asks him to wake Emma and then jumps in the shower—and the usual morning chaos in the Bradley home begins.

Forty-five minutes later, Ava is heading downstairs with her smartphone in her hand, consulting the day's calendar and scanning through emails. She is dressed and almost ready to leave. She finds Emma sitting at the table eating a bowl of cereal with her history book and her laptop open in front of her. Ben is pouring coffee in his travel mug, ready to dash out the door. His smartphone sits on the counter with his email open. "Emma, didn't you tell me you finished your homework last night?" asks Ava.

"I did, but Lisa texted me this morning that she heard there might be a surprise quiz today. I found a summary of the chapter on Google, so I just need to pull it off the printer before we leave. I'll memorize it in the car on the way to school." Ava, chagrined, has a fleeting thought about Emma making her *own* chapter summary, as her cell phone rings. Without bothering to look at the caller ID, "Hello, this is Ava," she answers, carrying Emma's cereal bowl to the sink. Ben pecks each of their cheeks and mentions something about dinner as he dashes out the door. Morning at the Bradley home. . .

## Who This Book Is For

If you're reading this book, you can probably relate to the Bradleys' busy life. Busy lives tend to be complicated. If you don't have too much going on, you could probably make some notes on a paper calendar and manage just fine; but if you have some combination of a career, a family, ambitious goals, outside obligations, and perhaps a hobby or two, you need a solution that matches the complexity of your life. Given this scenario, it's likely that a calendar and and address book, even the electronic versions, just aren't enough.

When your solution for managing the details of your life doesn't match the scope and complexity of your life, you have to work harder to keep track of everything. "Working harder," in this case, probably means depending on your brain and doing constant mental gymnastics trying to stay on top of everything. That causes stress—and stress makes you sick.[1]

A modern assumption of today's busy, driven professionals seems to be that more work equals more accomplishment. On the contrary, our "working" often means constantly dividing attention among unrelenting incoming demands, with little or no downtime. In addition to making us more impatient and irritable, we are also distracted more easily and frequently, all of which *prevent* focusing on achieving our significant results.

Many people try to solve this "working harder" problem by purchasing some new software, or a fancy device, or a new app, only to find that they are still struggling. In fact, their struggle is compounded because they now need to figure out how to *use* the new software, device, or app. The most important element of using these types of productivity tools successfully is the "how," or what I call the *process*. What these people don't realize is that the process is the missing piece to using any tool successfully.

Your brain is not the place to manage all the details necessary in the service of your life, so a tool is necessary; but the tool by itself won't help much. Consider these analogies: Buying a fancy set of clubs, the kind worthy of a PGA golfer, doesn't make you a better golfer, does it? Similarly, owning an expensive set of cookware and knives won't make you a better cook. Although I can't help with your golfing or your cooking, I *can* offer you a useful process for reaping the most productivity and efficiency from the tools you have available to you.

## What This Book Offers

I have been in the productivity industry for almost 20 years. In that time I have assembled and refined what I believe to be the most universally useful process for managing the details of a busy life. I've been fortunate to have the opportunity to study many different systems and learn from some of the brightest minds in the productivity industry. This education has enabled me to take the best tips and techniques from other experts and systems, create some of my own, and adapt the result to the changing technology of the twenty-first century. The result is my Empowered Productivity™ System. In giving the system a name I chose the word "empowered" because I have come to realize that the secret not only to peak personal productivity, but also to living the life you choose, is *control*. Specifically, gaining *control over your own attention*. Control over your own attention puts you back in the driver's seat of your life; you become *empowered*.

I've read all the most popular books about personal productivity and they all seem to fall into one of three categories:

▶ They are high-level theory about achieving your goals and include very little practical application.

▶ They include very detailed instruction but are ambiguous in terms of how to apply the instructions to anything but paper, note cards, file folders, and other outdated tools.

▶ They are specific to only one particular product or software and are not universally applicable.

I wrote this book with the intention of providing a resource that addresses all three of these deficiencies: It's full of instructions for practical application on the most common, current electronic tools.

*Personal Productivity Secrets* is divided into four parts: "Managing Your Attention," "The Empowered Productivity System," "Tools for Success," and "Appendices." In the first part, I demonstrate why you should stop worrying about "time management" and "information overload." Continuing to frame your productivity in these outdated ideas is the first hurdle to overcome in improving your productivity. I discuss the most common habits that sabotage your productivity and your attention, rather than support them.

The second part outlines the Empowered Productivity System methodology, which is a step-by-step process for managing your attention and regaining control over all the details of your life. This process is not dependent upon any specific tool—it is universally applicable, but this part also walks you through the steps to apply the process to several common software programs, devices, and apps that you might already be using.

Part III teaches you some techniques for getting the most out of the electronic tools available to you—probably many you already have, some that are free, and some that may have a cost associated with them. You don't need anything special to take advantage of the book; and you can skip to the sections that are most relevant to you. If you change to different software and devices, the book can still serve as a resource and help you get up and running quickly.

Part IV includes helpful books, websites, and apps to help you develop new habits that will support your productivity. It also includes a glossary to help you understand the many common words and phrases that have a specific meaning in the context of the

Empowered Productivity System and this book. The glossary provides contextual definitions plus the definitions, of general terminology, especially related to computers, that you might otherwise find confusing.

You can find additional information for the book at the companion website, www.personal-productivity-secrets.com, and on my company website at www.RegainYourTime.com.

## What's Your Significant Result?

Have you ever had the experience of going to work knowing that there are just two or three really important things you *had* to get done that day? They are weighing on you as you start your day, but before you know it, it's 4:00 p.m. and you're dismayed (and a little astonished) to discover that you haven't had a chance to tackle those things yet! This is a common scenario, and it means you've allowed other people's demands and priorities to dictate your day. At the micro level, it is detrimental to your productivity.

Now consider another common scenario: Have you ever reflected at the end of a year, or around New Year's Day, or on a birthday, and found yourself thinking, "Wow, another year has gone by, and I still haven't made any real progress on *X*." You haven't gotten the promotion, you didn't go back to school, you didn't start that side business, you've made no progress on your "bucket list." If you've ever found yourself a little disappointed that you haven't made any progress on those larger life goals, then you have experienced this lack of control at the macro level.

If you allow too much time to go by without exerting any control over your attention, not only does it affect your productivity on a daily basis, you may eventually realize that your life is not on the track you originally intended. Your days are the building blocks of your life. If you manage your attention and what it produces each day, then you can orient your productivity toward the larger, and more rewarding, goals of your life.

The goal of the book is to help you become more productive so that you can *accomplish more*. My approach, however, is not to help you just check more things off your to-do list every day; it is not "doing" just for the sake of it.

What does productivity really mean? The dictionary defines the word *productive* as "achieving or producing a significant amount or result." Isn't that the ultimate goal? If you're reading a book like this, it's probably because you are motivated to *accomplish* things: to "produce a significant result;" to aspire to lofty goals and achieve them; to make things happen, to design the life you enjoy living. That's how I define productivity, and that's why I love to study it and continually improve my own. I wrote this book to share with you what I've learned along the way, in the hope that it will help you *empower* your productivity and accomplish more than you ever thought possible with your time, your attention, and your life!

## Features and Icons Used in This Book

At the end of each chapter is a "Quick Tips" section that contains a short summary of many of the important points in the chapter. These tips each contain fewer than 140 characters so that you can conveniently share the productivity tips with your followers on Twitter. I'd love to know if you are finding the information worthy of sharing, so please include #Productivity Secrets and/or my username, @mnthomas, if you have room.

The following features and icons are used in this book to help draw your attention to some of the most important and useful information and some of the most valuable tips, insights, and advice that can help you unlock the secrets of personal productivity.

▶ Watch for margin notes like this one that highlight some key piece of information, that elaborate more fully on a point, or that direct you to other relevant information.

---

### SIDEBARS

Sidebars like this one feature additional information about topics related to the nearby text.

---

**TIP** The Tip icon indicates a helpful trick or technique.

**NOTE** The Note icon points out or expands on items of importance or interest.

**CROSSREF** The Cross-Reference icon points to chapters where additional information can be found.

**WARNING** The Warning icon warns you about possible negative side effects or precautions you should take before making a change.

## Endnotes

1. Emily Deans, M.D., "How Stress Makes You Sick and Sad," *Psychology Today*, March 27, 2011, www.psychologytoday.com/blog/evolutionary-psychiatry/201103/how-stress-makes-you-sick-and-sad.

# PART I

# MANAGING YOUR ATTENTION

## CHAPTER 1

# Stop Trying to Manage Your Time

## IN THIS CHAPTER

- ► Regaining control of your attention
- ► The lure of multitasking
- ► New kinds of ADD
- ► Focusing and choosing

"Time management" is a twentieth-century term that has far outlived its usefulness. The longer into the twenty-first century people continue to frame their productivity in terms of "time management," the less efficient they will be. That's because the traditional tools of time management are a calendar and a clock. However, rapid technological advances have made our lives far too complex to manage with these tools. Putting something on your calendar doesn't mean it will occur, and "making time" for something doesn't guarantee that you'll have the experience you intended.

For example, say you schedule coffee with a colleague, but while you are together, she can't keep her eyes off her mobile device because she's checking her email, texting someone, or searching the Internet for the answer to a question you posed. If she's doing all that, chances are good that she is not truly present in her experience with you. In other words, it would probably not be the meaningful dialogue that you intended when you scheduled the date, but rather an annoying waste of time. Does this scenario sound familiar? It appears to be a common occurrence in both social and business interactions of the twenty-first century; you "spent the time" together, but because at least one person's attention was lacking, it didn't have the desired effect.

It's hard to blame your coffee guest for her lack of focused attention. Today, many people carry "the world in their pocket" in terms of Internet access on their smartphones. With Internet access, you have at your fingertips the answer to virtually any question that pops into your head, random or otherwise. Whether you want to know about the weather or the theory of relativity, the answer is just a few taps away. And not only do you have to contend with your *own* curiosity and your *own* scattered attention, but advertisers know that human beings are evolutionarily wired to respond to lights, color, sound, and movement, which are all features that your smartphone offers. Every business in the world is currently studying how to use your smartphone to direct your attention to *its* service or product.

Advertisers attempt to steal your attention in myriad ways: music and messages played in public places, on-hold advertising, scrolling marquees, commercials and product placement in television, radio, and movies. Many of us make the advertiser's job easier by frequently having a screen in front of us, so that we are constantly subjected to banner advertising on virtually every single web page, in-app advertising on handheld devices and tablets, and even messages in our car from our navigation system or in-vehicle security device! Matt Richtel, technology writer for *The New York Times*, calls this "screen invasion." [1] Unfortunately, this invasion of screens, and the resulting distraction, is the cost of indulging in the conveniences and technological progress of the last 50 years.

Given all these demands on your attention, this book proposes that how you spend your time only matters to the extent that you also apply your *attention*.

The more I study productivity, efficiency, and effectiveness, the more I am convinced that the secret to defending against the constant demands on your attention is learning control—and the most important place for you to exert control is over your own attention. When you control your attention, you control your life. In the twenty-first century, "time management" and "information management" are no longer as important as *attention management*.

This chapter illustrates why this issue has serious implications for your productivity, and how this shift in your thinking from *time management* to *attention management* affects your effectiveness. This chapter also teaches you how and why to exert more control over your own attention.

# MODERN TECHNOLOGY: ADVANTAGES AND DISADVANTAGES

New communication technologies are vastly changing the landscape of human interaction. Social media is the latest incarnation of Internet communication that has volleyed the power back and forth from the hands of the powerful into the hands of the people. In medieval times, information was distributed from the seats of power. The invention of the printing press then provided access to creation and dissemination of information by citizens. The advent of radio and television created one-way media that have enabled those who can afford to broadcast to create "mass audiences" that are passive recipients of content, a scenario that enables powerful channels of propaganda.

Chat rooms were among the first Internet technologies that enabled *one-to-many communication*, and they have evolved into social media in its current form (blogs, Twitter, Facebook, and so on), which is the greatest opportunity yet invented for everyday people to have a voice and make themselves heard. These technologies allow back-and-forth communication in real time, literally shaping the evolution of events. The 2011 uprisings in the Middle East and the Occupy Wall Street movement are examples of situations that are propelled and nourished by social media.

▶ Social media can be defined as any type of public, two-way, one-to-many technology application or platform. Some examples are Facebook, Twitter, blogs, YouTube, Flickr, and the like.

Social networking has changed the face of business as well. Although the late 1990s marked the emergence of "corporate complaint" websites, consumer complaints gained even more power with the growth of Twitter. Now one person having a bad experience with a company can share his or her negative feelings with millions of people in a matter of hours. Tweets appear in Internet search results and end up as stories in mainstream media. As a result, many large corporations have employees dedicated to controlling bad press and resolving customer issues specifically on Twitter and use their corporate Facebook pages as interactive, public customer-service portals.

## More "Friends" = More Distractions

The explosion of opportunities to connect with real and virtual friends online has dramatically affected the number of people with whom we share our attention. One-to-many communication has changed the way we form relationships, removing the obstacle of physical distance. Millions of people now connect and share with others globally, creating "friendships" with people they have never met in person. It's increasingly common for relationships begun online to result in meaningful partnerships and marriage. Social media has even been credited with preventing suicides. Defining relationships has always been somewhat subjective, but an entire generation is arguably redefining what it means to be a "friend" and to "like" something.

Social media is changing not only our external realities, but our internal ones as well. The new capability for "live sharing," broadcasting experiences live and in real time, has led to a concept of self as "becoming externally manufactured rather than internally developed: a series of profiles to be sculptured and refined in response to public opinion. . . .Your *psychology* becomes a performance."[2] It's not uncommon these days to be at a concert, conference, or event and find more of the audience live-sharing their experience rather than fully absorbing it.

These changes in the breadth and depth of external relationships we keep updated online have increased the popularity of the field of "attention research." Journalists and academics alike are studying, discussing, and publishing information about the effects of being so frequently connected to a screen, whether we are in a car, at our desks, or walking down the street. Recent research has found that "when people keep their brains busy with digital input, they are forfeiting downtime that could allow them to better learn and remember information, or come up with new ideas."[3]

This advent of social media, which has created a seemingly endless variety of ways to communicate with vast numbers of people continuously and in real time through multiple technologies, is the most recent assault on our ability to control our own attention. The lure of the conversation, of news we might be missing, be it good or bad, often proves impossible to resist, making the task of managing our attention harder than ever.

## Digital Convergence

▶ Also called technology convergence.

Current studies on productivity and controlling your attention often contain the phrase *digital convergence*. Digital convergence describes the phenomenon whereby communication and media tools that used to deliver separate and distinct information now deliver the same things. For example, a newspaper used to be different from radio, television, the phone, and the Internet. Now, however, you can access all these technologies through a computer or handheld device. You can get radio programming as a podcast or live on the Internet, watch television via Netflix or Hulu, and read digital versions of print newspapers and magazines. You can even socialize with your friends through your device! That's convergence, and it makes it harder to manage your attention.

For example, if you commit to starting your day not by reacting to email, but instead listening to an educational podcast on the train to work, it takes an enormous amount of awareness and personal control to ignore your email inbox, which is accessible from the same device that delivers the podcast. Now that smartphones have become a central source of information about business, hobbies, socializing, entertainment, news, and recreation, focusing on and attending to only one of those things at a time has become more challenging. It's hard to be truly present in your leisure time if you are trying to relax with the same device that also brings you all that other information.

# THE TRUTH ABOUT MULTITASKING

New communication technologies and convenient access to the Internet hold great allure. Reluctant to miss anything, many of us jump from one thought to another, from one task to another, from one device to another. The result is split attention; we're seemingly doing several things at once, almost simultaneously. This ability to "multitask" was long considered a desirable skill. However, more than a decade ago, one of the first studies of its kind showed that multitasking actually increases the time it takes to complete a task and decreases the quality of output.[4] It's now widely accepted among researchers and scientists that constant multitasking even makes us worse at multitasking![5] In other words, the more multitasking we do, the worse we get. . . at everything.

You might be surprised to learn that there is really no such thing as *mental* multitasking. The human brain can only hold one conscious thought at a time. Common use of the word *multitask* actually has two distinct meanings. The first is physically doing two things at the same time, and it is hoped that neither task requires too much attention. For example, driving and talking on the phone simultaneously *might* not be a problem if the conversation is relatively light, you're on familiar roads, and the traffic isn't heavy. However, if the road conditions are difficult, such as encountering construction or detours, or the conversation is intense, many people find themselves abandoning one task in order to focus attention on the other. (Do you ever find yourself turning down the radio—or telling your caller you have to hang up—when you're lost, or when the traffic suddenly gets heavy?)

▶ Using a cell phone while driving, whether it's hand-held or hands-free, delays a driver's reactions as much as having a blood alcohol concentration at the legal limit of .08 percent!)[6]

The second, and more common, use of *multitask* describes the behavior of switching one's attention rapidly back and forth between tasks or ideas. The thoughts in our mind can change so fast that it *seems* like we're thinking about things simultaneously, but the process is actually linear, called *cognitive switching*.

Both types of multitasking, physical or cognitive switching, are subject to the finding that they cause an increase in time to completion and a decrease in quality of the tasks.

A study published by the American Psychological Association concluded that the ability to switch between tasks, termed *mental flexibility*, generally peaks in one's twenties and then decreases with age.[7] The extent to which mental flexibility decreases depends upon the type of tasks being performed. However, the findings of this study indicate that it decreases an average of almost 31 percent from a person in her forties to a person in her seventies.

Given all the data arguing against the effectiveness of multitasking, you might think that my advice would be to never multitask. Actually, I'm a big fan of multitasking, but the secret to successful multitasking is control. When you *choose* whether to multitask, instead of doing it out of habit, you're more likely to be efficient and effective. For example, I often combine tasks that don't require too much mental energy, such as catching up with a friend by phone while emptying the dishwasher or folding the laundry. Neither of these tasks requires much concentration, and the consequences of distraction are minor (for example, you might have to ask your friend to repeat something, or you might put a dish in the wrong cabinet). Conversely, if you are driving down the highway and you answer the phone out of habit simply because it rings, you have not decided to multitask. You inadvertently relinquished control over the situation.

Do you skim your email while you're on the phone simply because it's in front of you? Do you leave your email client open, with messages automatically downloading, all day, even while you're trying to do other things? How many application windows do you routinely have open on your monitor? If you're like most people, the answer might be in the double digits. These are all examples of *sabotaging* your own attention, rather than supporting it. You've created a situation where multitasking is virtually mandatory, rather than optional, and despite your intention to focus. Again, you are not deciding; you are relinquishing control.

You can also apply to productivity a useful lesson from martial arts that I have learned. It's called *eliminating chosa*—refining your movements to remove wasted effort. Efficiency is useful regardless of its application. In martial arts, conserving your energy by eliminating *chosa* can provide you with the extra burst you need to win a fight or escape an attacker. When you switch tasks, right in the middle, because something else grabs your attention, you greatly increase the time it takes to complete the task, and you decrease the quality of your output, just like wasted movement in martial arts. Even when the consequences aren't dire, you are still expending more effort to get less done. That's because when you are jumping from task to task, no task is getting your full attention; and it takes some percentage of brainpower to switch among them.

For example, have you ever been engrossed in a document or spreadsheet, and had a pop-up screen of a downloading email cause you to lose your train of thought or neglect to include something you intended? If studies prove that multitasking causes you to take longer and perform worse, yet you find yourself routinely multitasking, this probably means that most tasks you perform are taking you longer than necessary. More importantly, what you are putting out into the world might really be only a fraction of your true talents, skills, and abilities. It's up to you to decide if that's all right with you.

Clearly, multitasking has its time and place—the time and place you *choose* to engage in it. Otherwise, it is probably sabotaging your efforts.

# SELF-INDUCED ADD

*"All of a sudden, I realized that I had just one week to take my kids school clothes shopping and school supply shopping, get Butter [the dog] to the vet because he can't seem to stop scratching his ear, meet with the new web designer and get him the materials he's going to need, and find the time to make and ship two products which I wasn't expecting orders for. This is in addition to all the other stuff I have to do, like grocery shop, cook, clean up, and spend time with my family.*

*So what did I do? I freaked out. Instead of getting to work, I sat on the couch and watched talk shows."*

— From the case study of ADD patient "Anna"

Although the details and tasks are different for everyone, this is a familiar tale for those with Attention Deficit Disorder (ADD). Life seems to be rolling along fine and then, out of nowhere, the to-do list seems too big to handle. Panic sets in, and it's easy to shut down under the weight of the pressure.[8]

Symptoms of ADD include the following:

▶ Difficulty getting organized

▶ Chronic procrastination or trouble getting started

▶ Many projects going simultaneously; trouble with follow-through

▶ A frequent search for high stimulation

▶ An intolerance of boredom

▶ Easy distractibility; trouble focusing attention, tendency to "tune out" or drift away in the middle of a page or conversation

▶ Impatient; easily frustrated

▶ Physical or cognitive restlessness[9]

Given how easily we can access the plethora of communication tools at our disposal, it's easier than ever to indulge one or all of these tendencies. In addition, the more we do it, the more we are *tempted* to do it. An ADD diagnosis is typically made when a person exhibits at least 12 typical symptoms, and those symptoms remain evident regardless of the circumstances or environment.

In the field of psychology, there is a concept called *intermittent reinforcement* that helps us to understand the challenges created by twenty-first century technology. To illustrate this idea, imagine a mouse in a cage. If you drop a food pellet into the cage at the same time every day, the mouse eventually begins to look for the pellet *only* at the expected time. If, however, you distribute the food pellet at random times throughout the day, the mouse soon begins to look for the pellet virtually *all the time*. That's intermittent reinforcement. The mouse doesn't know when the reward will come, so it is driven to check frequently. Busy people with access to many communication tools exhibit the same type of drive. Email, voicemail, and other forms of communication bring good news, neutral news, and sometimes bad news, and we never know which it will be, or when it will come, which creates a strong temptation to check for updates continuously.

When professionals are feeling overwhelmed at work, similar to what Anna experienced, they often "shut down" by reaching for the most convenient distraction—email. Skimming email messages *seems* like work and satisfies us that we are "busy," which we mistake for productivity. The email actually serves as a procrastination tool, however, and a way to avoid that overwhelming to-do list. Patricia Wallace, a techno-psychologist who directs the Johns Hopkins Center for Talented Youth program, believes that part of email's allure—for adults as well as teens—is similar to that of a slot machine. "You have intermittent, variable reinforcement," she explains. "You are not sure you are going to get a reward every time or how often you will, so you keep pulling that handle. Why else do people get up in the middle of the night to check their e-mail?"[10]

Like babies, who quickly learn to shift their focus to new information, adults are also tempted to react to what is "new and novel." Because "new information" is constantly available, and constantly being pushed to us in ways that demand our attention, it's easy to indulge this behavior of constantly shifting focus. The more we do, though, the more our focus is undermined. Like any other skill, without practice, our ability to focus for any length of time declines. "The more we become used to just sound bites and tweets," says Dr. Elias Aboujaoude, director of Stanford University's Impulse Control Disorders Clinic at Stanford University, "the less patient we will be with more complex, more meaningful information. And I do think we might lose the ability to analyze things with any depth and nuance. Like any skill, if you don't use it, you lose it."[11]

ADD *is* a clinical condition, usually attributed to a genetic predisposition for lower dopamine levels in the brain, or to brain injury either before or after birth.[12] However, ADD is not diagnosed by testing the levels of dopamine in the brain *or* by determining evidence of brain trauma. ADD is diagnosed only through observing symptoms, but there is increasing evidence of a new cause of ADD symptoms.

Several years ago, Dr. John Ratey, a clinical associate professor of psychiatry at Harvard, began using the term "*acquired* attention deficit disorder" to describe the condition of people who are accustomed to a constant stream of digital stimulation and feel bored in the absence of it. Regardless of whether the stimulation is from the Internet, TV, or a cell phone, the brain, he maintains, is hijacked.[13] This means we may be actually *giving ourselves* attention deficit disorder. Another prominent attention researcher, Dr. Edward Hallowell, uses the term *attention deficit trait*. Unlike attention deficit disorder, or ADD, people are not born with ADT. Rather, he contends, it's the result of the modern workplace, where the constant and relentless chatter coming from our computers, phones, and other high-tech devices is diluting our mental powers.[14] He poses the rhetorical question, "How do you know if you have ADD or a severe case of modern life?"[15]

Dr. Hallowell notes that ADT isn't present when people are in a relaxed setting, such as on vacation. Therefore, not only can we *give* ourselves the symptoms of ADD, it seems that we can cure ourselves of them, too. However, it's not always as easy as just "putting down the devices." Both researchers point to behavioral, chemical, and societal influences that combine to make it not only difficult, but also *undesirable,* to be away from our devices for any length of time. Is it possible that we are actually *choosing* a state of being that most people consider to be an affliction, and take medication to alleviate?

The ability to control one's attention is required to achieve a state of "flow"—that single-minded immersion and focus described often by athletes or performers as being "in the zone." Flow is associated with achievement because performance is optimized, but being easily distractible is the antithesis of flow. Consider the control of attention as a scale, with flow at the high end and distraction at the low end (see Figure 1-1). If learning and achievement are maximized at the high end (flow), what does it say about our performance if we are spending more and more time at the low end (distraction), and perhaps even losing our ability to ever achieve the high end?

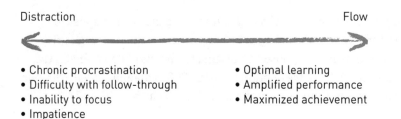

**Control over Your Attention**

Distraction                                            Flow

- Chronic procrastination
- Difficulty with follow-through
- Inability to focus
- Impatience

- Optimal learning
- Amplified performance
- Maximized achievement

**FIGURE 1-1**

# INFORMATION OVERLOAD IN THE ATTENTION AGE

The buzz phrase of the last decade of the twentieth century was "information over-load." Digital convergence, the idea that all types of different technologies are merg-ing into one ubiquitous "presence," means that it's almost impossible to escape the demands on our attention. It's true that more information is being created than ever before, and the rate at which this information is being created is faster than at any other time in history; because of this, its value has decreased, as Davenport and Beck so aptly describe in *The Attention Economy*.[16]

In fact, the volume of information is not the real problem. The real problem is that *this information is no longer passive*: It enters our world through multiple com-munication media, be it radio, TV, newspaper, blogs, tweets, emails, text messages, and many other ways. Each medium is pushed to us in ways that are designed to *command our attention*. After it has done that and the information has entered our consciousness, we need to do something with it. Otherwise, it stagnates and clut-ters our mind and our physical space.

Every technology has one or more features to get your attention, whether it's by visually attracting you on a monitor or handheld device, or by ringing, buzzing, or vibrating within earshot. Website creators speak in terms of *eyeballs* (to get you to look at something) and *click-throughs* (to get you to click on something). Marketers speak in terms of *taglines* and *calls to action* (to make you notice and then do some-thing). Have you ever noticed that commercials are louder than the programming? The ability to write "attention-grabbing headlines" is a valuable skill. New ways to get you to notice information are being invented and refined every day. The term "demands on your attention" has never been more appropriate. The following sec-tions describe how you can proactively manage this assault on your senses.

# THE IMPACT OF FOCUS

American social scientist Herbert Simon may have been the first to understand the implication of these increasing demands on our attention. In 1971 he wrote, ". . . in an information-rich world, the wealth of information means a dearth of something else: a scarcity of whatever it is that information consumes. What information consumes is rather obvious: it consumes the attention of its recipients. Hence a wealth of information creates a poverty of attention and a need to allocate that attention efficiently among the overabundance of information sources that might consume it."[17]

We've moved into a new era. The Information Age has been replaced by the "Attention Age," wherein *attention is becoming the most valuable commodity, and focus the most valuable skill.* However, the ability to focus is like any other skill: Without practice, it is lost. Children show signs of being easily bored without constant stimulation,[18] and teenagers are scoring poorly on cognitive functioning tests designed to determine their reasoning and critical-thinking skills, the kinds of skills that require deep thought and reflection.[19]

The benefits of focus are numerous, and focus is likely to be the competitive advantage in the coming decades. Whether you're reviewing sales data to create a strategic plan or helping your child with his homework, the ability to focus determines the quality of the interaction and the final output, sometimes with significant ramifications.

Children are becoming increasingly technologically savvy and more accustomed to media-multitasking; when they enter the workforce this will afford them some advantages in the business world. However, the current generation of adults grew up doing more reading, handwriting, and using their imagination—so they have had more practice focusing than those who are younger. This ability to focus also provides an edge.

When a person can focus for extended periods of time and be quiet, unplugged, and thoughtful, true learning takes place. Not "learning" in the sense of memorizing facts, but making connections between things, performing analysis, and deconstructing an idea.[20] For many of today's children, this high-quality "downtime" is simply no longer part of their daily activities. They acutely experience the "need" for constant stimulation and have the technology readily available to indulge it. "Scientists say juggling e-mail, phone calls and other incoming information can change how people think and behave. They say our ability to focus is being undermined by bursts of information. These play to a primitive impulse to respond to immediate opportunities and threats. The stimulation provokes excitement—a dopamine squirt—that researchers say can be addictive. In its absence, people feel bored."[21]

If deep thought, contemplation, and reflection are required for learning to occur, and yet our current technological climate makes it increasingly challenging to create the space for this contemplation, what does that say about the future of our ability to learn? Dr. John Dovidio, psychology professor at Yale University, describes it this way:

*There is a lot of evidence that suggests that part of learning is taking the time to consolidate, to reflect upon things, to make sure that what we know just has to reverberate enough in our head for it to stay there. That's a simple way of saying it. There's a lot of work that also shows that there are these times that we develop insights by not actively thinking about something, but different pieces, or different elements to the solution of a problem just appear to us through insight, and not in a logical fashion. And this insight comes usually during those periods following consolidation and reflection, where you have to become inwardly focused to start thinking about the thoughts, and then those thoughts can come to coalesce in some unique, synthetic way that becomes a creative insight. But if we're always focused outward, we're not going to do as much of that. . .we're going to rely on creativity coming from the outside rather than from the inside.*

This "quiet time," when the brain has an opportunity to grab hold of an idea and let it ruminate, consciously or subconsciously, has consequences that go beyond effectiveness or quality of output. It affects the very way we learn and grow as people.

## SIT! STAY! SLEEP.

Until this point, I've been describing all the *external* demands on your attention. However, *you* are actually the source of many demands—interrupting yourself with curiosity about unanswered questions, thrill-seeking/socializing/what-am-I-missing syndrome, incomplete tasks, commitments, responsibilities, uncaptured ideas, and things you *aren't* doing now. Many people are unable to sleep because they cannot silence their overstimulated brains. This is a symptom of these constant *internal* demands—the mental gymnastics we do daily in order to keep our busy lives flowing smoothly, to get everything done, to not let anything slip through the cracks, and to not drop any of the balls we're trying to juggle. Mental stress is a main contributor to the pressures of life that busy people experience—that underlying anxiety about all the things you are not doing, whether it's an expense report, the laundry, or starting that new business.

Compounding the problem is the fact that the brain is not very obedient. Thoughts flow in and out without prompting from the conscious mind. Often the very act of *trying* to recall something is the exact impediment to being able to do so. You can't reach into your mind and pluck out the exact piece of information that you need at exactly the moment that you need it. We have all experienced this when trying to remember the name of an acquaintance, or when we want to tell someone something but can't recall what at the moment. It is that annoying experience of having something at the tip of your tongue; but no matter how hard you try, your brain just doesn't obey.

Knowing how to minimize your own mental interruptions is one of the most important factors in controlling your own attention. It enables you to be in complete control of everything on your plate: what you are responsible for, what you want to get done, whatever commitments you've made, keeping any dates you've agreed on, any great idea you plan to pursue. The details you need to manage in the service of a busy life are endless and sometimes overwhelming. The way to exert control over these innumerable details—to achieve peace of mind, stop your brain from spinning, to reduce the stress—is to capture all of them, in the same place, in a logical way, that makes each one easy to access and act upon. This gives you a way to know, at a glance, what you *aren't* doing now, so that you can relax and give your complete attention to whatever you *are* doing. When you have captured everything in a reliable way that you can trust, your mind will quiet down, and your ability to focus will be enhanced. This enables you to *support* your own attention, rather than *sabotage* it.

▶ Capturing and organizing all of the details of your life are foundational processes of the Empowered Productivity™ System. You can find specific details and step-by-step instructions in Part II, "The Empowered Productivity System."

## STOP WORKING ON THE WRONG TO-DO LIST

One of the goals of managing both the external and internal demands for your attention is to give you the ability to be *proactive* rather than being constantly *reactive*. When we lack a clear understanding of the most important tasks to which we need to give our attention, we often succumb to the temptation of constant reaction. When there's no clear "master list" of your true priorities, it's tempting to work on whatever is easiest or most distracting at the moment—whether that's email, a ringing phone, or the beep of a text message. Surrendering to these demands means that you are spending too much time reacting.

When you are reacting, you aren't really choosing. Or, at best, you are choosing from a limited set of options, most of which typically reflect *other people's priorities*. In other words, you are relinquishing control. You're not making a decision based on *all* your options—including, most importantly, the things that *you* have determined are important. Instead, you are responding to a limited subset of options that reflect how other people want you to spend your time: answering their emails, solving their problems, satisfying *their* needs.

It's easy to spend your time simply *reacting* to all of the demands on your attention, but the result is simply activity, rather than productivity. If you work in a busy office, you are likely familiar with the following experience: You spend a morning, or an afternoon, or even entire days or weeks performing many tasks—answering emails, listening to voicemails, returning calls, attending meetings, dealing with co-worker interruptions, and so on. When you reflect on that time, however, you realize that you never had any unscheduled time to accomplish items on your *own* to-do list, leaving you with that unproductive feeling of having accomplished very little, despite the fact that you were always busy.

In the book *Rapt,* Winifred Gallagher discusses the fact that, like time and money, attention is a finite resource, and you must choose how you want to invest your cognitive cash. Expanding on this analogy, financial gurus often say that in order to gain control over your finances, you must "pay yourself first." I believe the same is true for your attention.

When you find yourself substituting busyness with progress, you might be inadvertently working on everyone else's to-do lists. This is certainly beneficial to your cooperation with co-workers, but constantly reacting prevents *your* to-do list from getting any shorter.

## CONTROL YOUR ATTENTION, CONTROL YOUR LIFE

In addition to its implications for learning, the ability to manage your attention can also influence your happiness. There is ample research showing that exerting control over the circumstances around us—and, indeed, even the *perception* of control—has a positive effect on happiness.[22]

The dictionary defines control as "command or mastery." The opposite is helplessness, powerlessness, or relinquishment. Another definition of control is to "have charge of," which is the opposite of abandoning, forsaking, or giving up. When you constantly react, you relinquish or abandon your own intentions for those minutes, hours, or days. What you want to achieve is results that have significance to *you*. To do that, it is necessary to be proactive, not reactive.

Twentieth-century philosopher William James said, "My experience is what I agree to attend to." Said another way: We have experiences based on the things to which we give our attention. For example, if you enjoy fishing, you probably spend time consuming information about fishing, in the form of magazines or blogs, talking with people about fishing, creating relationships based around fishing, and spending leisure time engaged in activities that include fishing. In other words, because you enjoy fishing, you give it your attention, and therefore you have experiences based on it.

However, your experiences determine your life, so if you don't exert the discipline to successfully manage all of the constant and increasing demands on your attention, you run the risk of never choosing where your attention goes. Instead, you squander your time by submitting to the external noise and clutter. Without even realizing it, you might inadvertently give your attention to other things and find many years later that the life you lived wasn't the one you would have chosen.

**FIGURE 1-2**

The bottom line is this: if you don't control your attention, you don't control your life. Because we are happier when we are in control of our lives, it follows that the more you *choose* what you attend to (that is, where your attention goes), the happier you are likely to be.

▶ Reacting is relinquishing control, which can lower your sense of well-being and negatively affect your happiness.

## SUMMARY

As we begin the journey of managing our attention, we spent Chapter 1 talking about all the forces we compete with to take back control. While the external distractions of smartphones and social media are true sources of self-induced ADD, internal distractions also play a significant role. From our own tendencies toward self-interruption to the temptation of multitasking, we are often the cause of much of the stress in our lives. What is becoming clear, however, is that the ability to focus may well be more than just the currency of success in the twenty-first century; it may also hold a key to our own happiness and well-being.

## QUICK TIPS

The following are some important points from this chapter (also suitable for tweeting). For more information on Twitter, including relevant usernames and hashtags, please refer to the "Read This First" chapter.

- ▶ Consider your "attention management" instead of your time management.
- ▶ If you feel like you have ADD, it might just be situational, caused by YOU!
- ▶ When you are always reacting, you are relinquishing control!
- ▶ Ability to focus may be 21st century's rarest and most valuable skill.

▶ Are you prioritizing your own to-do list, or someone else's?

▶ Constantly reacting means prioritizing others' to-do lists over your own.

▶ You have two types of distractions to manage for peak productivity: internal and external.

▶ Distraction completely prevents flow.

# ENDNOTES

1. Terry Gross, "Digital Overload: Your Brain on Gadgets," *Fresh Air*, National Public Radio, August 24, 2010, http://www.npr.org/templates/transcript/transcript.php?storyId=129384107.

2. Sherry Turkle, interview by Peggy Orenstein, "I Tweet, Therefore I Am," *The New York Times*, June 30, 2010, http://www.nytimes.com/2010/08/01/magazine/01wwln-lede-t.html.

3. Matt Richtel, "Digital Devices Deprive Brain of Needed Downtime," *The New York Times*, August 24, 2010, http://www.nytimes.com/2010/08/25/technology/25brain.html?_r=1&src=me&ref=technology.

4. "Is Multitasking More Efficient? Shifting Mental Gears Costs Time, Especially When Shifting to Less Familiar Tasks," *American Psychological Association*, August 5, 2001, http://www.apa.org/news/press/releases/2001/08/multitasking.aspx.

5. "Distracted by Everything," *Frontline: Digital Nation,* February 2, 2010, http://www.pbs.org/wgbh/pages/frontline/digitalnation/view/.

6. U.S. Department of Transportation, Distraction.gov, http://www.distraction.gov/stats-and-facts/#did.

7. Nancy S. Wecker, Joel H. Kramer, Bradley J. Hallam, and Dean C. Delis, "Mental Flexibility: Age Effects on Switching," *Journal of Neuropsychology* 19, no. 3 (2005): 345–52.

8. Jennifer Koretsky of ADDManagementGroup.com, http://ezinearticles.com/?An-ADD-Case-Study:-When-the-Pace-Picks-Up,-Learn-to-Slow-Down&id=18854.

9. Dr. Edward Hallowell, "ADD/ADHD Overview," http://www.drhallowell.com/add-adhd/.

10. Claudia Wallis, "genM: The Multitasking Generation," *Time* Magazine, March 19, 2006, http://www.time.com/time/magazine/article/0,9171,1174696,00.html.

11. Kevin Parrish, "Technology May Lead to Attention Deficit Disorder," November 16, 2009, http://www.tomsguide.com/us/Attention-Deficit-Disorder-Technology-Internet,news-5122.html.

12. Ben Martin, Psy.D., "Causes of Attention Deficit Disorder (ADHD)," June 26, 2011, http://psychcentral.com/lib/2007/causes-of-attention-deficit-disorder-adhd/.

13. Matt Richtel, "It Don't Mean a Thing if You Ain't Got That Ping," The New York Times, April 22, 2007, http://www.nytimes.com/2007/04/22/weekinreview/22richtel.html.

14. Alorie Gilbert, "Newsmaker: Why Can't You Pay Attention Anymore?," Cnet, March 28, 2005, http://news.cnet.com/Why-cant-you-pay-attention-anymore/2008-1022_3-5637632.html#ixzz1LnpQCMBd.

15. Edward Hallowell, quoted in *Distracted: The Erosion of Attention and the Coming Dark Age*, Maggie Jackson (Prometheus Books, 2009), 17.

16. Thomas H. Davenport and John C. Beck, *The Attention Economy: Understanding the New Currency of Business* (Harvard Business Press, 2001).

17. H.A. Simon, "Designing Organizations for an Information-Rich World," quoted by Martin Greenberger, *Computers, Communication, and the Public Interest* (Baltimore: The Johns Hopkins Press, 1971).

18. Marilyn Elias, "So Much Media, So Little Attention Span," USA Today, March 30, 2005, http://www.usatoday.com/news/education/2005-03-30-kids-attention_x.htm.

19. "Is Technology Producing a Decline in Critical Thinking and Analysis?", *Science Daily*, January 28, 2009, http://www.sciencedaily.com/releases/2009/01/090128092341.htm.

20. *Researcher Interview Part 5*, with Dr. John Dovidio, November 3, 2010, http://regainyourtime.com/interviews/researcher-interview-dovidio-part-5/.

21. Matt Richtel, "Your Brain on Computers: Attached to Technology and Paying a Price," *The New York Times*, June 6, 2010, http://www.nytimes.com/2010/06/07/technology/07brain.html.

22. Shelley E. Taylor and Jonathon D. Brown, "Illusion and Well-Being: A Social Psychological Perspective on Mental Health," *Psychological Bulletin* 103, no. 2 (1988): 196.

## CHAPTER 2

# Changing Your Mind: Attention Management

**IN THIS CHAPTER**

▸ Focusing on the *real problem*
▸ Taking control
▸ Analyzing your habits
▸ Changing behaviors
▸ Discovering your starting point
▸ The big picture versus the details
▸ Getting real

In Chapter 1 you learned about external distractions and internal distractions. These are two big challenges to managing and controlling your attention so that you can be "productive" in the sense of the relevant definition of "achieving or producing significant results." External distractions are the constant demands on your attention created by other people and technology. Internal distractions are the mental gymnastics you do on a daily basis to stay on top of all the necessary details that enable your life to run smoothly.

▸ The process is the secret to using any tool successfully.

The solution to successfully managing internal distractions is the Empowered Productivity™ System methodology (explained in Section 2), plus the efficient use of the right set of tools (discussed in Sections 2 and 3) for capturing, storing, and controlling all the details necessary to manage your busy life. Combining the right tools with the right process for using them successfully will keep you organized, in control, and productive.

If you plan to follow along with implementation, in addition to using this book as reference, you can immediately begin using what you learn. For extra support along the way, consider registering for the free *Empowered Productivity System Implementation and Follow Up Program*, a series of 18 emails that coach you as you implement your new behaviors. Sign up at www.personal-productivity-secrets.com as soon as you're finished reading Chapter 6.

Continuing the discussion begun in Chapter 1, the way to successfully manage external distractions is to stop worrying about how you manage your *time*, and start noticing how you manage your *attention*. The solution described in this chapter is about truly internalizing the shift from the idea of "time management" to the idea of "attention management," and mastering this concept. As the following sections describe, and as you might be aware if you have read about time management or productivity in the news, the media is focusing on the wrong problem.

## SOLVING THE *RIGHT* PROBLEM

Many times in my productivity work with companies, clients tell me that the problem is that there's just too much information for them to process.

The truth is, there has always been more to know than one person could ever learn. It's been said that high school graduates learn only one billionth of what there is to know. Every two days we create as much information as we did from the dawn of civilization up until 2003, according to Google CEO Eric Schmidt.[1] With the increased pace of information generation in the last 50 years, this is perhaps more true now than ever before, but it doesn't change the fact that too much information has always existed.

As I discussed in Chapter 1, information overload is not the problem. The problem is that the information is *no longer passive*. We used to be able to go through life blissfully unaware of information that we didn't actively seek. Now, however, the technological advancements of the last several decades mean that information confronts us virtually constantly. Communication and technology have changed so quickly that it's necessary to learn new behaviors just to keep up with the changing environment.

Fretting over the fact that there is "too much information" means that you aren't focusing on the real problem, which is how you're going to take control over technology and defend yourself against this constant onslaught of demands on your attention.

If you feel overwhelmed by all the details that are necessary to keep your life running smoothly, it's important to explore the reasons why you are feeling this way. I've found that many people have unintentionally created habits that *sabotage* their own

▶ It's not just that you're busy.

attention and productivity, rather than support it. This chapter asks you to pay attention to these behaviors. Being productive and effective, and learning to control your attention, are skills just like any other: If you learn them and practice them, you'll see results. The goal of the book is to help you start to *support* your productivity and attention, rather than *sabotage* it.

# SUPPORTING VERSUS SABOTAGING

The secret to working at peak productivity is *attention management*. It's not until you can control your attention and where you direct it that you can make informed decisions about how to spend your time. For example, you can practice "time management" and tell yourself that you're allocating an hour to pay bills, but if you're also taking phone calls or keeping one eye on email, you're not practicing "attention management." It's likely that the quality of your work will suffer, and you won't finish in that hour.

▶ Not only what to spend your time doing, but also how to allocate your attention to it.

Mastering attention management and gaining control over where you focus your attention is not about specifically what you *do* every minute; it's about staying on top of all the details you need to manage your life with a minimum of effort and stress so that your internal distractions are kept to a minimum. The Empowered Productivity System explains how to handle all manner of commitments, communication, and information, which collectively are the details necessary in the service of your life:

- ▶ **Commitments** that you've made to someone else, or that someone else has made to you, whether it's some place to be or something to do.

- ▶ **Communication** that you send or receive in any of the various ways we communicate (email, phone, voicemail, instant message, text message, fax, snail mail, social media, and so on).

- ▶ **Information,** which includes all the data that you want or need—and much that you don't—whether it's physical, electronic, or ubiquitous. You need to actively decide what information to accept or reject. If you accept it, you need to know what to do with it.

▶ Ubiquitous information often reaches you subconsciously. It is all around you, in the form of billboards, on-hold advertising, banner ads in your browser and the apps on your smartphone, and so on.

A great example of the value of control comes from martial arts. A sensei once said to me, "control or be controlled." This valuable advice is true not only in martial arts, but also in controlling your attention. With so many things competing for your attention, if you don't exert control, you risk spending all your time just "blowing in the wind" of reaction, instead of purposefully choosing how you focus your attention.

Three areas of control are key to supporting your attention management:

▸ Control over the information you receive

▸ Control over the technology that brings you the information and communication

▸ Control over your own behaviors (which is the hardest part to control)

The secret, not only to working at peak productivity, but to living the life you *choose*, is control. I call my system "Empowered Productivity" because it is designed to put you *back in the driver's seat* of your life and your work. In fact, the dictionary defines *empower* as "to make someone stronger and more confident, especially in controlling their life and claiming their rights." That is my goal for you. The following sections describe each of these control components.

## Controlling Your Information

When you consider the various kinds of information you receive, ask yourself the following question: Does it serve me? The rate and volume of information most of us receive means that there is an abundance of noise in our lives. For example, if you engage in social media, can you identify some of the benefits you get from it? Or do you often find yourself wondering why you bother? Do you get a lot of email spam? How about "junk" email, things that you may have requested at one time but no longer read? Are you subscribed to online groups that result in many unwanted messages collecting in your inbox? Do unread magazines or newspapers pile up in your home or office? If you answered yes to any of these questions, you are ready to exert more control over the information you receive.

An easy place to begin is with the "unsubscribe" button in your email for some of your unread messages. Start culling down the information you allow to interrupt you with the knowledge that you can usually find that information manually if the need arises. Reducing the information that automatically comes to you enables you to spend more time focusing on the more important information that remains.

> **CROSSREF** You can find resources to help you manage the information you receive in Chapters 12 and 16.

## Controlling Your Technology

No matter how you use the current technology, there is something new on the horizon. Whether it's the iPhone or another smartphone or whether you're a gamer, a photographer, or a music or video buff, many of us have that sinking feeling that we can't keep up. While it's true that many gadgets can make your life easier, they also have a downside: their ability to interrupt you and steal your attention—if you let them.

For a simple example, have you configured your computer and your smartphone to automatically download new email, rather than manually retrieve it? When I see clients who use automatic download, they seem to be drowning in a tidal wave of email—it just keeps coming. No matter how often they read it, no matter how hard they try to stay on top of it, it's relentless! You can't get people to stop sending you email, but you *can* shut off that automatic download so that the messages arrive only when *you* decide you're ready for them.

> **CROSSREF** You can find instructions on how to shut off automatic downloading in various tools in Chapter 12.

Here's another example: Do you ever set your phone on silent (or, heaven forbid, off), but *not* vibrate? We are often courteous enough to realize that our ringing phone can rudely interrupt others, but switching it to *vibrate* means it still interrupts someone— you! Maybe on some level you welcome the interruption the phone provides. Remember the "Self-Induced ADD" section in Chapter 1? The less you allow yourself the opportunity to focus, the less focused you will be. How often do you truly work on *one* thing, with no interruptions? If you're like most people I encounter, the answer is "not too often." Remember that multitasking both increases the amount of time it takes you to do things and decreases the quality with which those things are done. If your normal work style is to allow every device you own to ping, beep, vibrate, or otherwise interrupt you at the whim of virtually anyone in the world who is trying to contact you, then your technology is controlling *you,* rather than the reverse. If you were asked to choose between "control- ling" or "being controlled," which would you choose? Remember that your technology exists for *your* convenience.

*▶ Do you welcome the interruption? What does this say about your work and how you approach it?*

## Controlling Your Own Behavior

The hardest part of attention management is controlling your own behavior. If you *do* shut off that automatic email download but you can't keep yourself from pushing that send/receive button every 30 seconds, then the fact that it's off doesn't help much. Do you find yourself flitting from task to task but having trouble finishing any of them? Are you leaving tasks half done because you got distracted in the middle of doing them? If these behaviors sound familiar, you probably have room to exert more control over your own behavior—control that leads to productivity gains. You can likely complete all of those partially completed tasks, and in less time.

*▶ If these behaviors seem truly debilitating, you may have a clinical case of ADD, and not just a situational one. You can find many self-assessments online to help you determine whether you should consider consulting a doctor. A good starting point is http://psychcentral .com/addquiz.htm.*

All of these behaviors and practices I've just described are examples of sabotaging your own productivity and attention, rather than supporting it. You just may be your own worst enemy! As I mentioned earlier, though, you can't change unproductive habits until you recognize them. After you do that, you can begin to notice when you are sabotaging yourself, and *that's* the first step toward replacing those behaviors with more productive habits that support you.

So far this chapter has covered two important components of successful attention management:

▶ Control over information, technology, and your own behaviors

▶ Supporting your attention and productivity versus sabotaging it

Now read on to take a closer look at changing your behaviors.

# LEARNING TO INCORPORATE CHANGE

We all know that changing a behavior is hard. Whether it's trying to keep to a diet, quit smoking, or exercise more, giving something up or adding something new is a constant struggle, at least at the beginning. Knowing you should exercise isn't necessarily enough to get you into the gym or out on the trail every day. That's why most New Year's resolutions don't last beyond January. The following sections discuss three components of changing behaviors that can make it easier for you to incorporate new habits and processes into your life.

## Awareness

As I mentioned earlier, the first component is *awareness*. Most habits are so ingrained in your life and behavior that you probably don't even recognize them anymore. Becoming aware of the behaviors that aren't serving you is the first step in changing them. For example, if you want to incorporate more environmentally friendly habits into your lifestyle, it's important to understand what you're doing that doesn't serve that desire. Do you leave the water running when you brush your teeth? Do you participate in your city's recycling program? Do you buy recycled products?

Try to identify behaviors and patterns that you could change or improve, and even make a list. That way, the next time an opportunity presents itself to change a behavior, you'll be more likely to remember it, instead of just being on "autopilot" as you move through your day.

As you go about your day, do you pay attention to how you work? Do you know how often you check your email? Do you allow people to interrupt you? Do you have a process for managing your workload, or do you just respond to whatever calls your attention throughout the day? The answers to these questions might surprise you. Give some thought to your existing behaviors. People often forget that communication is a two-way street; if you feel that you are always being interrupted, then you need to take some responsibility for that pattern.

▶ You can exert more control without being insulting or alienating people. It's about setting boundaries.

Become aware of the behaviors you want to change—not just with a vague idea in your mind, but to the extent that you can actually articulate them to someone else. Once you do that, you create opportunities to change those behaviors. It's been said that you can't improve what you don't measure; the first step to measuring your level of attention and focus is to identify when it's being sabotaged.

▶ You can find a tool to help you analyze your work habits at www.rescuetime.com.

## Education

Educating yourself is the second step in changing your behavior. Often we exhibit a bad habit because we're not exactly sure how to change to make it better. Let's say you've become aware that you spend too much time on your email, and you know it's having a detrimental effect on how much you get done every day. But what choice do you have? You seem to get an endless amount of email; and if you aren't checking it all the time, it just piles up on you, right? You can't change a habit until you know with what will replace it. The Empowered Productivity System is full of education on behaviors that support you instead of sabotaging you. The purpose of this book is to give you the knowledge you need to accomplish that. Thus far, you've looked at several ways to support your own attention:

▶ Creating an environment for focus and flow

▶ Prioritizing your own tasks, not constantly reacting to others'

▶ Considering how you're managing your attention, not your time

▶ Single-tasking

▶ Allowing fewer interruptions

▶ Learning a process to use with your software or technology tools

## Overcoming Internal Barriers

The most difficult component of creating change is addressing your thoughts. We all have internal barriers to changing our behaviors, and often we can't even identify them. We are so good at rationalizing! When it comes to tackling a big goal, for example, it's very hard to get started, so it's easy to convince ourselves that we're too busy this month, but next month will be better, or one of 100 other excuses. Often, we just avoid thinking about a task until months have passed, and then we find ourselves thinking again, "Man, I still haven't made any progress on that. . . ."

▶ If you think your thoughts are really holding you back, you may be interested in learning about the impostor syndrome at www .impostorsyndrome.com.

To get yourself out of the trap created by internal barriers, you need a crystal-clear idea of what you want to achieve (awareness), *and* you have to identify exactly what you have to do next to move in that direction (education). Big goals seem daunting, but remember this important principle: You don't have to convince your-self to do everything; you only have to convince yourself to do the next thing.

> **NOTE**  Don't forget about the email follow-up program that can coach you as you implement new behaviors. Refer to the first section of this chapter for more information.

At this point, improving your productivity might seem like just another challeng-ing task. Don't worry. It won't happen overnight; but if you work the steps in this book, practice, and remain committed, it *will* happen. Before setting out on your own, you'll receive complete instructions on how to take each step; and if you sign up for the email follow-ups, you'll also have plenty of reinforcement along the way.

# RECONCILING YOUR "PLANNER" AND YOUR "DOER"

Even with the best of intentions, awareness, and education, you might still have a bar-rier: the internal conflict between your "planner" and your "doer." In order to implement the third step of overcoming internal barriers and be successful at creating the change you desire, you must do two things: create a plan and take action.

▶ You can find a suggested reading list in Appendix A.

In their excellent book about decision making, *Nudge*, Richard Thaler and Cass Sunstein describe the concept of the *planner* and the *doer*. The planner and the doer exist within each of us. For example, the authors describe the planner as the part of us that sets the alarm clock at night with the intention of getting up early in the morning to exercise. The doer is the part of us that in the morning either hits the snooze button four times or gets out of bed to implement the planner's plan.

Many of us have set our alarm again and again with great intentions, only to have our sleepy doers foil our attempts to accomplish something good for ourselves. We tend to blame our doers for this lack of well-intentioned action. It is our doers, after all, who are ineffective at getting us out of that nice, warm bed and into our running shoes or to the gym. It seems like the doer is at fault when we fail at implementing our plans and achieving our goals; but the real problem may lie with the planner. Successful leaders and managers can tell you that motivation is one of the most important keys to getting things done. In addition, they know that part of their job is understanding exactly what motivates each of their employees. Therefore, a critical part of our planner's job is understanding what motivates our doer to take action. This is especially true when the action to be taken is challenging.

Going back to the example of getting out of bed early enough to exercise before work, let's add the aspect of motivation. Getting out of bed to exercise in the morning can be especially difficult for anyone who is unaccustomed to the gym. One of the most significant barriers to exercise is a lack of experience or knowledge. Recognizing that you lack the sufficient experience or knowledge to feel comfortable using the gym equipment provides you with a good indicator of the motivation necessary to get you to the gym. In this case, it would be best for you to have a plan in place, such as meeting with a personal trainer who can guide you through the best exercises for helping you meet your goals. With the added motivation of having a knowledgeable personal trainer waiting to provide you with assistance, and the commitment you made to meet her, you stand a much better chance of getting yourself out of that comfortable bed.

You can apply the same technique used in the example about exercising to improve your productivity, combined with what you've learned so far about what it takes to get you there. First, identify the kinds of work currently being done by your internal planner and doer.

If you can identify some things you have wanted to accomplish for some time but have not successfully achieved, then you have identified a problem for your planner to solve. Your next step then is to identify what will ensure that your doer has the proper motivation to take the right actions and get things done. After you have identified the proper motivation, ensure that it is completely incorporated into your plans; you will soon find that you are finally making progress toward achieving your goals.

The following are some examples of common symptoms of decreased productivity that you may like to change:

▶ Working too many hours

▶ No vacation

▶ Cluttered work space

▶ Hundreds or thousands of messages in your email inbox

Now get your planner busy finding what is preventing you from changing these energy-draining habits and patterns, and start motivating your doer to take action toward your goals!

# IT MATTERS WHERE YOU START

Before you figure out where you're headed, it's helpful to assess where you are now. I generally see three different stages of productivity in my clients. See if any of these sound familiar to you.

## Stage One

We all have days that seemingly fly by and at the end of which we know that we were busy, but we can't really articulate exactly what we accomplished. I call this mode of working "stage one" productivity. For some of us, many days go by like that. For still others, it's a way of life. When you're at stage one productivity, you are almost exclusively in reactive mode. Being reactive doesn't necessarily mean that you aren't being productive; it means that you are dealing with the other people in your world, and we all have to do that sometimes: going to meetings, answering emails, returning phone calls, putting out fires, and so on. In fact, you may have a job that requires you to be reactive.

▶ Other types of very reactive jobs include firefighter and receptionist.

For example, if you are a manager whose only responsibilities are managing your employees—that is, keeping them on track, making sure they are meeting deadlines, and dealing with interpersonal issues—then your job is to be reactive. However, if you have even *one* responsibility that isn't dependent on your staff, at least one project or task for which you alone are responsible, and which can't be delegated to other people, then you must find some time to be proactive in order to get that project or task done. You can't do that, however, if you're stuck in stage one productivity.

## Stage Two

In stage two productivity, you are making time, every day, to be proactive. You are knocking things off your to-do list, and you finish each workday with at least some sense of accomplishment—that is, you actually completed something you set out to do that day. This is a great place to be.

If you are having a hard time getting to stage two, my suggestion is to break the habit of checking your email in the morning, a particularly insidious habit to break.

If checking your email is the first thing you do when you start your workday, you're setting the day's tone as reactive. It puts you on a "hamster wheel" of answering emails and responding to people and situations. Before you know it, you're reading blogs, checking your Twitter stream, and reviewing your Facebook notifications. You then have to rush off to a meeting, then to lunch, and when you come back, you're back on email, and the cycle starts all over again.

Break that cycle by checking your to-do list first thing in the morning, not your email. Work for an hour or 90 minutes checking items off your to-do list, and then check your email. The result is that you'll have a sense of accomplishment at the end of the day, even if the rest of your time was spent being reactive. You'll be able to point to some concrete tasks that you completed that day. There are more specifics about managing email in Chapters 11 and 12.

▶ There are exceptions to every rule, including the "don't check email first thing in the morning" rule. You can find those exceptions in the "Developing a Better Process" section of Chapter 11.

## Stage Three

There are two components to stage three productivity: consistently making progress toward your goals and being not only proactive, but *preactive*. Many people's to-do lists contain important items that need to be done but whose completion would not significantly affect their work or life. In other words, your to-do list is filled with items that do not bring you closer to the "big picture" goals you are trying to achieve. In the third stage of productivity, you are not only marking things off your to-do list, but adding and completing those that bring you closer to your goals.

You are working at stage three productivity when you accomplish one or more goal-dependent things in your day, things that are steps toward achieving your major goals or initiatives. My suggestion for reaching stage three productivity is to ensure that you always keep your "big picture" objectives visible to you so that you can stay focused on them.

And that brings me to the second component of stage three productivity: being *preactive*. OK, preactive might not be a real word, but one of the first books I was introduced to when I started my career in productivity is a book that was published only in German. The title, *Das Vorsprungs-Prinzip,* translates to *The Principle of Lead*. In it, authors René Marchand and Stefan Boëthius describe preactive as the state in which you have created the space to think, to plan, to use your own creativity to get an edge in your work and your life; the time when you are gaining insight and solving problems. In the fast-paced world that most of us live in, you may have reached a place where you feel like taking the time "to stop and think" is a luxury you can't afford. Is that really how you want to live your life? Stage three productivity is the level I strive to consistently attain.

In the following sections, I share more details about how to attend to your goals, and discuss two other skills necessary for successful attention management:

▶ Controlling the details

▶ Being realistic about your responsibilities and commitments

## ATTENDING TO YOUR GOALS

▶ Productive (adj.): achieving or producing a significant amount or result (definition courtesy of WordReference.com)

Do you know what you're trying to achieve? Have you written down your long-term goals? Proponents of *positive psychology* and the *law of attraction* will tell you that if you can see and articulate your goals, you can achieve them. I remember hearing Tony Robbins say something to the effect of, "If you give your brain a destination, it will find a way to get you there." Stephen Covey advised, "Begin with the end in mind." A common adage is "what is measured is improved." I firmly believe that all these ideas are true, and I've seen ample evidence in both my own life and the lives of my clients that clearly understanding and keeping an eye on your "big picture" is a key component to being productive—that is, "achieving your significant results."

A productivity methodology like the Empowered Productivity System gives you a way to make your goals visible and take action to move toward them. First, however, you have to know what your goals are. What I teach with regard to productivity is its practical application, what some people might consider the "nitty gritty"—the actual set of habits and behaviors to implement when you are sitting at your desk or otherwise need to actually *accomplish* something so that you can gradually move toward your bigger, more long-term goals. It's the way you act when you're looking for that satisfaction that comes at the end of a day you spent actually moving things forward, knocking things off your list, and relieving your burden.

In some ways, applying a productivity methodology is not very "high-level." On the other hand, deciding what's important to you, laying out a plan for your life, describing what you hope to achieve in one year, five years, ten years, or more, is important work; but only you can outline those goals. If you need help, you might want to first consult with someone who specializes in that kind of soul-searching, such as a life coach, business coach, or counselor. A good productivity methodology picks up where those professionals leave off.

For example, perhaps you have attended a conference or seminar that really motivated and inspired you, but the next day when you're back in your office, you have no idea where to begin. It is this type of scenario for which this book is precisely what you need. After you've assessed your goals and determined *your* "big picture," you need to keep your attention on those high-level goals, map out plans, take appropriate action, and eventually achieve success. Examples of high-level goals include all manner of "big picture" activities, such as the following:

- ▶ Starting a business
- ▶ Creating the budget for the next fiscal year
- ▶ Running a marathon
- ▶ Hiring the new staff member
- ▶ Implementing the feature upgrade
- ▶ Writing a book
- ▶ Running for political office

You get the idea. Some goals are important to you personally, some professionally, some are less consequential, some are life-changing, some are those you really *want* to do, whereas others you are required to do. The common denominator is that they are all "big," in that you can't simply take an action and check it off your list.

The expression "I can't see the forest for the trees" is often used to describe a situation in which one gives too much attention to small details, thereby failing to make enough progress on the important things. The "big picture" is the high-level view of what's on your plate at the moment: the large, time-consuming projects, activities in the areas of planning, problem prevention, relationships, professional or personal development, health and well-being, and those goals and aspirations that you plan to pursue. Remember the words of French writer Antoine de Saint-Exupery, who said, "A goal without a plan is just a wish." Make sure that your big picture is clearly defined, because wishes can only be granted. Goals must be achieved.

▶ S.M.A.R.T. goals: Specific, Measurable, Attainable, Realistic, Timely.

It's easy to avoid the big picture because the tasks involved in achieving it can seem overwhelming when you consider the amount of work they require. However, successful people have a clear view of their big picture: the things that *they* have determined are important. Differentiating the forest from the trees helps you to control your attention, so that the choices you make regarding your attention and how to spend your time are the *best* choices for moving you closer to your goals. Any effective productivity methodology requires the ability to focus on the big picture, reminding you of your important goals and helping you keep your attention on them. Chapter 4 contains more specifics about attending to your goals.

# CONTROLLING THE DETAILS

Could you list, right now, everything you're committed to, everything you need or want to do, every goal you have, everything you owe someone else, and everywhere you're supposed to be in the coming days and weeks? Usually, determining your commitments requires a lot of thought, a review of outstanding messages, checking both work and personal calendars, gathering a bunch of scattered notes, and flipping through piles of papers. If this describes you, then you don't yet have a grasp on all the details necessary to run your life.

In this situation, how do you know if you're overcommitted? How do you know if you can *really* meet your deadlines? Sure, you can work late if you have to; you can cancel some plans; you can pull an all-nighter. But wouldn't it be better to know *in advance* when you might need to do those things? How can you make informed decisions about the best use of your time and attention if you don't really know which things truly *need* your time and attention?

▶ *The constant juggling is also stressful!*

People often make a list of things that need to be done in order of their importance; but in the day, or two, or more that it takes to work down the list, practically everything has changed: new emails, new voicemails, new sticky notes. Constantly re-prioritizing is not an efficient use of your time.

The brain is not very good at memorizing little details. It is said that Einstein claimed he never bothered to memorize information that was easily accessible. Because keeping track of details is not your brain's strong suit, it makes sense that when you use your brain in this way you are not using your brain most effectively. Most of us have a limited capacity to recall the large amounts of information stored in our brains, so cluttering it with details that are not easily remembered is not a good idea.

In order to make the optimum use of your brain, it's best to free it from as much "clutter" as possible, making space available for creative, high-level thinking that can't be achieved with only pen and paper or an electronic tool: such as brainstorming, problem solving, and imagining.

As you read on, you will learn how to use the Empowered Productivity System to do the following to manage the details of your life:

- ▶ Capture all those details
- ▶ Store them in a way that makes them easy to track
- ▶ Organize them in a way that gives you clarity
- ▶ Avoid procrastination to make progress toward your goals

It will also do the following:

- Prevent you from "dropping the ball" by forgetting to follow up
- Reduce your stress by easing the burden of your "mental gymnastics"
- Enable you to be more proactive than reactive
- Compel you to act on the *right* things at the *right* time

These are the ingredients necessary to create a productivity methodology that is logical and useful; one that is sophisticated enough to handle the complexity of your busy life, but is not overly burdensome; one that becomes integral to your workflow, rather than being a separate and additional process in which to engage.

▶ *If your life is complicated, it takes some effort to keep it running smoothly.*

## BEING REALISTIC ABOUT "ONE MORE THING"

Do you often find yourself scrambling to get things done? Do you think you work better under pressure? Do you find yourself burning the midnight oil more often than you prefer? Do you regularly need to work evenings and/or weekends to complete work left unfinished? These are symptoms of failing to have a firm grasp of all the details necessary to run your life. When this is the case, it's easy to delude yourself about how much you can realistically accomplish in the time frame you expect. When we don't fully grasp how much we have committed ourselves to, we tend to just assume that we'll "figure out a way."

If you're dedicated to having a balanced life, the only way you can achieve it is if you know whether or not you are overcommitted. Even if you manage to get everything done by working evenings and weekends, wouldn't it be less stressful to realistically anticipate from the beginning whether you can successfully finish what you want to accomplish in the time you allotted? Although it can be hard to estimate how much time everything is going to take, it isn't that difficult to recognize when too much is squeezed into too little time. If you have enough time and resources, even "too much" can be done on time, but knowing in advance if you need extra time and resources can prevent a great deal of stress.

In fact, this is what causes anxiety for most people: knowing that they have a lot to do, and worrying every day about whether or not they can get it done, consciously or unconsciously fretting over what will happen if it doesn't get done, and feeling pressured in general.

A process that gives you control over everything on your plate enables you to be realistic about what you can and can't get done in a particular time frame, giving you a clear sense of how much is "too much." It helps you to set yourself up for success when asked questions like "Can you chair the event this year?" or "Is now a good time to start remodeling the house?" or even "Can I really get that report out by the end of the day?" When you can look at incoming projects, activities, or opportunities within the context of things to which you've already committed, you can make informed decisions about what to accept, when you need help, and what kind of due dates are achievable and realistic.

What can and can't be done in a specific time frame often depends on how much time you are willing to devote to it. For example, maybe you *could* finish that report before you leave today, if you work until 10:00 p.m. If you can't, or prefer not to work until 10:00 p.m., then perhaps saying that you'll finish it today is a bad decision. It's hard to find balance when you are constantly overcommitted; in fact, the two are mutually exclusive.

The idea of achieving "balance" is two-fold. First, you want to ensure that one aspect of your life doesn't completely eclipse all others; but there are nuances to consider. Someone might think that an inventor who is always consumed by his inventions doesn't have a balanced life. However, an inventor likely gets more than just professional satisfaction from spending time on that invention. It might provide him energy, inspiration, and relaxation, so perhaps this life is not as unbalanced as it seems from the outside.

▶ You'll learn more about being realistic to achieve balance in Chapter 6.

Another perspective on balance is the idea of being "present"—both in your personal life when you are trying to enjoy some recreational activity and in your professional life when you are trying to work and be productive professionally. This is a common challenge, especially for people with careers who also take the lead in managing a busy household. This is especially so for those in the so-called "sandwich generation," carrying the bulk of the responsibility for not only their own family, but their parents' and/or in-laws' as well. This creates challenges in trying to focus on work when at work, because they may be worrying about what's going on at home. Also, professionals often have business responsibilities that weigh on them even when not at work, which makes it hard to be "present" in a personal life and certainly to find an opportunity to really relax and unwind. I believe that you achieve balance when you can successfully be in control of all the details related to your personal life and your professional life, so that you can truly devote your attention to the moment at hand, regardless of where you are or what you are doing.

# SUMMARY

In this chapter I addressed how most people focus on the wrong problem—productivity is not dependent on how much information is out there, but on how you manage and control the attention you give to that information. I provided some simple tasks to begin managing your information, your technology, and your behavior. Because changing your behavior is one of the most challenging steps of the Empowered Productivity System, I went into detail about how to become aware of your habits, learn better methods to replace bad habits, and remove internal barriers to change so the "planner" in your mind can motivate the "doer" to start accomplishing your goals.

Regardless of whether you're at stage 1 or stage 3 of productivity, you might suffer from being overcommitted, so the chapter ends with some checkpoints to help you recognize whether you're trying to squeeze into one too many tasks into your day.

The next chapter introduces the methodology—the *Empowered Productivity System*—and sets you up to begin to implement the specific habits and behaviors that will help you regain control over the details of your life and work.

## QUICK TIPS

The following are some important points from this chapter (also suitable for tweeting). For more information on Twitter, including relevant usernames and hashtags, please refer to the "Read This First" chapter.

▶ The real challenge is not "information overload"; it's intrusive & distracting technology. Control is necessary!

▶ Your "planner" wants to be productive, but it's your "doer" that might be getting in the way!

▶ "Empowered Productivity" comes from being in control. Are you working on YOUR to-do list?

▶ My ringing phone distracts everyone; a vibrating phone distracts me. Why is distracting myself OK?

## ENDNOTES

1. MG Siegler, "Eric Schmidt: Every 2 Days We Create As Much Information As We Did Up To 2003," TechCrunch, August 4, 2010, http://techcrunch .com/2010/08/04/schmidt-data/.

# PART II

# THE EMPOWERED PRODUCTIVITY SYSTEM

## CHAPTER 3

# Empowering Your Productivity

## IN THIS CHAPTER

▶ What you might have in common with a lion

▶ What you can learn from Dwight D. Eisenhower

▶ Getting rid of the "shoulds"

▶ Managing crises

▶ Being responsive versus reactive

▶ Focusing on goals

▶ Why control matters

If you've looked at the list of topics covered in this chapter, you're probably wondering what lions and Eisenhower have to do with your productivity—with your ability to achieve your *significant results*. This chapter introduces you to a behavior that lion tamers know that lions possess, and that busy people share. Learning how to recognize it in yourself helps you "tame" the feeling of being overwhelmed that sneaks up on us all.

Eisenhower was known for staying focused on the most important things and not letting himself get caught up in the (often false) sense of urgency that sometimes infects behavior in fast-paced environments. In this chapter I introduce you to Eisenhower's mantra and present you with ideas and techniques for handling different types of situations that might present themselves in the course of your busy day.

# AVOIDING THE LION SYNDROME

Because of the volume and speed of technological advances, managing communication alone has become an overwhelming job. Consider this: Do you have more than one place where you get phone messages: cell phone, work phone, home phone? Do you have more than one email address? Perhaps your profession or industry is still using faxes. If you work in an office, you might get "snail mail" (postal service, FedEx, UPS, and so on) at more than one location—home and office. You might also have at least one place in both your personal life and your workspace where unfinished tasks accumulate, making you a member of the "file by pile" club. You probably also deal with some combination of instant messages, text messages, blog/picture/video comments, Facebook, LinkedIn, Twitter, the Internet, radio, and television. The list is seemingly endless.

▶ Remember your goal of being proactive, and working on your priorities from "Stop Working on the Wrong To-Do List" section from Chapter 1.

That's a lot of incoming information to process. Consequently, it's easy to simply spend all your time just reacting. The result? You end up working according to everyone else's time schedule, responding to everyone else's priorities, and fulfilling everyone else's needs and wants. In short, you are no longer in control. Using the techniques presented in this chapter, you'll learn to save time and achieve peace of mind. In particular, you'll be able to do the following:

▶ Have a complete understanding of everything on your plate at any moment, including its priority

▶ Know exactly what to do next

▶ Act on any number of things immediately

▶ How often do you currently know exactly the best thing to do when you have a few minutes or a few hours to get things done?

When you *empower* your own productivity by learning and implementing the Empowered Productivity™ System, you know the best use of your time at any moment, and can take immediate and appropriate action. One of the biggest wastes of time is sitting down at your desk and wondering, "What do I need to do now?" and then going through the exercises to try to figure it out. For most people, the sheer number of potential answers to that question is completely overwhelming. It probably causes you to retreat into some sort of busywork—something that is easy, familiar, and doesn't require a lot of thought. For most people, this means email. It's easier to go look at new business coming down the pike than try to figure out what to do about the pile of old business.

The old work is probably that to-do list you made and stored somewhere. It contains things that *you* put there, that *you* decided were important, that *you* wanted to accomplish. I've learned to call that overwhelmed feeling you get when you contemplate all the possible things you should be doing the *Lion Syndrome*.

If you have ever seen a lion tamer at the circus or zoo or on television, you know that they always bring two tools into the cage: a whip and a stool. The whip's purpose is obvious, but you might not realize why a stool is used. Most people assume that its purpose is to keep some distance between the lion tamer and the lion's sharp teeth, but the stool actually serves a different purpose. If you notice, lion tamers always grab the stool by the seat, and aim the legs at the lion. The animal perceives four separate threats and tries to focus on all four legs at the same time, which makes it confused. When the lion is confused, it becomes passive and retreats.[1]

In my productivity research, I find that people react to multiple inputs just like lions. For example, it isn't unusual for all of the following to be happening simultaneously in a workspace:

- ▶ Emails are downloading.

- ▶ The phone is ringing.

- ▶ The voicemail light is flashing.

- ▶ Paperwork is piled all over the desk's surface.

- ▶ A co-worker pops in to ask if you can spare just a minute.

It's not unusual to shut down when the volume of things that are demanding your attention is so overwhelming and distracting. Typical responses, with which you might be very familiar, include checking email, making a list, getting a cup of coffee, or chatting with a co-worker about your plans for the weekend—none of which will get you any closer to productivity. It's time to learn how to avoid the Lion Syndrome: how to be in complete control of all of the details of your life. When you're caught up and have processed and prioritized demands on your attention *as they come in*, then the only things that need to be recognized, organized, and prioritized are the *new* items that have just arrived. It's much easier to deal with *only* the new things, trusting that previous items are being handled by your system.

# PICKING THE RIGHT SPOT ON THE EISENHOWER MATRIX

Dwight D. Eisenhower has been credited with saying, "What is important is seldom urgent and what is urgent is seldom important." Apparently, he was notorious for applying this to the prioritization of his workload. Even in Eisenhower's day, productivity students recognized the value of this wisdom and developed what was known as the *Eisenhower Matrix*. Decades later, Steven Covey adapted it in the *Seven Habits of Highly Effective People*, where he called it the *Four Quadrants*.

It has now become common time-management advice to use this matrix with the understanding that you should spend the most time working on items that fall in the quadrant of Important, rather than Urgent, which is easier said than done. I use a different approach to this matrix; the following sections explain all four quadrants and some specific techniques for optimizing your attention within each of them.

**Eisenhower Matrix**

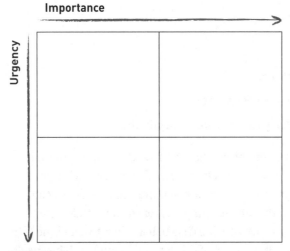

**FIGURE 3-1**

## Unloading the *Shoulds*

The Eisenhower Matrix essentially considers all the demands on your attention in terms of only two factors: importance and urgency. The top axis measures importance from low to high, and the side axis measures urgency from least urgent to most urgent. For example, in the upper-left quadrant, you have low importance, low urgency.

▶ For the definition of terms within the specific context of this book, refer to the Glossary.

Low importance, low urgency items are the tasks that I call the shoulds (see Figure 3-2). These are typically the things that have *very little* effect on your life and your work if you actually complete them. However, knowing this does not free your mind from worrying about them. As things that you feel you should do, they languish on your to-do list and weigh on your mind. We all have these nagging items to attend to:

- ▶ "I should download the pictures off the camera. What's the point of even taking them if they just sit there?"

- ▶ "I should mow the lawn. The neighbors will be upset with me if my yard looks bad."

- ▶ "I should organize the files from that project. If we need to refer to them in the future, we won't be able to find what we need."

- ▶ "I should fix the leaky faucet. I know it's increasing my water bill, and isn't there a water shortage?"

**Eisenhower Matrix**

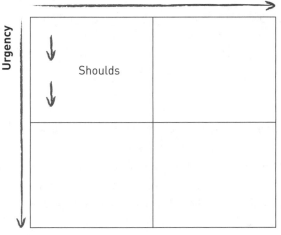

FIGURE 3-2

These are the nagging tasks that you might think of as the "monkeys on your back." If you were prioritizing your list by A, B, C, these are the items that would get a C priority or even lower, which means you'll never get to some of them. In the meantime, however, a little part of your brain still nags you about them. After all, it's not like your life is going to change if you actually organize your vacation photos.

To get the *shoulds* off your list, you need to get help. Items in this quadrant are perfect items to delegate because they don't necessarily need your specific expertise or input. If you are a busy person with a full life, but don't have help—whether it's a cleaning person, a babysitter, or an administrative support person—then you are missing an opportunity to manage your life more easily and more productively. There are many ways to get support in small increments, often for a lot less money than you think. Furthermore, the money you invest in having help could pay dividends many times over in terms of time, decreased stress levels, and the opportunity to achieve your significant results.

For example, let's say you're having the floors redone in your home. The flooring installers will move the big furniture, but the smaller items are up to you. You need to empty the larger pieces of furniture of all the picture frames and knickknacks so they are not broken when the installers move the furniture. Packing knickknacks is probably not the best use of your time.

Instead, consider working at home for a day while you supervise a college student. A reliable young person (perhaps your own child or relative) would probably be thrilled to do this for $8 or $10 per hour—maybe less. Your time is likely worth more than that, and probably a lot more. Ask yourself this: Is it worth $20 or $30 to get my afternoon back?

▶ How much is your time worth? The answer is often both objective and subjective. It can be partly calculated based on your salary; but when you strongly dislike doing something, paying someone else to do it can be a smart use of your resources.

> **NOTE** Something isn't a should if you love to do it. If you enjoy the mental break that working with your hands provides, or the connection to nature you feel when mowing your lawn or weeding your garden, then by all means do these things yourself. Something is a should only if it 'is nagging at you *and* you don't relish the thought of doing it yourself.

If no one in your own family or neighborhood is able to help you out, check your local community paper. If you are part of a neighborhood association that issues a newsletter, it may contain the names of individuals willing to do part-time work, or maybe your workplace has an online bulletin board. Another option is Craigslist (http://craigslist.org); and if you live in a college town, the school might have a job office or website where students looking for extra income post their services.

If you have shoulds on your list that require a more specific set of skills, you can find numerous websites offering all manner of assistance, most of which provide support on an on-call basis. TaskRabbit is a new service that is expanding rapidly and has a very promising business model.

For even more specialized expertise, websites such as www.elance.com for business skills and www.angieslist.com for trade skills provide a quick and easy way to find a data entry expert, a reliable handyperson, or whatever services you may need to get these shoulds off your list. The benefit of investing a bit of time to find these types of service providers is that you can begin to develop a network of people to call on when you need some help shortening your to-do list. Timothy Ferriss, author of *The 4-Hour Workweek*, is a master of this type of delegation, and his book offers numerous examples.

The more shoulds you get off your list, the more free you are—to do the things you're best at; to do the things that offer you the highest payoff in your life; to do the things you truly love to do—your significant results. For example, maybe you've been longing to start a part-time business doing something you enjoy. If you didn't have to mow the lawn, organize the garage, or fix the leaky faucet on the weekend, you could devote the time instead to generating extra income from your hobby. What have *you* been wanting to do as soon as you "find the time"? Is it time to unload some of your shoulds to create the time you need?

## Handling Crises

The lower-right quadrant of the Eisenhower Matrix contains items of high importance and high urgency. This is the quadrant of *crises* (see Figure 3-3).

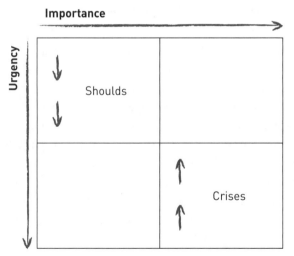

**Eisenhower Matrix**

**FIGURE 3-3**

Crises are usually outside your control, you don't see them coming, and there is nothing you can do to prevent them. They could be serious—true crises—or they could be something minor like the fender-bender you had on the way to work. You had a whole day of appointments scheduled, but instead of crossing them off your list you're watching your car being towed away.

▶ Crises are unanticipated events that change your schedule and your priorities for the day or the week.

Because these crises are outside your control, and you often can't see them coming, the best way to handle them is to have the flexibility in your schedule to absorb them. For example, if your calendar is stuffed front-to-back with appointments, meetings, and commitments, then you have no room for a crisis. A full calendar combined with an unexpected situation (you or your child come down with the flu, you throw out your back, you car doesn't start, and so on) causes your plans to topple like dominoes.

On the other hand, a calendar that isn't overscheduled offers you two benefits. First, in the event of a crisis or unexpected situation, your day or week can absorb the new issue needing your attention without too much disruption, making it much more manageable, and perhaps not even a crisis at all. Second, during those times when you don't have an unexpected situation, crisis, or changing priority, that room in your calendar provides the opportunity to get some things done—to be proactive. The appointments and commitments you schedule on your calendar are likely to be reactive time—somewhere that someone else wants you to be, doing something other than crossing items off your to-do list. In other words, when your schedule is constantly booked, with 80 percent or 90 percent of your week committed to other things, not only will you be unable to absorb a crisis, you are leaving yourself no time to be proactive.

In order to efficiently and effectively handle crises, consider your week in terms of *productive time*—that is, when you are awake and taking action. This time might begin just after you've woken up in the morning—for example, checking your smartphone as you get ready to go exercise or make some breakfast. It's the point at which your day begins. This is not necessarily your "workday," but your day in general. It ends when you have decided you are done for the night—maybe before you go to sleep, but after your downtime begins. For example, my productive time begins around 7:00 a.m. I may not be showered, dressed, and out the door yet, but I'm up and about, checking the weather, gathering my belongings for the day. My productive time ends around 8:00 p.m., as this is the point at which I'm typically "spent" for the day. I'm not going to sleep but I am relaxing, unwinding, perhaps reading a book or watching television. Collectively, those 13 hours times 5 business days equal my productive time per week.

When you have calculated your productive time, check whether more than about 60 percent of that time is *scheduled*. It could be work activities or personal activities, but if you are committed to do something or be somewhere (not just "at work" but in a meeting or other appointment) for more than that 60 percent of your time, then you are probably overcommitted. The consequences of being overcommitted are that you can't effectively absorb an unexpected situation, change in priorities, or crisis, *and* you have too little time to be proactive and get things done.

For you, 60 percent might not be exactly the right percentage, but it's a good starting point. You can do this whether you work 9:00 a.m. to 5:00 p.m. at an office or are self-employed. If you share calendars with co-workers, protect some times from having a meeting added. Limit your commitments to 60 percent of your productive time, and see how your week goes. Are you being more proactive? More productive? Feeling less stressed? Dealing better with changing priorities? Assess the situation and adjust your calendar if necessary.

## Mastering the Difference between Reactive and Responsive

The lower-left quadrant on the Eisenhower Matrix contains items that are low importance and high urgency. In this case, urgent refers to those items that are constantly demanding your attention, such as the ringing phone, the instant messages and text messages, and the co-workers waiting for "just a minute" of your time. These are the items that feel urgent but likely are not that important, or at least not important enough for you to drop everything at that moment to deal with them.

▶ Remember the concept from martial arts: control or be controlled.

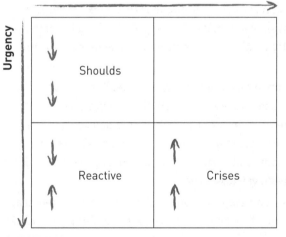

**Eisenhower Matrix**

FIGURE 3-4

When you work at peak productivity by using the Empowered Productivity System, you spend as little time as possible being reactive, instead being proactive. As this book has emphasized thus far, it's very easy to spend all your time reacting to things, and it *is* important to be responsive; but it's also important to understand that there is a difference between being responsive and being constantly reactive. A client once said

▶ When you need to respond to people, it's OK to do that according to your schedule instead of their schedule.

to me that he felt like his email was "his to-do list to which anyone in the world could add things." While it is often true that your email contains new work, that doesn't mean you necessarily have to drop everything every time a new message arrives. Nor do you have to drop everything every time the phone rings. Unless you work in an industry or job that *truly* requires immediate responsiveness, there are very few situations in which you have absolutely no control, or no ability to exert any control, over your own time, your own attention, and your own workload.

I understand that other people in your life sometimes require your attention, and I would never suggest that you don't respond to them. However, there is an important distinction between being responsive and being reactive, and that difference has a significant effect on your productivity. According to *Webster's New World Dictionary*, *react* means "to act in return," whereas *respond* means "to reply." We typically have a responsibility to reply to the many communications we receive on a daily basis, however they arrive. We *don't* have an obligation to constantly and immediately *act* on the relentless stream of communication we receive daily.

It's courteous and responsible to respond to the communication you receive in a timely manner. Of course, the definition of timely varies according to the specific request, and it's something you need to determine for yourself; but it's probably longer than you assume. As stressed throughout this book, given the relentless stream of communication you receive virtually all day long in some form or another, if you constantly react to all of them you can never get anything important done.

▶ Refer to the discussion of "flow" in Chapter 1 for more information.

There is an additional drawback to being constantly reactive. The more you allow yourself to be distracted and to immediately act on every thought you have and every new request you receive, the more you reinforce that behavior. When you become conditioned to constant distraction—constant *reaction*—you eventually become bored in the absence of that constant stimulation. Focus and concentration are skills like any other: If you don't use them, you lose them.

▶ These times should occur between the times when you're working on key items from your to-do list.

My suggestion is this: Rather than stop what you're doing to immediately react to (take action on) every communication that reaches you, set aside specific times in the day when you respond to communication. The action required by the communication might fit into your plans for your day. If you expect that it will take longer than you have time to allocate that day, based on the priorities you've set for yourself, then *make the conscious decision* to either rearrange your priorities or simply respond that you will take action later. This is thoughtful action, not reaction.

One of the secrets to exerting more control over your time and your attention is noticing when you are most productive. For example, some people get the most done in the morning but are not so effective in the afternoon or evening; for others, the opposite is true. Think about the time of day and your natural energy patterns when planning out appropriate times to block for responding to communication versus accomplishing your proactive tasks.

▶ Either way, you should honor your body's natural rhythm. For more information about the body's natural rhythm, do a quick Internet search using the phrase "larks versus owls."

## Accomplishing More

The fourth quadrant of the Eisenhower Matrix, in the upper-right, is high importance and low urgency (see Figure 3-5). These are tasks that you've intentionally put on your list of goals, or things that you've decided to do in your lifetime, whether it's start a business, go back to school, start a family, run for office, write a book, or ski the Alps. These are the types of big picture goals that are covered in Chapter 2. None of those tasks are likely very urgent, so they tend to fall to the bottom of your list. Even work-related items, such as "hire a new staff member," "write the marketing plan," or "revamp the website," can fall into this category. Because these kinds of things aren't urgent, they somehow don't get done; until they become urgent, and suddenly you have a crisis.

**Eisenhower Matrix**

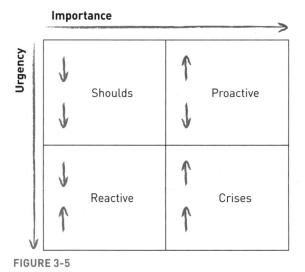

FIGURE 3-5

These high importance, low urgency items often reflect things that can have the biggest effect on your life and work if you actually accomplish them (contrary to the shoulds). This is the quadrant of being proactive. This is where you take control. This is where the stuff that's on *your* list, that *you've* decided is important, happens. Whether or not you accomplish these goals is all about your discipline in exerting control. When you control your work, you free your mind of clutter and make room for your creativity to flow, which enables your best problem-solving abilities to manifest themselves.

A quote that really drives home the importance of being proactive versus reactive is the following, from author Rita Mae Brown: "A life of reaction is a life of slavery, intellectually and spiritually. One must fight for a life of action, not reaction."

One definition of *genius* is the ability to make connections that other people don't make. That ability to make connections—true learning—happens at quiet times. Did you ever have a great idea in the shower? Perhaps it was because you don't bring all your gadgets and devices into the shower with you. Most of us have had the experience of waking up with a great idea or the solution to a problem because we weren't distracted while sleeping, giving the brain an opportunity to take hold of the ideas it pushed aside during the day. The more time you allow yourself those moments to use your brain for what it's good at, the more often your best (most productive) self emerges, which is why the quality of your work increases when you single-task.

## SUMMARY

This chapter has provided you with some of the foundational concepts of the Empowered Productivity System, including techniques to help you identify when you are sabotaging your own attention and productivity, rather than supporting it. Can you now recognize when you might have the Lion Syndrome? Can you find the quadrant on the Eisenhower Matrix where you spend the majority of your time? Is it where you want to be? Are you exerting enough control over your own attention to keep your day, your week, and your life on track to facilitate your own happiness, and reduce your stress levels?

In Chapter 4 I show you how to harness these ideas to take control over your to-do list, and make consistent progress toward your goals.

# QUICK TIPS

The following are some important points from this chapter (also suitable for tweeting). For more information on Twitter, including relevant usernames and hashtags, please refer to the "Read This First" chapter.

- ▶ "Lion Syndrome"? Lions view 4 stool legs as 4 threats & shut down. Faced with too long to-do list, so do we!

- ▶ Phone is ringing, emails pinging, text messages dinging. . . do you grab a cup of coffee instead? Classic Lion Syndrome!

- ▶ Stop "should-ing" on yourself! Delegating is a great option for low-importance/low-urgency tasks.

- ▶ "What is important is seldom urgent and what is urgent is seldom important." Wise advice from President Eisenhower.

- ▶ Only cure for a crisis? Having enough time in your calendar to deal with it.

- ▶ Your calendar should only be ~60% booked, to allow room for the unexpected.

# ENDNOTES

1. Dr. John Maxwell, *The 21 Indispensable Qualities of a Leader*, (Nashville: Thomas Nelson, 2000), p. 31.

# Controlling the Constant Chatter

Regaining control of all the demands on your attention enables you to be proactive, but first you need to be organized. You must get the details necessary for running your life out of your head and into an organized system; and to most people, "organizing" means grouping items and information in ways that are logical. Often organization is intuitive, but sometimes you need to think specifically about the discrete ways you could organize various things, and the most appropriate and efficient use for each organization method.

# ORGANIZING YOUR MENTAL CLUTTER

▶ A big source of stress is having to mentally keep track of things for which you're responsible.

To create an effective organizational system, it is important to have a comprehensive understanding of *all* the things that need to be included in your system. If you are like most people, all the commitments, communication, and information required to keep your life running smoothly are scattered in many different places. Many people carry the bulk of their responsibilities in their heads, perhaps supplemented with a digital or paper calendar, scraps or pads of paper, sticky notes, and items scribbled on business cards, cocktail napkins, and random envelopes! Writing things down can be helpful, but where you write them matters. When you lack an organized capturing system for thoughts, ideas, and tasks, some part of your brain recognizes that you may lose a business card, or not have that piece of paper when you need it. Therefore, you are unable to release things from your mind because you feel that you still have to remember them.

Unfortunately, because your brain is not obedient, as discussed in Chapter 2, it's not the most efficient location to store these details. Your brain doesn't offer you the opportunity to reach in and "pluck out" exactly the thought you need at exactly the moment you need it. At any given moment, you can remember only a fraction of all the information stored in your brain, and the extent to which you can choose what you can access is limited. Equally unfortunate is the fact that any ability you *do* have in this regard tends to decline with age.

Storing too many details in your brain is inefficient, but it also causes stress. It can be hard to sleep or relax when you feel like your brain is spinning as a result of the "mental gymnastics" required to keep your life running smoothly. It is also stressful when you *know* you aren't remembering everything, because you worry about what you *can't* remember and what you *aren't* doing right now. Consequently, it's harder to focus on what you *are* doing, which makes it tempting to jump from task to task, leaving them incomplete and/or poorly done. Again, you are *sabotaging* your own attention and productivity instead of supporting it.

# GAINING CLARITY

The antidote to the anxiety caused by what you aren't doing now, and by what you need to do that you can't remember right now, is to get everything out of your head and into a place where you can see it and therefore effectively manage it. You are most efficient when all the details you have to manage are corralled in one place, but that place should not be your brain.

The secret to gaining clarity over the details of your life, so that you can best manage and control them, is the following: You can only manage what you can *see*, and you can only see what is *outside* of your head.

Your brain cannot simultaneously remember multiple tasks and effectively deal with them. In order to organize all the details you must manage, you need a level of clarity that can only be achieved by offloading the "remembering" responsibility to another tool. After you've freed your mind from the job of juggling details, you can use the brainpower you've freed up to make progress on the actual work to be done.

Perhaps you're someone who has previously learned in a time management class that you should spend time at the beginning of each day, or the night before, writing down all the things that you would like to accomplish that day. This tip is usually followed by the advice to prioritize the list using A, B, C, or some other hierarchy, and then simply spend the day working from your list. The theory behind this advice is that the list keeps you focused on the important tasks.

That advice was probably useful 30 years ago or more, when the business environment was simpler than it is today, but I believe that this advice has far outlived its usefulness. Making a long list every day virtually guarantees that you will forget some things, leading to that collection of random scraps. There is simply too much to remember for a human brain not wired for details.

► This concept is one of the foundations of the Empowered Productivity™ System. Recognizing and applying this principle provides an opportunity for improved efficiency virtually anywhere it is applied.

► Instead of reinventing the wheel every day, a running list ensures everything is captured.

# FIVE WAYS TO ORGANIZE

I agree with Richard Wurman, the author of *Information Anxiety*, that there are only five ways to organize anything. The following sections describe these five ways and give you examples of the most appropriate and effective times to use each of them.

## Organizing Alphabetically

One common way to organize is alphabetically. Alphabetical organization can be useful for many scenarios—for example, it is how many people organize their files. (Read Chapter 8 for more information on filing.) Alphabetical organization can also be effective when you have a static list and you need to easily find specific items on it. Typically, alphabetical organization is useful for reference information, such as your address book or an inventory list.

► Reference information is information that does not require action in and of itself. The reason you keep reference material is because you might need it later.

## Organizing by Size

Another way to organize information is on a size continuum, such as smallest to biggest. A continuum is useful for organizing physical items. For example, many people organize areas of their homes using a continuum. You may have the dishes and pots organized in your kitchen with small items in one cabinet and large items in another. Similarly, a warehouse might have large inventory stored in one area, and smaller parts in a separate section.

## Organizing by Location

The third way to organize is by location, which can be useful for both physical items and information. At home, for example, you might use different locations for summer clothes and winter clothes. Or you might store all the items you need to take with you when you leave the house—your keys, wallet, and phone—close to the door.

At work, it can also be useful to store information by location: If your company has both domestic customers and international customers, the files of the domestic customers might be located in one file cabinet or folder on your computer, while the files of the international customers are kept in a different file cabinet or folder on your computer.

Alphabetical, size-, and location-based organizing all have their place, but following are the two most critical organizing methods to regain control over a busy life: time and category.

## Organizing by Time

Organizing by time usually applies to information and commitments. Time-based organization is the method used most often by busy people, because everyone knows how to use a calendar. In fact, until we had sophisticated electronic tools to help us organize, a paper calendar was the primary tool for keeping track of a busy life. We all still have a tendency to organize by time, despite the fact that our lives today are often too complex for simple time-based organization.

Things that will happen on a certain day or at a certain time have a strong relationship to time, and time-based organization is perfect for these situations. Day-specific activities are things such as someone's birthday; the day a bill is due; or a commitment that you made, such as, "I'll call you on Tuesday." Other activities are specific to both a day and a time, such as meetings and appointments—for example, a meeting on Monday at 3:00 p.m., a doctor's appointment on Wednesday at 4:00 p.m.

Meetings and appointments only fill a portion of our time. The majority of our daily time is spent managing information, sending and receiving communications, and meeting non-time-based commitments, all of which is *discretionary time*. For example, if your workplace requires that you occasionally attend meetings but the rest of the time you are left alone to do your work, then you have discretionary time. The work you do during discretionary time has a *weak* relationship to time, so using a time-based tool to manage it (such as a calendar) means that you are working harder than is necessary. Consequently, using a calendar as the foundation of any organization system just doesn't cut it, which is why many people also keep some sort of "to-do" list.

> ▶ Time-based events with a strong relationship to time.

Information has a weak relationship to time if it isn't associated with a due date, or if the due date is very far away. For example, suppose you decide to update a page on your website. It's something you'd *like* to do, something that you may be *planning* to do, but visitors to your website are unaffected by your inaction. You could pick a due date, but it would be arbitrary; and if you aren't able to update the page by the date you selected, you could still update the page later. This task has a *weak* relationship to time.

Similarly, if you have a report due on Friday and today is Monday, it probably doesn't matter whether you complete that report on Tuesday at 11:00 a.m. or Wednesday at 2:00 p.m. or Thursday at 7:00 p.m., as long as you meet your deadline of Friday. This task also has a weak relationship to time. Items that have a weak relationship to time are usually activities one would find on a task list.

> ▶ You may refer to your task list as your to-do list. For the purposes of this book, task list and to-do list are interchangeable.

## Organizing by Category

Organizing by category is the fifth option. Categorical organization is more useful for organizing your task list than time-based organization is. Mentally processing uncategorized information takes more effort and is more time-consuming than understanding categorized information.

A compelling reason to use categorical organization is that your brain works categorically. A simple visual example demonstrates how information that is categorized is easier and faster to digest than uncategorized information. Figures 4-1 and 4-2 show some images of fruit. First, look at Figure 4-1 on the next page and note how long it takes you to determine two things:

▶ How many different types of fruit are there?

▶ Which fruit is there more of?

Then, see Figure 4-2 and do the same exercise. I'm willing to bet that it is easier and faster for you to answer the two questions using the second image than it is with the first. In this example, the fruit is a metaphor for the details of your life, and hopefully you can see that if you use categorical organization, those details will become much more manageable and actionable.

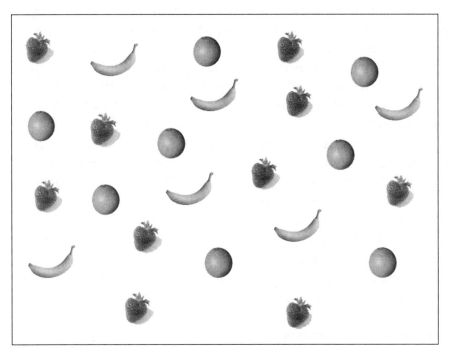

FIGURE 4-1

## Organizing Tasks for Action

As I discussed earlier, you can only manage what you can see, and you can only see what's outside your head. Therefore, the first step in organizing the details of your life is to get everything out of your head, which might result in a very long list of all of the things you need to do. Having everything listed in a place where you have to flip or scroll through several pages in order to select the most appropriate item to complete at the present moment is not very effective, and it will still give you the Lion Syndrome described in Chapter 3. You need a system for managing things after you get them out of your head, and an organization system is most effective when you combine the five different ways to organize. An external list is absolutely necessary, but it's only the first step.

For example, after you make a list of the details you need to manage, you can sort them into three groups:

▶ Those requiring action that have a strong relationship to time (calendar events and appointments)

▶ Those requiring action that have a weak relationship to time (task list items)

▶ Those that serve as reference information (no action required)

Flag the time-based events and appointments for your calendar, and the reference materials for your Notes, which are both addressed in Chapter 5. Next I explain the best and most effective categories for your task list.

# CATEGORIZING AVOIDS CHAOS

After you've determined your tasks—or to-do list items, which are the items that require action and have a weak relationship to time, you need to organize them into effective categories.

If you are a list maker by nature, you probably have some experience with this. As you start to write things down, you begin to realize that the list is going to be very long, so you begin to sort it in some way, or keep separate lists. The problem is that the categories most people choose—either business and personal or urgent and not urgent—are not particularly effective:

▶ Business and personal are not particularly helpful because many people do personal tasks at work, and vice versa. Small-business owners often have an exceptionally difficult time distinguishing between business and personal.

▶ Urgent and not urgent is similarly ineffective because priorities often change so quickly that constant reorganization is necessary.

I suggest using the following categories to organize your task list in a way that makes it logical, manageable, and actionable.

## Next Actions

Give your tasks the category of Next Action if they are single-step activities for which you have all the information you need to complete them. Other than time or opportunity, nothing prevents you from completing a Next Action. Examples include the following:

▶ Call the tax advisor (you have the number, the necessary papers, and you know what you need to say)

▶ Email the book club members (you have their addresses and the subject clearly in mind)

▶ Write the marketing proposal (you have done your research and collected your thoughts)

These are tasks that could take a minute or two, or an hour or more, but what they have in common is that you *can* get them done completely if time allows. Consult this list during your discretionary time when you have the opportunity to be *proactive* and get things done.

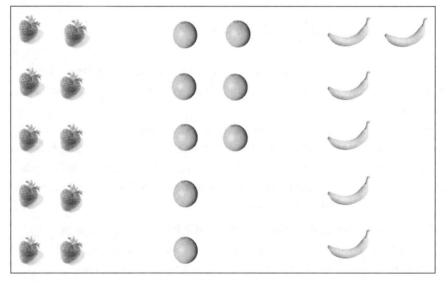

FIGURE 4-2

## Projects

Projects happen in multiple steps, over multiple time periods. These are big-picture activities that you are actively working on or about to begin. Also, in order to be a Project, the activity must have a definable beginning and end. Be careful not to confuse a category of your work, which is ongoing, with a Project. For example, if you are an attorney and also manage employees, "Manage Staff" is not a Project; it is just a category of your work because it has no beginning and end dates.

If an activity requires more than one step but you will complete them back-to-back, they are Next Actions, not Projects. For example, if you are going to brainstorm the components of a client proposal, write the proposal, and then email it to the client, and you intend to do all these things sequentially in the same sitting, then that is one Next Action. It would only be a Project if some time were going to pass between tasks.

▶ Remember, Projects involve multiple steps over multiple time periods and have a definable beginning and end.

Each Project probably has one or more Next Actions associated with it, but not every Next Action relates to a Project. The following are some examples of Projects:

- ▶ Plan a birthday party
- ▶ Develop next quarter's goals
- ▶ Write a company benefits guide

For each Project, you must define the *next* thing that has to happen in order to move that Project forward; otherwise, it becomes stagnant and you do not make progress on it. The next thing that needs to happen in order to move a Project forward *could* be a Next Action, but it could also be something from another category, or it could be a calendar appointment. For example, for the Project "Write a company benefits guide," the next thing that will move the Project forward could be a meeting with the head of HR, which is on your calendar. Or it could be "assemble documentation from the shared folder," which would be a Next Action. Deciding on the Next Action helps you avoid procrastination if you remember that you don't have to tackle *everything*; you only need to tackle the *next* thing.

> **NOTE** Projects are "big picture" activities that you have specifically defined, as described in the section "Attending to Your Goals" in Chapter 2. For example, "make more money" is a goal or a wish, but it is not a Project per se in this context because it is too vague—it lacks a starting point, and stating it this way gives no indication when it will be over, or achieved.

Consult your list of Projects when you are assessing your current responsibilities, when deciding to take on a big new project, or when you need to "come out of the trees" and "see the forest." Use the list when you need a high-level view of your current major initiatives.

Other advantages to keeping a Projects list include the following:

- ▶ Track accomplishments for your résumé
- ▶ Track accomplishments for your annual review with your boss
- ▶ Better control your workload

Regarding this last item, you can think of your Projects list as your "ammunition" to use if you work in an environment where priorities change quickly and frequently, and you feel like you are always getting new work and new responsibilities without regard to your existing work.

When a manager drops a major new initiative or responsibility into your lap, you might assume that you can't possibly take on one more thing—and maybe you can't. However, without a clear and trackable understanding of your current workload, you won't be able to articulate why; that is, you won't have the necessary information to support your claim. For most managers, a simple "I'm too busy" (with no backup information) is not a sufficient reason for not taking on more work. As a result, you end up taking on more work than you can realistically accomplish.

A Projects list provides the immediate ammunition you need to confidently respond, "I'd be happy to take on that new project. Here are the things you have currently assigned to me. Which one would you like me to bump in order to make room for this new project?" This empowers your productivity at work and gives you control over whether or not your workload is manageable and realistic.

Remember from Chapter 1 that exerting control contributes to your happiness. Maintaining a Projects list helps you to control your workload. Always identifying the next specific action that's necessary to move the project forward lowers your stress levels by making even the biggest projects seem manageable and actionable.

## Waiting For

Waiting For items are responsibilities of yours that are currently out of your hands. Therefore, your only responsibility with them is to ensure that you don't forget them! Managing Waiting For items without an effective system in place requires a lot of mental effort because your brain can't always easily recall things the way you wish it could. Wouldn't it be nice if you could always think of exactly what you wanted to say to someone just at the moment you see that person? All of us have had the maddening experience of saying, "I can't remember what I wanted to tell you."

Some examples of Waiting For items include the following:

▶ Hearing back from your co-worker regarding information requested by the client

▶ Receiving information from the client in order to start the new assignment on time

▶ Waiting for the sales figures in order to complete month-end reports

If you collect everything you're waiting for in one place that you can consult when you're feeling uneasy, you can eliminate a great mental burden. It's especially helpful if you maintain this list using an electronic tool that can remind you of responsibilities at just the right moment. Some electronic tools even take advantage of geo-location services, so you can get a reminder to buy bread when you arrive at the grocery store!

You can consult your Waiting For list before you leave the office for the day, for the weekend, or before a vacation, and you'll know exactly where everything stands while you are away. This helps ensure that nothing falls through the cracks, that you keep your commitments to others, and that you hold people accountable their commitments to you.

## Talk To

When you have a lot of recurring interaction with someone, personally or professionally, you often think of things that you want or need to share with that person the next time you talk. When these items occur to you, most people exercise one of the following options:

- ▶ Call or email that person every time you think of something, which could result in multiple messages back and forth for both of you.
- ▶ Go to see that person (if he or she is in close proximity) every time you think of something.
- ▶ Tuck the thought away with the intention of sharing the information the next time you see the person.

The first two options are disrupting, distracting, and inefficient for both of you. The third option puts an unnecessary burden on your brain, and probably won't go according to plan anyway.

A more effective option is to create a Talk To list that includes the people with whom you work closely or communicate frequently. As you think of things you need to communicate to a person, create tasks that start with his or her name (in the subject line if you're using an electronic tool) along with whatever you need to say to them. For example, a Talk To task might look like the following: "Joe: Ask his opinion on the pricing for the client proposal."

When you see that person throughout your day, you can refer to your Talk To list to ensure that you have covered all the items you thought of while you were not in his or her presence. If the other person has a list for you as well, this process results in very efficient and effective communication. This is especially helpful if you have people reporting to you.

> **NOTE** If you think of something you need to communicate to someone you will *not* likely run into during your regular daily activities, then the item is a Next Action, not a Talk To.

## Future

Future items are those activities (Projects or Next Actions) that you have decided you are definitely going to do, but you're not going to do them right now. Capturing items on your Future list is an effective way to avoid forgetting them while still maintaining your focus in the *present*. As time goes by, you can capture details related to Future items in the Notes section of the task (assuming you are using an electronic to-do list), so all pertinent information is ready and waiting for you when it comes time to move that Project or Next Action from Future to the appropriate list.

## Someday/Maybe

Someday/Maybe items seem like a good idea at the moment, but you haven't decided if you actually want to take action on them, and you know that you definitely are not going to take action anytime soon. A Someday/Maybe list gives you a place to capture dreams, ambitions, interesting ideas, and so on. Keeping a Someday/Maybe list helps you live your life purposefully—you do things or you don't do things based on actively deciding, rather than remembering or forgetting about them.

## Location

The final category, Location, is used for tasks that can only be completed while you are in a specific location. Your Next Action list should only contain items that you are able to complete while you are in the physical location where you typically work, but you probably spend time at other places besides where you work.

> **NOTE**   If you work in an office, your Next Action list might include items that are personal in nature, but because you can complete them while you are in your office, they belong on your Next Action list (for example, making a phone call to your child's school).

If there are tasks that you can only complete when you are physically in a specific location, then categorize these tasks by each location where you spend time.

For example, a list of tasks categorized as Home should not contain a phone call that you can make from the office, but it would contain an item such as "Change the light bulb in the garage." This is because if you put "change the light bulb in the garage" on your Next Action list, but you typically complete items on your Next Action list when you are at work, then it is inefficient to see a task when you're at work that you can't complete unless you *aren't* at work.

Perhaps your company has an office in another city to which you frequently travel. If you want to complete some tasks that can only be done while you are there, it would be helpful to categorize tasks by that location. Here are some examples that are categorized by location:

Home

- ► Change light bulb in garage
- ► Collect food to donate at soup kitchen
- ► Clean filter in HVAC unit

Cleveland Office

- ► Take sales manager out to lunch
- ► Update software on Cleveland server
- ► Drop in on Cleveland's top three clients

Categorizing by location ensures that you don't waste time looking at things you are unable to act on, helps maintain your focus in the present, and prevents you from forgetting to complete activities that need to be done when you are at another location. One example of a location list might be Errands—those tasks that require a trip to a specific location to complete, such as "pick up dry cleaning." Removing errands from your Next Action list allows you to ignore them in moments you can't complete them (like while you're at the office) but keep them handy to make your trips around town efficient.

Organizing your to-do list using the categories described in this section enables you to continually and consistently take immediate and appropriate action—whether you have 5 minutes or 5 hours of proactive time.

The next section gives you the last piece you need to understand about your to-do lists before you can move on to actually *making* these lists and learning where to store them.

# GETTING SPECIFIC

As you get details out of your head and into your lists, one very important point to remember is to be specific when you enter the items. Otherwise, you are less likely to take action on them. If you're not careful, how you record to-do items might be another way that you sabotage your own productivity instead of support it.

When most people write things down, they often use a personal shorthand to trigger the exact action they need to take. This trigger is usually abbreviated because you only have a vague idea of the action that needs to be taken. Take a look at the following example of a typical to-do list:

expense report

Joe – budget?

bday card

order shirts

check to school

deal with the study

plan the meeting

garage!!

clients – W9s

▶ Speed bumps are habits that interfere with your productivity by slowing you down. They sabotage rather than support you.

You probably move quickly through your busy day in a hectic environment. A list like this example reflects what I call speed bumps. Remember from the last chapter that in order to empower your productivity, you need to be aware of the best use of your time at any moment in order to take immediate and appropriate action.

If your workday is full and hectic, your opportunities to get things done probably occur in very short windows—10 minutes before the next meeting, 30 minutes in the early morning before everyone else arrives, a relative lull during the lunch hour. If this is the case, a list like the preceding one slows you down because the time it takes you to read all these items, figure out exactly what needs to be done, and then choose one will eat up some or most of the time you had to complete a task! Also, having to stop and think about a list like this contributes to the feeling of being overwhelmed because taking the time to decipher something seems like a luxury you can't afford. Even if you do relish the idea of a few minutes to stop and think, deciphering your to-do list is not the best use of that brainpower.

When you add an item to your list, take a few extra seconds to enter it in a way that will enable you to take immediate action on it as soon as you decide to do so. This is one way in which categorization is helpful. When you find yourself with unscheduled, proactive time, you can consult your Next Action list, which should contain *only* items that you can take immediate action on. However, you can only take immediate action if you have already determined *exactly* what action needs to be taken. In other words, you need to ensure that the items on your Next Action list are *actionable*.

Compare the previous list to the following updated version, which now contains items entered in a way that enables you to take immediate action:

| BEFORE | AFTER |
| --- | --- |
| Expense report | Enter receipts into spreadsheet |
| Joe – budget? | Email Joe for budget numbers |
| Deal with the study | Put a link to the study on the website |
| Bday card | Look up address for the envelope in phone book |

Note how the second list is much more actionable than the original list, whose items are hard to decipher. Conversely, in two minutes or less, you could very likely dash off an email to Joe or look up the address for the birthday card. When you eliminate any obstacles to completing the tasks on your Next Action list (speed bumps), you greatly increase the likelihood of getting more things done.

Do this by ensuring that every item on your Next Action list starts with an *actionable* verb. Eliminate vague words such as "plan," "implement," and "develop" because vague words act like speed bumps, which means you're likely to skip the item. Save those vague words for your Projects list, which should contain items that aren't immediately actionable by themselves. For example, "implement new order entry system" is a Project and by itself is not immediately actionable, whereas "call the software company to set date for training on new order entry system" might be a Next Action for that Project, and it *is* immediately actionable. The following two lists show a few examples of the difference. The column on the left contains vague verbs that suffice for your Projects list but not your Next Action list; and the column on the right contains actionable verbs that are appropriate for your Next Action list.

| PROJECTS LIST VERBS | NEXT ACTION LIST VERBS |
| --- | --- |
| Plan | Call |
| Develop | Write |
| Implement | Email |

# SUMMARY

I find that most of the items that keep people from sleeping at night are the things that need *doing*—the things that don't lend themselves well to a calendar. An effective and logical to-do list is often the weak link in an individual's efforts to keep their lives organized and on track.

Remember that you can only manage what you can see, and you can only see what's outside your head. You must first empty your mind of all the things that "you need to remember." All the commitments, communication, and information that you must manage to keep your life and work running smoothly must be stored in some external location, so that you can view, organize, sort, and otherwise manage it.

After getting the information out of your head, you must organize it categorically and enter it on your lists using specific language in order to make it manageable and actionable.

This chapter has given you the information you need to control the constant mental chatter, stop your mind from spinning, and ease the burden on your brain that causes stress and anxiety. Time-related things belong on a calendar, action items belong on a to-do list, and reference information belongs in appropriate locations such as email folders, contact lists, and computer and paper files.

There is more detailed information about effective use of your calendar and efficient storage of your reference information throughout the book, specifically in Chapters 5, 7, 8, and 13.

## QUICK TIPS

The following are some important points from this chapter (also suitable for tweeting). For more information on Twitter, including relevant usernames and hashtags, please refer to the "Read This First" chapter.

- ▶ The brain is a lousy file cabinet—quit trying to remember!

- ▶ You can only manage what you can see, and you can only see what is outside of your head.

- ▶ Your best thinking doesn't come from a stressed-out brain! Control the mental chatter to lower stress!

- ▶ Organizing categorically is the best option to bring peak productivity to your to-do list.

- ▶ Is your calendar full of things you keep moving to next week? Weak connection to time = not on calendar!

## CHAPTER 5

# Supplementing Brainpower with Technology

The last chapter made the case that your head is not the best storage mechanism for all of your life's details. Our brain is not good at memorizing and accessing details on demand. We can't always remember exactly what we need, exactly when we need it, and the constant mental gymnastics only add to our stress. Therefore, a "tool" is necessary—someplace reliable where you can store all these details.

Until the late 1990s, most professionals relied on paper tools to organize their work—typically some combination of one or more calendars, address books, and note pages. Some people carried all those items in one paper-based system, often zipped up inside a binder, while others made do with a desk or wall calendar, a separate address book, and some pads of paper or notebooks. These days, the accessibility of electronic devices has rendered most of these systems obsolete. And the complexity of your life demands processes and tools that are equal to the challenge.

These tools, often called *personal information managers (PIMs)*, are available in many different forms, and finding the one that is right for you can be a challenge. Indeed, merely looking at all the options can send you scurrying back to your tried-and-true system. Most of us have very ingrained habits regarding how we deal with commitments, communication, and information, but the rapidly changing pace of business and technology can send those old habits into a tailspin. In this chapter, you can assess whether the tools you are currently using are actually working for you; and if they aren't, you will learn about some useful alternatives.

# NECESSARY COMPONENTS OF A GOOD SET OF PRODUCTIVITY TOOLS

The first factor to consider when choosing a PIM is that you are most effective when you can store everything in one place. By "everything," I mean the following:

▶ Calendar

▶ To-do list

▶ Contacts

▶ Notes

Calendar items and task (or to-do list) items are described in the previous chapter, but in this section I'm sharing a few more factors to consider for each, including the specifics of *contacts* and *notes*.

## Calendar

There is a distinct difference between calendar items and task (to-do list) items. As mentioned in Chapter 4, tasks have a *weak* relationship to time. A calendar is a time-based tool for organizing items that have a *strong* relationship to time, such as birthdays or meetings.

Events or tasks that involve someone other than yourself typically have the strongest relationship to time. You might skip a workout to sleep in on Saturday morning, but you probably wouldn't leave a friend stranded on the racquetball court. Conversely, some tasks have a weak relationship to time. These are tasks that you would *like* to do today, and which you might intend to do today, but in fact there would be no consequences if you did them tomorrow, or the next day, or even later.

Because busy people have many responsibilities that have a weak relationship to time, this is the weakness of relying heavily or exclusively on time-based organization for your life. Everyone has meetings and appointments, certainly, so a calendar is necessary. However, using *only* a calendar requires you to work much harder to manage your life than necessary. You probably have many more things on your to-do list than appointments on your calendar. You can tell when a task has a weak relationship to time if you find yourself moving it to the next day on your calendar to remind yourself to do it "today."

You should certainly use a calendar to manage items that have a strong relationship to time. An electronic calendar has many advantages over a paper calendar, as it enables you to easily move things around, set reminders and alerts, and share your schedule with others.

# Tasks

Unlike calendar items, which happen at a specific time, you probably have many things to do that have a weaker relationship to time—meaning you have some discretion as to when they get done. They might have a due date at some point in the future, or no due date at all, but they are still important to complete. I find it useful to treat these items as tasks and add them to your list, which is grouped by the categories covered in Chapter 4.

Even if you do this, however, you might still end up with a very long, and very overwhelming, Next Actions list. This is common because we often feel like everything needs to be done, and everything is important! The following sections describe three specific ways you can make your Next Actions list manageable.

## TASK CATEGORIES: NEXT ACTIONS VERSUS FUTURE

Just because you can do something now doesn't mean that you *need* to do it now. When you review all the things that you are tempted to put on your Next Actions list, ask yourself, "Given everything else that's important, is this task something that I should, or realistically can, accomplish anytime soon?" If you decide that the task needs to be done but realistically you can admit that it's not pressing enough for you to be considering right now, then give it a category of Future, instead of Next Actions. If you fear forgetting that it's there, then simply create a reminder.

For example, suppose you read about a great new sales technique that you'd like to implement. When you assess your priorities, you realize that you really don't have the opportunity to give it the attention it deserves for at least a couple of months. In that case, add the item to your list with a category of "Future," and a reminder date for perhaps two months from now. When the reminder pops up, reassess whether or not it realistically fits into your workload in the next month or so. If it does, then change the category from Future to Next Actions. Otherwise, leave it with the Future category, change the reminder to another point in the future, and follow the same process when it pops up again. This practice helps to keep your Next Actions list manageable and realistic, and is closely related to the next technique I recommend.

## SORTING BY PRIORITY: ABC DOESN'T WORK

Many people prioritize their work using a rating system such as ABC (or 123, or High-Low-Medium), assuming that it provides a quick way to decide what needs to be done next.

Unfortunately, chances are good that everything you write down is important to you. In fact, the main reason you write tasks down (or enter them on an electronic list) is because they are weighing on your mind and you don't want to forget them. The things that aren't important don't even make it onto your list, so almost everything gets the highest priority; and if you do happen to assign a lower priority to some items, they never get done, unless and until something happens to make them a higher priority. In other words, ABC doesn't work.

When you want to prioritize your work, order your tasks by due date, using the date you'd like to have the task completed by. Although a given date may be arbitrary, using due dates helps you see when the amount of work you've assigned to a day is unrealistic, therefore enabling you to spread them out appropriately over the coming days and weeks.

> **WARNING**  Some people make the mistake of assigning the task to an appointment on the calendar for the arbitrary due date they selected. Picking an arbitrary due date for a task does not give it a stronger relationship to time, so entering that task on your *calendar* just artificially clutters your calendar.

Some people make the mistake of then entering the task on their calendar for that arbitrary due date they selected. If you pick an arbitrary due date for a task, and then enter that task on your calendar, it creates several problems:

- ▶ It artificially clutters your calendar.
- ▶ It's common to be overly optimistic about all the things you can get done in a day, so you're faced with the task of having to remember to move the things that you neglected to do on a given day. But your other days have their own agendas, and your undone tasks start to pile up.

▶ It sets you up to start the day focusing on the things you failed to accomplish yesterday, which is not very motivating.

▶ There will come a time when you forget to move something that you didn't do and then it won't get done. This is called "slipping through the cracks," and you want to minimize the potential for that to happen. So, prioritize by due date, but do it on your task list and not your calendar.

Chapter 6 includes specific instructions for creating your lists. In that chapter, I'll remind you to assign a due date to all of the tasks on your Next Actions list. You'll be tempted to put "today" for many things, but it will quickly become apparent that there are only so many hours in the day. Inevitably, you'll assign too many tasks to a given due date, and after that dates passes the task will turn red (in most electronic tools), but that's okay. The next day, re-assess your overdue (red) tasks in the context of the items you've assigned to that day. What seemed really important yesterday might seem less so today. In some cases, though, an item might still seem very important, and you'll realize that you have to bump one or more of the tasks that were scheduled for today.

After a few days' time, you'll realize approximately how many things you can complete in an average day, and you can parse out your to-do list accordingly. For example, let's say you have 25 things on your Next Actions list, indicating that all of them are high-priority tasks. However, now you know from experience that because of meetings, interruptions, and other things that need your immediate attention, you can actually complete only four or five tasks in an average day. Therefore, planning for five tasks today, five tasks tomorrow, and so on means that some of those high priorities won't actually get done for *at least five days*.

This rather shocking realization forces you to recognize that you have to make some adjustments, whether that's canceling some meetings to buy more time for tasks, working more hours—at least for a short time to get caught up—or getting help and/or requesting extensions on deadlines.

Knowing whether reality is likely to conform to your expectations about what you can accomplish gives you many advantages. It helps you to head off potential crises, enables you to plan appropriately, and reduces your stress, which is often caused by the pressure of trying to get everything done, wondering whether you will, and imagining what bad things will happen if you don't.

Prioritizing by due date helps you manage a long (and sometimes overwhelming) list by focusing only on the most critical things for that day. You can relax because you are in control of not only what you are currently doing, but everything else that *isn't* being done.

## CREATING POSITIVE HABITS

In order to keep your task list and your calendar manageable, it's important to recognize that there is a difference between a recurring task or appointment and a habit.

Are you trying to remember to do a random task that must get done periodically, or are you trying to create a new habit for your work or personal life? For example, what's the best way to remember to do a weekly expense report, get yourself to exercise as much as you think you should, or find the time to read those books piling up on your nightstand? Unfortunately, simply putting something on your calendar or your task list doesn't mean that it will definitely happen.

▶ For more on minimizing the energy it takes to get things done, check out The Power of Full Engagement by Tony Schwartz, and this article from the Harvard Business Review: http://blogs .hbr.org/schwartz/ 2011/05/the-only-way- to-get-important.html.

The best way to remember to do something new is to make it as automatic as you can. Find creative ways to ensure that the new behavior occurs. Studies show that it takes at least 30 days for a new behavior to become a habit. It's also much easier to do things that don't require any thought, because those take less energy. Ask yourself, "What's standing in the way of this happening?" and set yourself up so that any new behaviors happen as automatically as possible. Trying to create a habit of working out in the morning? Set your alarm clock on the shelf across the room. Lay out your exercise clothes the night before. Make plans with a friend to meet you at the gym. Pay for a class or a personal training session. All of these things increase the likelihood that you will actually do the workout you scheduled on your calendar; and every time you do something you scheduled, the more likely you are to do it again—and again—until it becomes a habit just like brushing your teeth. Brainstorm other ways to make your new behaviors routine, easy, and requiring no thought. Creating a new habit is not as easy as creating a recurring appointment in your calendar or on your task list, but there *are* ways to bring new and beneficial habits into your life.

## Contacts

The contacts section of any productivity tool is primarily a storage place for contact details. Some tasks relate directly to contacts, such as making a phone call or sending an email, and these should be captured in your task list.

Be careful, however, not to store vital contact information *only* in your task list. Otherwise, when you've completed and checked off that item, you could lose easy access to information you might need in the future.

Certain professions may require more sophisticated tools, such as a Customer Relationship Manager (CRM), like Act! or SalesForce, to track sales opportunities, call histories, and complex organizational charts. If you are considering a contact management solution, I suggest that you look at it within the context of your overall productivity and the three other areas of your process: your calendar, tasks, and notes. Before you consider a complicated CRM, consider how your process for using this tool will work within your overall productivity methodology.

Whatever electronic tool you select, be sure you fully understand how to use all the features. You may find that the features you were seeking in a CRM are already available to you in your PIM. There is more about CRMs in Chapter 15.

▶ For a "how-to" video on some of the features of the Contacts section of Microsoft Outlook, visit http:// regainyourtime.com/ outlook/do-you-need- a-crm/.

## Notes

The important thing to remember about notes is that they serve as reference material. Reference materials are things that do not currently require action. Notes give you a place to capture ideas, instructions, lists, even project details; but if an item requires action, it belongs on your task list.

Like the other types of information, you first organize reference information by location. You probably store it in different locations depending on the type of information. If it's contact information, for example, you organize it in your address book (paper) or contacts (electronic), and then you add the next level of alphabetical organization. You probably also have reference information located in your email folders, your computer folders, and your paper files, to name a few.

Some notes are useful to have on hand at all times, such as instructions, lists (shopping lists, books to read, movies to watch, and so on—in case you unexpectedly find yourself at the grocery store, the bookstore, or the movie rental location), and any information you haven't memorized that you require to complete your tasks. Therefore, it's handy to have a Notes component in your PIM.

# CHOOSING THE MOST RELEVANT TOOLS

In the past, paper-based planners and planning tools, such as calendars and address books, were the only option for managing the details of our lives. Today, in addition to paper, the options for electronic tools are overwhelming. This section is designed to help you make the selection that's best for you.

## Drawbacks of Paper

Those paper-based productivity binders described earlier are still around as an option, but the vast majority of paper-based planners available today are basically a calendar with a few other simple organizational aids, such as memo paper. Although a calendar is necessary, as I outlined in the last chapter, most of the details that you need to manage in order to run your life smoothly are not time-based.

Therefore, using a task list with categorical organization improves efficiency. If you are determined to use a paper-based tool, then there is one on the market I can recommend that is organized categorically, instead of by time. This paper-based planner is from Time/system International (www.timesystem.com). Although you can run your life successfully with a Time/system planner, I still believe that the disadvantages of paper far outweigh the advantages of electronic tools, and those advantages are growing quickly.

A handwritten list on paper is simply no match for all the ways in which modern technology has conspired to distract us. In your work environment, you are probably facing at least one computer screen (maybe two), a screen on your handheld device, and maybe even a screen on your desk phone and a television or two, depending on your industry—all cleverly designed to steal your attention. Unfortunately, your handwritten list cannot compete with fun and engaging technology.

Other drawbacks of paper include the following:

▶  You can't "back up" paper.

▶  You typically have only one "copy" of your paper system.

▶  A paper system is bigger and heavier to carry around.

In addition to addressing the problems of a paper system, an electronic tool enables you to easily assign categories to your items, shuffle priorities, modify due dates, and quickly handle other details more easily than you can using paper. Perhaps the most useful benefit of an electronic task list is reminders that can flash/ring/vibrate or otherwise compete with all the other *unwelcome* distractions you are subjected to daily, reminding you to focus on your significant results.

## Considerations for Choosing Electronic Tools

For the reasons I outlined in the preceding section, I suggest an electronic tool—along with a growing list of new features and improvements they include. However, the difficulty is that there are many tools on the market, and most of them are very specialized, meaning they focus on only one or two of the four components mentioned earlier (Calendar, To-Do List, Contacts, and Notes). In addition, the tools vary based on operating platform, so it is important to select a product that integrates with your needs: PC-based, Mac-based, or even cross-platform, which might be better served residing "in the cloud" (online). Although this plethora of options can seem overwhelming when you are faced with the task of assembling your own set of tools, take a deep breath and relax. The following sections put these options in perspective.

## LOCAL OR CLOUD?

Your first consideration when selecting an electronic tool is your computing platform. If you will be storing the information locally, then you'll most likely be choosing from tools for the Windows operating system or the Mac operating system, which are the two platforms we'll focus on in this book.

The qualities that are advantages to storing your information locally on your computer can also be viewed as disadvantages. For example, when you store your information in the cloud, you are dependent on a remote server that you don't control. In theory, your data is accessible to you anywhere you have an Internet connection. In reality, there could be times when it's unavailable to you, either because the server is down or because you don't have Internet access. If your information is stored locally, it is in your control, and you have it as long as you have your computer or access to your computer. However, you are responsible for backing it up and keeping it secure from "hacking" and information theft. Similarly, it might be harder to share your information with family or co-workers if you store it locally, but that could also mean you're able to keep your information more private.

The bottom line is that there is no right or wrong solution when deciding between local or online storage of the information necessary to manage your life. The many factors involved in the decision are changing rapidly with advances by Google, Microsoft, and Apple. Factors such as safety, security, access, features, and personal preference will all affect your decision-making process. In this chapter I talk about some important considerations when selecting your tools, and in Chapter 7 I give you specific instructions for implementing the Empowered Productivity™ System with each of your likely electronic choices.

## SMARTPHONE VERSUS DESKTOP

The next thing to consider is how and where you're going to input your data. Will you rely on a desktop computer or a handheld device as your primary entry tool? You are most productive when you can refer to your details on the go, which means something small, light, and portable, such as a smartphone, increases your productivity.

However, I don't recommend using your smartphone or similar device as your only tool, or even your primary tool, unless you are rarely at a desk or workspace. Currently, smartphones are still designed as data-reference tools, not data-entry tools. Until we have smartphones that offer easy entry of large quantities of data, I suggest that you use a computer as your primary entry device, and access the information on your smartphone when you are on the go.

## SEPARATE OR INTEGRATED PROGRAMS

As I mentioned earlier, storing everything in one place increases your efficiency. Some people consider the "one place" to be anywhere on their computer, but you can do better than that. If everything is on your computer but it's located in several different programs and/or documents, that's not as efficient as having everything in one place. The fewer places you have to look to keep track of the details of your life, the easier and more efficient it is to manage.

If you're using an electronic tool, be sure to consider incorporating the four components listed earlier:

- ▶ Calendar
- ▶ To-Do list
- ▶ Contacts
- ▶ Notes

and also a fifth component:

- ▶ Email

Although email is only one of many different communication methods, it's still currently the one most frequently used. Despite new social media platforms and applications designed for the business community, their popularity has not yet overtaken or replaced email.

Because so many tasks arrive via email, it's helpful if your email client can integrate seamlessly with your task list and your calendar, which is why it's helpful if all these items are in one program.

Microsoft Outlook is a powerful tool, although most users only access a fraction of its potential. Not only does Outlook handle all five components very well, you can

▶ This might sound like I am recommending Outlook. Not necessarily—read on.

easily integrate them (creating a task from an email, or creating birthdays in the calendar from the contacts, for example.)

If you're using the Windows platform, I think that Microsoft Outlook is currently the best option. In addition to the advantages just listed, it's virtually free for most people because Microsoft Office is such a widely used product, and Outlook is included with popular versions of Microsoft Office. I explain exactly how to implement the Empowered Productivity System into Outlook in Chapter 7.

Microsoft offers a version of Outlook for the Mac platform, but it is not quite as robust as the Windows version. In addition, I have found that there is a greater potential for problems when Mac users stray from tools that are designed specifically for the Mac.

If you're a dedicated Mac user (like me), don't worry! I've devised a way to implement the Empowered Productivity System using tools that are part of the Mac operating system, and it doesn't lack any of the important components that I've outlined. Because these tools are native to the Mac operating system, they have the added benefit of a lower potential for technical problems. This gives you the best of both worlds: the ease and technology of a Mac computer and an integrated set of tools that supports your personal productivity needs.

> **NOTE** If you prefer the Mac platform, my recommendation for tools includes Apple Mail, iCal, and Address Book, which are all part of the Mac OS.

For those people who prefer to work in the cloud, Google Apps is a common choice. The program includes Google Calendar, Tasks, Contacts, and Gmail, and is relatively simple to use. Provided you have an Internet connection, you can access them from anywhere and easily share them with others. Google Apps does have some drawbacks (which I discuss in detail in Chapter 7) that makes it a little less efficient than Outlook and the Mac tools, so you should compare each product's features with your own requirements.

I explain how to implement the Empowered Productivity System into Outlook, Mac, and Google tools in Chapter 7, where I clearly illustrate the advantages and disadvantages of each set of tools.

See Figure 5-1 for a summary of these tools and my opinions of each component.

| As of January 2012 | Outlook | Apple OS X Tools | Google |
|---|---|---|---|
| Calendar | Good | Good | Good |
| Ease of syncing with a smartphone | Good | Good | Good |
|  |  |  |  |
| Tasks | Good | Good | Poor |
| Ease of syncing with a smartphone | Good | Good | Poor |
|  |  |  |  |
| Contacts | Good | Good | Good |
| Ease of syncing with a smartphone | Good | Good | Good |
|  |  |  |  |
| Notes | Good | Fair | Poor |
| Ease of syncing with a smartphone | Fair (depends on phone) | Fair (depends on phone) | Poor |
| Email | Good | Good | Good |
| Ease of syncing with a smartphone | Good | Good | Good |
|  |  |  |  |
| Easy integration of above with each other | Good | Fair* | Fair |
| Share calendars and contacts with others | Fair (paid option) | Fair | Good |
| Accessible from anywhere | Fair (paid option) | Good | Good |
| Easy to back up and restore | Poor | Good | Poor |
| Control | Good | Good | Fair** |

*The integration of each of the OS X tools with each other is rather clunky. However, a third-party software called MailTags makes this integration very easy and smooth. I discuss this in more detail in Chapter 7.

**I suggest that your control over Google tools is fair because Google has recently released an app that allows you to access your Google tools when you're offline, but only if you are using the Google Chrome browser.

**FIGURE 5-1**

# WHY TOOLS ARE NOT ENOUGH

Having the right support tools is obviously important, but what really matters is the process: specifically how, when, and why you use the tools. To use an analogy, having the fanciest set of clubs on the course doesn't make you the best golfer. You can think of adopting a good process in terms of having a good golf swing; it's what you do with the clubs that makes the difference. The better your process, the farther your tools will take you in a given workday.

The process is the secret to using any tools successfully. You could have all the latest gadgets and a whole arsenal of apps, but unless you have a methodology—a step-by-step process for using these tools to effectively manage all the details—you'll be just another hacker on the golf course. The process is often the part of a productivity system that's the most difficult to learn, which is why the majority of this book is dedicated to the methodology instead of just being a software how-to guide. Having a methodology means that when you do feel overwhelmed you know exactly how to quickly regain control.

# SUMMARY

At this point, I hope you are convinced that your memory is not the best place to manage the details of your life. I hope, too, that I have inspired you to think about how to organize those details in a meaningful and logical way. This chapter outlined the information you need to assess your own situation and determine which set of productivity tools will meet your needs.

In the coming chapters, you learn how to implement the Empowered Productivity System methodology that puts the support tool of your choice to work.

# QUICK TIPS

The following are some important points from this chapter (also suitable for tweeting). For more information on Twitter, including relevant usernames and hashtags, please refer to the "Read This First" chapter.

▶ If you'd like to do it today, but could still do it tomorrow or the next day, put it on your task list, not your calendar.

▶ Productivity Tip: Put "Future" tasks (beyond a month) on a different list to enable yourself to focus on your "right now" goals.

▶ Productivity Tip: Prioritize your tasks using due dates–forget flags, ABC, and High-Med-Low.

▶ Smartphones make better data-reference tools than data-entry tools. Plan your productivity process accordingly.

▶ Mac add-on MailTags integrates iCal + Apple Mail into a productivity rock star.

## CHAPTER 6

# Clearing Your Mind *Now*

By now I hope you are convinced that the secret to peak personal productivity is *not* memorizing all the details of where you need to be and what you need to do. Removing this mental burden is a key factor in lowering your stress levels, and there is another important technique—taking vacation so you have some "down time"! The first part of this chapter illustrates just how necessary down time is to being more productive and achieving your significant results. I also share some ways to minimize the disruption when you are out of the office and maximize your opportunities to unplug.

The Empowered Productivity™ System can be broken into two parts: clearing your mind and clearing your space. The sections of this chapter teach you to implement the "clearing your mind" phase of the process, which is the first step to getting started. I give you the specific instructions to clear your mind using the *brain dump* technique to begin shifting the management of your details from your brain (and whatever collection of things you've been using until this point—sticky notes, pads of paper, random notebooks, etc) into your new "personal information management" tools.

## YOU NEED A VACATION. . .

A "spinning" brain that keeps you awake at night is one of the more noticeable symptoms of the effort it takes to mentally manage the details of your life, and the pressure it causes is insidious. Most people don't recognize how much stress they are under until they *aren't* under it anymore, which is usually when they are away on vacation. American workers have less paid vacation time than virtually all of our European counterparts, and we *use* far less available vacation time than workers in any other country.

According to a 2010 study, only 57 percent of Americans use all their vacation time.[1] This means that most of us are not taking nearly enough time to recharge, refresh, and rejuvenate. Studies show that vacation is good for your cardiovascular health and your waistline, lowers your cortisol levels and your blood pressure, and may aid in recovery from diseases such as cancer. It's clear that skipping vacation can actually put your physical, mental, and fiscal health at risk.[2] Tim Ferriss, author of *The 4-Hour Workweek*, sums it up best when he says, "The average American spends more time in the bathroom than on vacation."[3]

If you are part of the minority who do manage to take a week-long break from time to time, you might feel like one week isn't enough. Most people rush around in the days before leaving to complete all the tasks necessary to prepare to be out of the office, which means beginning vacation with heightened stress. Consequently, it takes longer to unwind. Often, it's hard to leave the office completely behind, and for the first few days you might worry about what you've left unfinished. (Even worse, many people continue to check their voicemail and email.) It might be day three or four before you start to relax, which might last until day five or six, when you start to stress over what will be waiting for you when you return! All of that is assuming that you *don't* work while you're away, which many people do!

If you're the type of person who has a hard time unplugging and getting the most out of your time away from the office, consider the following productivity tips to help you clear your mind when you *are* out of the office:

▶ Be sure to put an out-of-office message on your voicemail and email—even if you are only out for a day or two—to relieve the pressure you might feel to stay on top of messages while you're gone. If you know that you have alerted people to your absence, you're more likely to allow yourself some breathing room and actually take a break from your work communication.

► If you're going to be out for more than a day or two, change your voicemail and email out-of-office messages to say that you'll be gone one day *before* you actually leave. This gives you a little cushion to temper the increased stress before you leave. It might give you a few extra undisturbed hours to tie up loose ends.

► Program your messages to also say that you get back one day *after* you actually return, to help alleviate the pressure you feel on the last day or two of your vacation. Knowing you have one extra day upon your return to get up to speed before people expect to hear from you makes your reentry quite a bit less chaotic. It's always better to under-promise and over-deliver; people would rather hear from you before they expect to than not get a reply until days after they know you have returned.

► *These suggestions for cushioning your out-of-office reply are not meant to deceive people; they serve to set appropriate expectations with others.*

# BEGIN YOUR MOVE

I explained in Chapter 4 why it's important to empty your mind of all of the details necessary to keep your life running smoothly. Because your brain is not obedient, thoughts jump into your mind unbidden and often at inopportune moments when you can't act on them.

Perhaps you're trying to focus on a client proposal, but you suddenly find yourself thinking about an expense report you need to submit. Or you're having dinner with your family and you realize that you forgot to respond to an important email message. For most people, these nagging thoughts are the the typical way they remember important tasks. These are the *internal* distractions that keep your mind racing and prevent you from being able to do the following:

► Control your attention

► Be present in the moment

► Focus on the task at hand

The only way to quiet your mind is to capture these thoughts and enter them into your workflow management process so that you can take action at the appropriate time. This is the first step to getting started with the Empowered Productivity System.

It's a challenge to empty your brain, and it takes an organized process to create a habit of keeping your commitments, communication, and information somewhere other than in your head.

An analogy for undertaking this new productivity process is the time I moved out of my apartment and into my new house, which was close to where I currently lived.

I had almost two months left on the lease for my apartment, and I had already closed on the house. I thought this overlap would allow me to leisurely move things a little at a time, and then call a mover for the big furniture after I'd moved the smaller items.

It only took me a week to learn what a bad idea that was. First I moved the things I didn't use often or currently, such as holiday decorations, winter clothes, infrequently used appliances, beach chairs, and tools. The closer I got to the things I used often, the more disruptive the move became. It was hard to prepare meals at either location because half the kitchen supplies were in each place. It was hard to dress properly because somehow one specific article for every outfit was in the wrong location. It never failed that whatever I needed at the house was at the apartment, and whatever I needed at the apartment was at the house. It quickly became very frustrating to be "in between homes."

You can apply this analogy to the task of moving from your old way of managing your life to the Empowered Productivity System. Being "in between" two ways of doing things is inefficient, and it makes it harder to create habits of the new process. Therefore, get started when you have some time to devote to the process. Don't worry; you won't need *days* to get started. After selecting your tool (refer to Chapter 5), you might need two or three hours to complete the first exercise—the brain dump—and then organize your information into your tool or tools of choice.

# UNLEASHING YOUR INNER GENIUS

Because you can only manage what you can see, and you can only see what's outside your head, the first step to regaining control over the details of your life is to pull all those nagging to-dos, commitments, and other things you're trying to remember out of every corner of your brain. I suggest you do this through what is called a *brain dump*. You may choose to use a pad of paper and a pen, a word processing document, or a spreadsheet to complete this exercise; but if you use a computer program, disengage from the Internet to avoid the potential for distraction.

Go to a quiet place and create a list of anything that comes to mind with regard to things you need to do or remember. Capture your free flow of thoughts, using one line per item. Don't censor the items and don't try to organize them; just write down all the things that are weighing on your mind as they come to you.

At first you'll probably be able to capture quite a bit before you even start to slow down; but keep in mind that our brains don't organize our thoughts in such a way that we can remember exactly what we need to remember, exactly when we need to remember it. Consequently, the initial geyser of items eventually turns into a trickle, and at that point you may need some help.

When your thoughts start to slow down, and you feel like you could use a little help peeking into those recesses of your brain where you've stuffed everything, it's time to make use of some personal and professional Brain Dump Prompts. You can find them in the Resources section of the book website at www.personal-productivity-secrets.com. As you read each item on the lists, pause to see if it prompts anything for you. If so, capture anything that comes to mind on your list. If not, move on to the next item.

After completing the activity with the Brain Dump Prompts, you'll feel like you have truly captured everything you're responsible for, everything that's been weighing on your mind, and everything you've been trying to remember about things you need to do.

Next, you can start to organize it, to make sense of it—to *control* it. It's hard to break old habits, so for a while these items may still weigh on your mind; but after you begin to use and rely on the Empowered Productivity System, you'll find yourself relaxing. When you free your brain of nagging details, you lower your stress levels.

Getting these details off your mind has added benefits, such as more clarity, more patience, and more ability to manage your attention. You may also notice more energy and motivation for higher-level mental processes—your "inner genius" activities—such as problem solving, brainstorming, idea generation, and critical thinking. The next section gives you a little more information about your brain dump, and then Chapter 7 explains exactly what to do with your list, and how to migrate it into your tool or tools.

## MANAGE ONE LIFE, NOT TWO

The brain dump prompt lists are designed to help you remember all your commitments, communications, and information related to both your personal life *and* your professional life. This is because you are most efficient and effective when you recognize that you have one life rather than two separate lives. The implications of global business and advanced technology mean that professionals often find themselves handling work responsibilities on personal time and handling personal responsibilities during work hours. If you're self-employed or a business owner, you probably can't even see the line where your professional life ends and your personal life begins!

Given this merging of our personal and professional commitments, communication, and information, when you try to segregate personal from professional you work harder than necessary to stay in control of everything. If you work at a company where information is very tightly controlled, highly regulated, or subject to open records laws, you may not feel comfortable storing personal details on your work computer. In that case, unfortunately, you may not have any choice but to separate your information. However, if you feel comfortable keeping track of personal tasks within your professional tools, I highly recommend that you treat all of your details the same and keep everything together in one place.

## KEEPING TRACK OF IT ALL

The next step to implementing the Empowered Productivity System is to organize and censor your brain dump list. Having everything out of your head is a good beginning, but creating a new long list without any further handling will probably give you the Lion Syndrome described in Chapter 3!

After everything is on your list you can "process" each item for entry into your tool, such as Outlook, iCal, or some other tool. For each item, consider the following:

▶ If an item must happen on a certain day (for example, you promised someone you would call on Tuesday) or on a certain day *and* at a certain time (for example, you have a meeting at 3:00 p.m. on Thursday), then it has a *strong* relationship to time and belongs on your *calendar*, not on your task list.

▶ If an item requires action but that action doesn't have to happen at any specific time, or if an item has a due date for some time in the future, it has a *weak* relationship to time and belongs on your task list. Following are some guidelines for proper item categorization:

▷ If an item requires action on your part and it's going on your task list, do you plan to do it soon, such as this week or next week? If so, assign it to the Projects category (if it will happen in multiple steps over multiple time periods) or the Next Actions category (if it's a single-step activity).

▷ Is it something you definitely want to do but you don't want to do it right now? If so, assign it to the Future category.

▷ If you think you *might* want to do it someday, but you haven't really decided yet, assign it to the Someday/Maybe category.

▷ If you can't do anything yet because you are waiting for something else to happen first, assign it to the Waiting For category and record exactly what you are waiting for in the Notes section of the task. Use the features of your electronic tool to assign a reminder if it's important that you follow up.

▶ Refer to Chapter 5 for a reminder about the various relationships to time that different items have and for a refresher on using categories.

▶ When adding something to your Next Actions list, be specific and use an actionable verb, such as *read*, *call*, *email*, and so on. Vague verbs such as *develop*, *implement*, *plan*, and *organize* are only allowed on your Projects list.

▶ As you decide what to do with items on your list, either discarding them or entering them into your tool, highlight them on your paper list so you know what you have already processed. It gives you a sense of accomplishment (and peace of mind!) after you've evaluated everything and captured it all in one place. If the item is important and you fear forgetting it, set a reminder. Be judicious with reminders, however; if many go off all the time, or all at the same time, you start to ignore them—and ignoring them isn't helpful.

▶ Set a due date for each item that you enter; just be mindful of how many things you are marking "due" on any given day.

CROSSREF  Refer to the "ABC Doesn't Work" section in Chapter 5.

▶ When processing your list, "highlighting" an item is better than crossing it off—for two reasons. First, you can still see it if necessary. Second, the highlighting emphasizes what's been done, rather than what has yet to be done, which is more motivating.

# CAPTURING THOUGHTS

When your mind is free from all of these details, it's important to determine how you're going to keep it that way. You need a tool for "capturing" thoughts and ideas when you are on the go. Because ideas, responsibilities, and other important thoughts pop into our heads unbidden, it's vital to your peace of mind to be able to capture these thoughts whenever they come up, ensuring that they don't fall into a void where you never see them again. This is often the sad or dangerous fate of thoughts jotted down on sticky notes, business cards, and napkins.

One popular way to capture thoughts is to carry a voice recorder or utilize the voice recorder feature of a smartphone. Voice recordings are a good way to capture ideas if you remember to listen to the recordings; otherwise, this technique can become another black hole of thoughts and ideas that never see the light of day again.

Some people leave themselves a voicemail message. This method is okay, but it's not without its drawbacks. If you leave yourself frequent reminders on voicemail, your voicemail inbox can become cluttered with messages, and messages from other people tend to be buried under the messages you leave for yourself. Furthermore, having to skip over all the messages you leave for yourself (to get to the real messages) can be an annoying waste of time.

▶ A voicemail service that emails messages to you is also a good solution.

If you use some sort of voice recording, it's helpful if you can send the recording to your email, which ensures that you see it again and are able to capture it appropriately into your system at the time you process your email messages. If you're using a smartphone, many built-in voice recorder apps offer an option to email the recording. Sending your voice recordings to email enables you either to take the action while you're sitting at your desk or to simply drag them to your to-do list for action at an appropriate time. Emails seem more tangible, and therefore more actionable, than voice recordings.

A smartphone offers several options for sending email to yourself, and I suggest you take advantage of all of them. In some situations it's appropriate to type, but not to speak. In those cases, use your smartphone to send yourself an email.

Investigate the options discussed in this book and decide on the best capture tool or tools for *you*. This is an important piece of developing the habit of keeping things out of your head. Back in the days of paper-based planners, we used to say, "If you think it, ink it," and paper notes are still an option. However, electronic tools now eliminate the extra tracking those paper notes require, and you should carefully consider the way you'll best be able to manage your workflow.

## SUMMARY

If you're impatient to start implementing what you're learning in this book, stop reading now and carve out some time to do a brain dump. Just as you must find a new home before you can move out of your current home, these exercises are exactly what you need to start the process of moving from your old habits, which sabotage you, to the new personal productivity habits, which support you.

After you've moved all the details necessary to manage your life out of your brain and into one place—your brain dump list—the next step is to get them into a system that helps you manage them. Chapter 7 shows you how to migrate these items, and any items you subsequently start capturing with your new capture tools, into the "hub" of your new system—your PIM of choice.

# QUICK TIPS

The following are some important points from this chapter (also suitable for tweeting). For more information on Twitter, including relevant usernames and hashtags, please refer to the "Read This First" chapter.

► Two secrets to productivity: clearing your space and clearing your *mind*.

► #Productivity Tip: Set out-of-office messages for an extra day before and after vacation to minimize chaos and stress.

► You can't unleash your inner genius if she's busy remembering to pick up the milk & submit the expense report. Clear your mind!

► #Productivity Tip: Highlight completed tasks instead of crossing them out. They'll still be visible and this emphasizes accomplishment.

► A smartphone voice recorder is great for capturing random thoughts when out of office—email the recording to yourself.

# ENDNOTES

1. Scott Mayorowitz, "Americans Afraid to Take Full Vacations," ABC News, August 10, 2010, http://abcnews.go.com/Travel/americans-refuse-vacation-days-lag-rest-world/story?id=11361600.

2. Wednesday Martin, Ph.D., "Gone Fishin': Why You Can't Afford to Skip Another Vacation," July 7, 2010, *Psychology Today*, www.psychologytoday.com/blog/stepmonster/201007/gone-fishin-why-you-cant-afford-skip-another-vacation.

3. Tim Ferriss, "The Truth—Stats and Research," The Blog of Tim Ferriss, accessed January 21, 2012, www.fourhourworkweek.com/blog/the-truth/.

## CHAPTER 7

# Capture, Store, Act

► The four skills for using any productivity tool successfully
► Recommended support tools: Microsoft Outlook and Apple iCal & Reminders
► Instructions for Google fans

Chapter 5 should provide all the information you need in order to choose a tool. In this chapter I provide instructions for implementing the Empowered Productivity™ System methodology into the most common electronic PIMs: those from Microsoft, Apple, and Google.

# GETTING STARTED WITH ELECTRONIC PIMS

If you've decided to use an electronic PIM, the odds are good that you chose one of the following popular options for each platform:

▶ Microsoft Outlook for those most comfortable with the PC platform

▶ The productivity suite built into the Mac OS: iCal, Reminders, Apple Mail, and Address Book

▶ Google Apps, including Calendar, Tasks, Contacts, and Gmail for platform-neutral tools

Regardless of which electronic PIM you choose, there are four basic steps to get started with each:

1. Learning the features of the tool (for this chapter, the Task feature specifically).

2. Setting up the Task List section to support categorical organization and custom views.

3. Entering tasks.

4. Handling completed tasks.

First, I elaborate a bit on each of these steps, and then I explain how to actually complete each one in Microsoft Outlook, the Apple OS X tools, and Google Apps.

## Learning the Features

To fully benefit from your tool, you need to learn as much as you can about its available features. For example, I have found that most people who use Microsoft Outlook use only a fraction of its capabilities. Electronic PIMs offer a wide range of benefits, and investing the time to learn how to use each feature usually pays big dividends. One of the fastest and easiest ways to learn about a particular feature of some software or an app is to do a video search on that feature. In most cases, you can find several short videos on the developer's website or on YouTube that walk you through the feature in a few minutes or less. You can also find several on my website at RegainYourTime.com.

Of course, what's important about each feature is not only how to use it, but when and why to use it. This is where a good methodology such as the Empowered Productivity System comes in; it provides you with the missing piece that enables you to use your tools successfully and efficiently.

▶ If you haven't decided on a tool yet, review Chapter 5 for help on narrowing down the options.

## Setting Up Your Tool and Using Its Views

You may have tried an electronic task list in the past but found yourself reverting back to paper. In my experience, this is typically because the Task List feature is much less useful without the proper categories and views. One long list in an electronic tool is no less overwhelming than a long list on paper. Using the categories I outlined in Chapter 4 and having the capability to view each of them individually or all of them together is what puts you in control of those details, enables you to manage them effectively, and helps you avoid the Lion Syndrome. Later sections in the chapter cover how to set up custom views in each tool.

## Entering Data in Your Tool

Task List tools can be very comprehensive, offering many more fields than you will likely need. Therefore, take the time to learn which options, such as Start Date, Due Date, Reminders, and so on, will provide enough benefit to offset the time it takes to enter them. In addition, keep in mind that the wording you use to create a task can affect whether you actually do it, and how quickly. The clearer and more action-oriented the wording, the more likely you are to successfully complete the task.

CROSSREF  Review the "Getting Started" section in Chapter 4 for a refresher on how to be specific when entering items in your task list.

## Managing Completed Tasks

It won't take long for all the tasks you mark as complete to clutter your list, and you might find it tempting to delete them as you check them off. However, keeping track of the things you've completed and viewing them in an organized manner maximizes your effectiveness. The following are some benefits of keeping your completed tasks in a specific view:

- ► For reference during a formal review related to your job performance
- ► To help you "take stock" at the end of a designated time period (for example, quarter, year)
- ► To avoid work duplication by chronicling what you've already done
- ► For progress or status reports required for your job

- ▶ To assist in updating your résumé to the more desirable "accomplishments" (rather than "responsibilities") format

- ▶ To aid in career advancement

The following sections provide instructions for completing each of these steps using Microsoft Outlook, Apple iCal, and Google Tasks. You might want to skip to the section that is relevant to you.

# SETTING UP OUTLOOK

Following are the steps to first prepare Outlook for the Empowered Productivity System and then use Outlook's Task List feature to manage all the items from your brain dump that have a weak relationship to time.

> **CROSSREF** For a refresher on Task items (weak relationship to time) versus Calendar items (strong relationship to time) you may find it helpful to review Chapters 4 and 5.

## Outlook: Learning the Features

Microsoft Outlook uses some confusing terminology and also offers several different ways to accomplish the same thing, which some people find confusing. I clarify both of those issues in the following sections.

### OUTLOOK TERMINOLOGY: TASK VERSUS TO-DO

The details in this section apply to the most recent version of Microsoft Outlook 2010 for Windows. However, these instructions do not differ much from Outlook 2011 for Mac or Outlook 2007 for Windows, so you should be able to apply these instructions to your version of the software. Even if you're using a newer version, the following instructions might still apply.

Between the release of Outlook 2003 and 2007, Microsoft picked up on the inefficient way that many people were handling their email for later follow-ups—marking them with the Flag feature. In Outlook 2007, Microsoft added a To-Do List section. Anything you mark with a flag, such as an email, appears in your To-Do List, and you can also manually add any Task item to the list.

> ▶ Later in the book you learn a much more efficient way of dealing with your email than using the Flag feature.

Take note that when you click the Task icon you may find yourself in To-Do List view, rather than Tasks view. I suggest you get used to using the Task view (see Figure 7-1) instead of the To-Do List because of the way I'm going to show you to customize the view in the "Manipulating Your View" section later in this chapter.

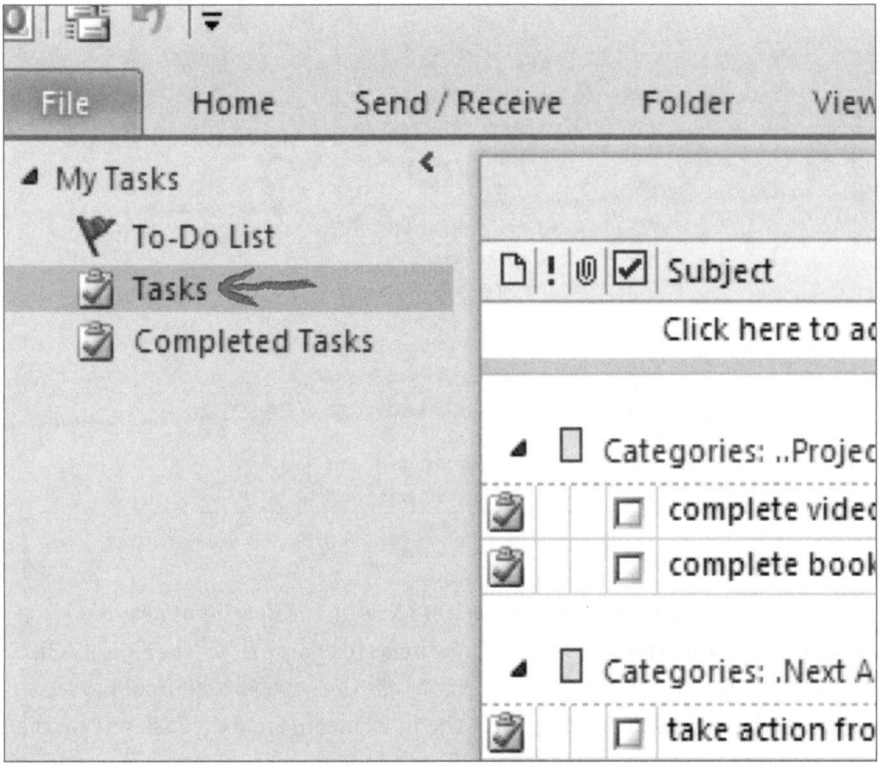

FIGURE 7-1

If you right-click on Tasks and select Move Up in List, Outlook defaults to the Task view when you click the Tasks icon.

## USING THE TASK LIST PLUS SHORTCUTS

Before setting up your task categories, you must first open a new task. There are several ways to do this, depending on the screen from which you are starting.

From the Home tab in any screen, select New Task. Alternatively, from the Tasks view, double-click in the field that reads Click Here to Add New Task. Both methods open a new Task window (see Figure 7-2).

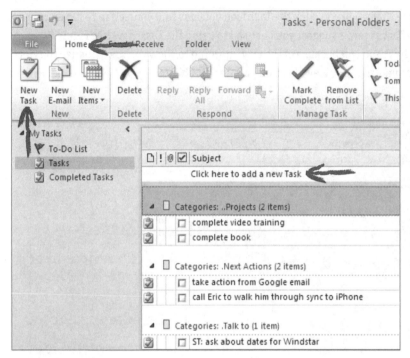

**FIGURE 7-2**

▶ Holding the Ctrl key while pressing the N key always presents a new item for that particular screen. For example, you get a new calendar appointment window if you press Ctrl+N from the Calendar view.

Notice the tiny down arrow next to the word New on the New Items button. Clicking that arrow also presents a list of new items to choose from (see Figure 7-3). Another alternative for creating a new task is to use the keyboard shortcut keys—Ctrl+Shift+K—from any screen view *except* the Task screen. From the Task screen, the keyboard shortcut is Ctrl+N. When the New Task window opens, you can set up your categories, as described in Chapter 4. All of these options produce the same result of opening a New Task window. (See Figure 7-4.)

## Preparing for Categorical Organization

From the Untitled Task window, select Categories to add new categories or rename the existing categories. The Color Categories window enables you to delete or rename the categories you're not using and add the ones you want. There are a few things to note with regard to setting up your categories. First, categories are the same for all Outlook items, so if you are already using any of the existing categories for another feature in Outlook—such as Contacts, for example—be sure not to delete them.

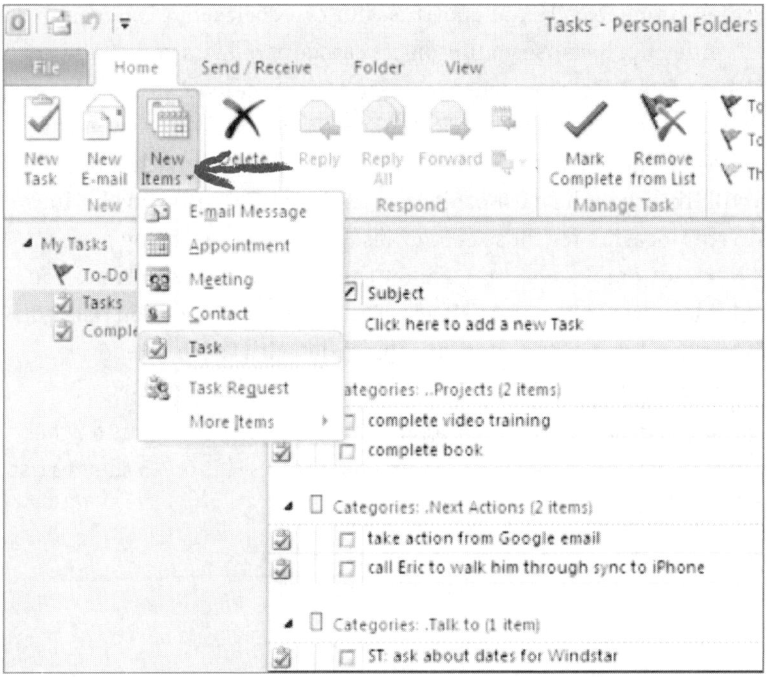


FIGURE 7-3

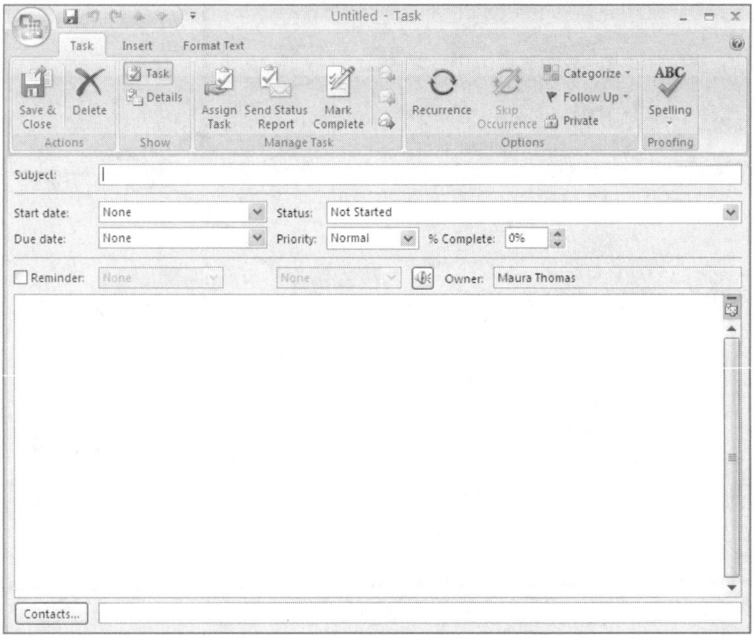


FIGURE 7-4

▶ This sorting method is called an ASCII sort (pronounced "ask-ee") in computer terminology.

Second, Outlook automatically alphabetizes your categories, but I suggest using a different ordering. Because your Projects category reflects your "big picture, 30,000-foot view," it makes sense for your Projects category to be at the top of your task list. To force your Projects category to the top of the view prefix the name with two periods (that is, "..Projects"). Follow ..Projects with those categories you will likely use the most often: Next Actions, Talk To, and Waiting For. To maintain this location for those categories, prefix them with one period (for example, ".Next Actions," and so on). Follow these categories with those you will likely use a bit less often: Someday/Maybe, Future, and any location lists you have, such as Home and Errands. To maintain this order with these categories, begin them with an @ symbol (for example,"@Someday/Maybe," and so on).

Lastly, I suggest you make all the Task categories gray, saving the colors for the Calendar categories (you learn more about that in Chapter 13). Figure 7-5 shows a list that has been set up following these guidelines.

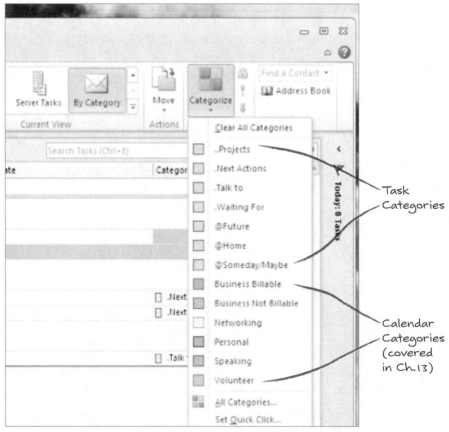

**FIGURE 7-5**

## Manipulating Your View

The Outlook Task view has many columns available for viewing and sorting, but I believe that in this case less is more. Clean up your Task List view by selecting View → View Settings. The Advanced View Settings window appears (see Figure 7-6). Select the Columns option and include only the options you need to have visible. I suggest the following:

- ► Complete
- ► Attachment
- ► Subject
- ► Due Date

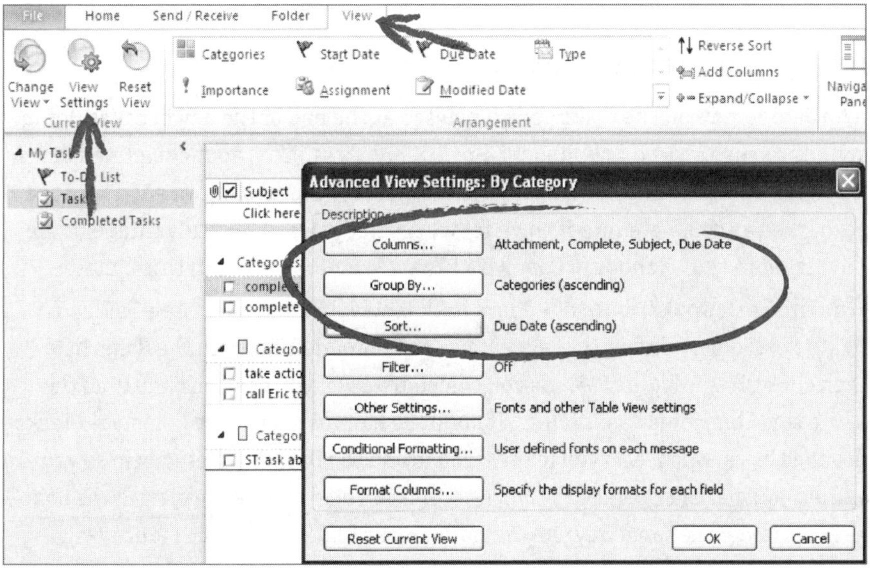

FIGURE 7-6

You've already set up categories for your tasks, so you probably don't need Category as a column, but it's okay to include it if you think it might be useful.

Next, click the Group By button to specify how Outlook should organize your items. Select Categories, Ascending.

Lastly, click the Sort button and select Due Date. It doesn't matter whether you choose Ascending or Descending. Try each option to see which View you prefer. Sorting by due date helps for prioritizing, as discussed in Chapter 5.

The other options in the Advanced View Settings window are probably not relevant, but feel free to click through them to familiarize yourself.

## Entering Tasks

Begin to transfer the items from your brain dump list by creating a new task for each one. In the Untitled Task window, you have the option to use a variety of fields. The most important is the Category field. In addition to that, I suggest you consider, when applicable, the Start Date, Due Date, and Reminder fields. In my opinion, the other fields are not particularly helpful. As discussed elsewhere, assigning due dates is helpful for prioritizing, even if the dates are somewhat arbitrary. Use reminders only for very important items, as they lose their value when they are not set judiciously. Be sure to set them to go off when you are likely to take action, not when you are out of the office, for example. In general, I find that the Start Date field is only helpful when it's truly relevant to know when you added the item to the list.

## Handling Completed Tasks

It's helpful to review all the tasks you completed at the end of the day because doing so provides a sense of accomplishment. However, very quickly, your completed tasks clutter your list. At the end of every day, it's therefore helpful to move each task that you've marked as complete into its own folder so that you can take advantage of the benefits listed in the "Managing Completed Tasks" section earlier in this chapter.

To do this in Outlook, right-click Tasks in the folder list and select New Folder. In the Create New Folder window that appears, type **Completed Tasks** in the Name field and then click OK (see Figure 7-7). As you complete tasks, you can click and drag the items into this Completed Tasks folder. It might be helpful to view the Completed Tasks also grouped by category, and you may decide to add the Date Completed field so you know when you marked the task as complete. You can manipulate the view in the Completed Tasks folder the same way you did in the Tasks folder (reference Figure 7-6).

# SETTING UP ICAL

Apple's operating system (OS) comes with a set of built-in productivity tools: iCal, Reminders (the to-do list app), Apple Mail, and Address Book. The advantage to using these tools, as with many Apple applications, is that help is always available at the Genius Bar in any Apple store. The main drawback is that it takes at least four programs to do what Outlook does in one. Taken together, I think the advantage of having the tools built into the operating system, along with the ease of syncing to other devices via iCloud, outweighs the disadvantage of using several tools, making Apple's tools a good solution to use as your PIM, if you use a Mac as your primary computer.

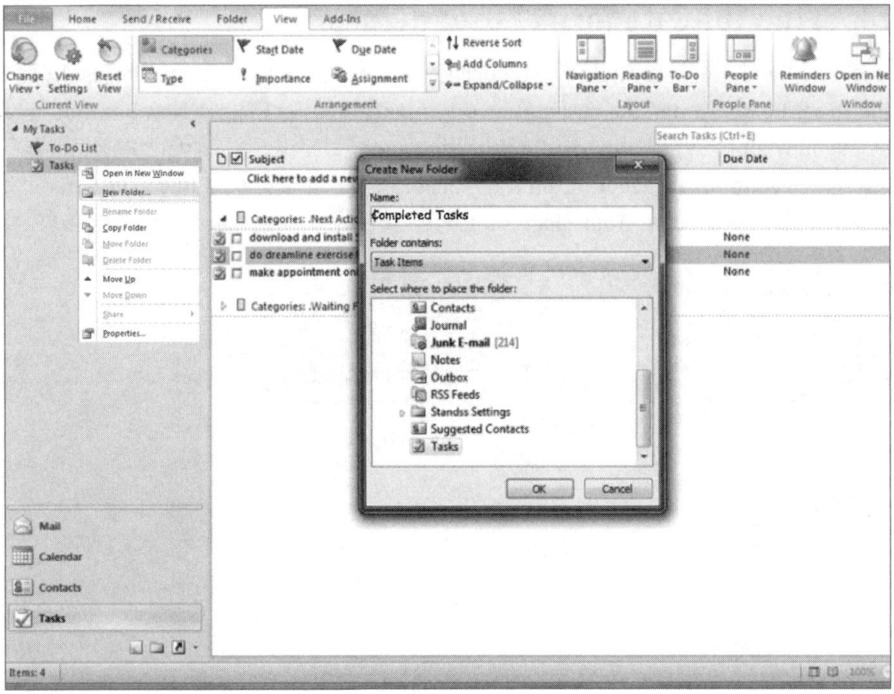

**FIGURE 7-7**

Apple's iCal has many of the same features as Microsoft's Outlook, but they're implemented differently. Also, as of this writing, some things aren't as easy to do in the Apple tools as I wish they were, so adding one or two extras is helpful. This section explains how to set up iCal and Reminders for use with the Empowered Productivity System. Chapters 12 and 13 cover some of the extras.

## iCal: Learning the Features

One slightly confusing aspect of iCal and Reminders is that Reminders is part of iCal in the desktop version, but it's a separate app on the iPhone, iPod touch, and iPad. Other than that, iCal is very straightforward and does not require much clarification.

In iCal, if you don't see a list titled Reminders on the right side of the window, click the View menu and select Show Reminders. Anything you enter in the Reminders section of iCal appears in the Reminders app on your handheld devices (iPhone, iPod touch, and iPad).

## Preparing for Categorical Organization

In iCal and Reminder terminology, you use Reminders Lists for task categories. In order to set up Reminders for categorical organization, select File → New Reminders List. If you want to sync through iCloud, which automatically sends your Reminders list items to your online account, plus any other Apple devices you may have (I recommend this), select your Apple account instead of On My Mac (see Figure 7-8).

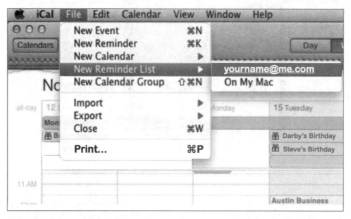

FIGURE 7-8

Syncing through iCloud enables you to access your Calendar, Reminders, and Address Book contacts from any computer with an Internet connection, in addition to any of your other Apple devices. However, you must first enable this in System Preferences → iCloud. Figure 7-9 shows that Mail & Notes, Contacts, and Calendars are all enabled for syncing to iCloud.

FIGURE 7-9

The iCal Reminders feature automatically alphabetizes your categories, but I suggest you use a different order, which you can do by dragging items as you make each Reminders list. Because your Projects category is your "big picture, 30,000-foot" view, it makes sense for your Projects category to be at the top of your task list. To force your Projects simply drag to the top category to the top of the view. Follow ..Projects with those categories you will likely use the most often: Next Actions, Talk To, and Waiting For. Follow these categories with those you will likely use a bit less often: Someday/Maybe, Future, and any location lists you have, such as Home and Errands.

After typing the name of the list, right-click or control+click it and select Get Info. This enables you to choose a color for the list. I suggest making all the Task categories gray, saving the colors for the Calendar categories (more on that in Chapter 13). Figure 7-10 illustrates what your Reminders Lists look like after you've followed these instructions.

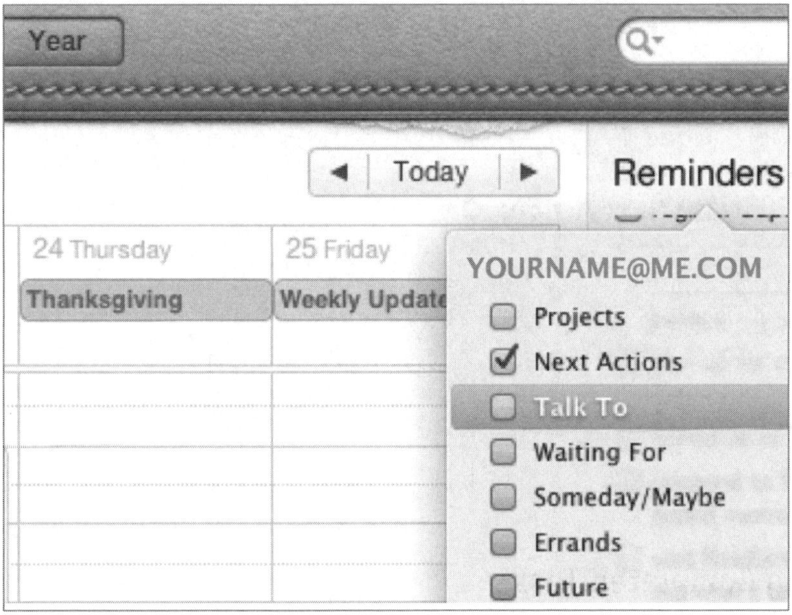

FIGURE 7-10

## Manipulating Your View

In order to view one, several, or all of your Reminders lists in iCal, simply click Reminders on the right side of the screen, and check the box next to the list(s) you would like to view. To prioritize the lists by due date, select View → Sort Reminders By → Sort by Due Date.

▶ For a refresher on why it's helpful to sort by due date, review the "ABC Doesn't Work" section in Chapter 5.

## Entering Tasks

To enter the tasks from your brain dump list, press Command + K and then press Command + I to open the New Task window and then choose More Information. You always need to view More Information (see the New Reminder—Info window in Figure 7-11) in order to select the correct category (Reminder List), add the due date, add a reminder (if applicable), and add any notes you'd like to include.

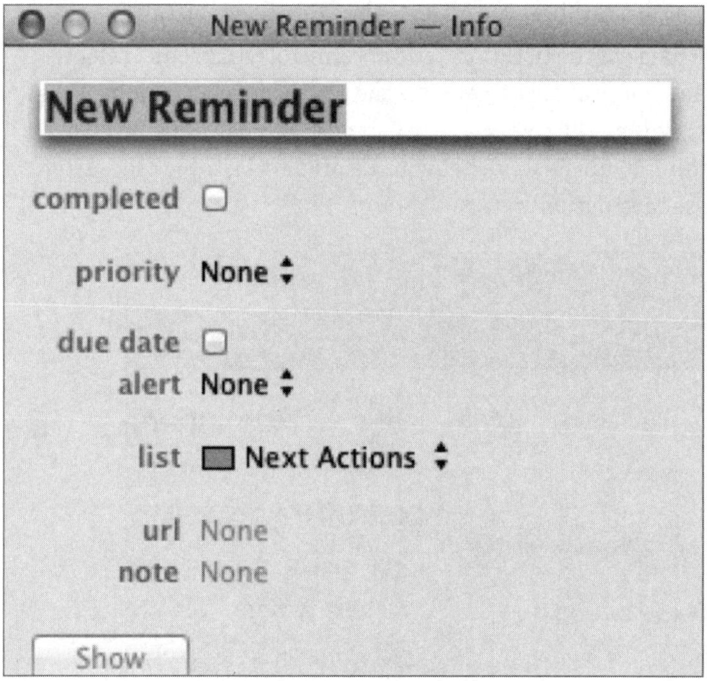

FIGURE 7-11

## Handling Completed Tasks

In iCal, you can specify what you'd like to do with your completed tasks: hide them or delete them. If you hide them, you can always find them again by running a search, and you can view them if desired by selecting View → Show All Completed Reminders. You can set your own options for handling completed tasks by selecting iCal → Preferences → Advanced (see Figure 7-12). I recommend that you do not delete them so that you can take advantage of the benefits outlined in the "Managing Completed Tasks" section earlier in this chapter.

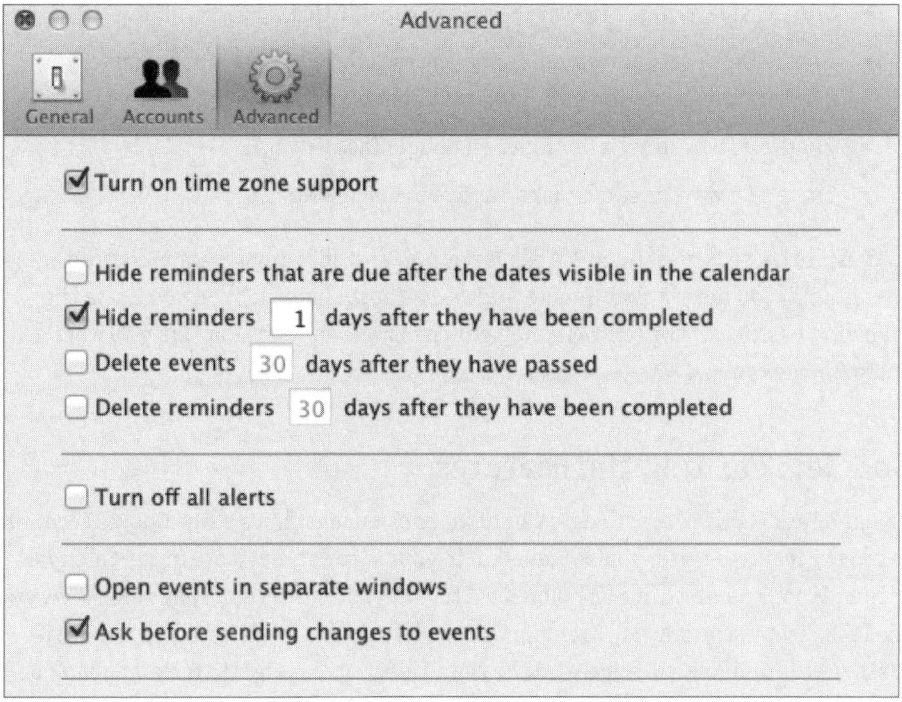

FIGURE 7-12

# SETTING UP GOOGLE

I am convinced that as of this writing, it's more effective to manage the details of your life on your computer rather than "in the cloud" (that is, on a remote server). That is, I recommend that you use a PIM application such as iCal/Reminders or Outlook locally (on your computer), rather than something such as Google Apps. At one time, Google Calendar was the only solution available if you needed to share your calendar with others, but that is no longer the case. I believe that the drawbacks of using Google as your PIM are substantial, and they include the following:

► Accessing your data when offline requires that you are using the Google Chrome browser and have the app installed on your computer.

► At least one extra step is required to synchronize all the various Google apps with most handheld devices. Tasks don't synchronize with iPhone or BlackBerry without a third-party app.

▶ The Task feature is seriously lacking in capabilities.

▶ Google Tasks only allows you to see one task list at a time. For example, you can periodically review your Projects list but you can't keep it visible.

▶ There's no way to set a reminder on Google Tasks.

▶ There's no way to search tasks—active or completed.

▶ *A few of these issues are addressed by using a plug-in task application for Google called Remember the Milk. See Chapter 16 for more information about this app.*

Despite these issues, Google Apps is popular and adds improvements often. Therefore, if you decide that Google Apps is the best choice for your PIM, use the following basic instructions to implement the Empowered Productivity System using Google tools.

## Google: Learning the Features

Google's Task List is part of Google Calendar, and you must have a free Google account to use the features. After you've signed in to your account, navigate to the Calendar option. If you're a first-time user you need to enter your name and time zone. View the Task List by selecting My Calendars on the left side and putting a check mark in Tasks. A task window will appear on the right side. Google refers to different categories of tasks as Task Lists. You may see a default list titled *Your Name* List. As of this writing, you cannot delete this list.

Create your own categories as outlined in Chapter 4 by clicking the List icon in the bottom-right corner and selecting New List (see Figure 7-13).

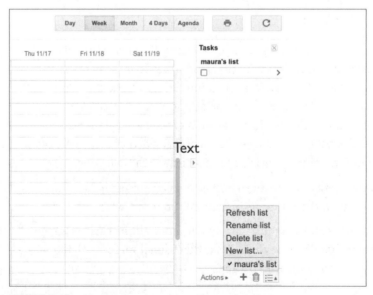

**FIGURE 7-13**

# Preparing for Categorical Organization

Google automatically alphabetizes your categories, but I suggest you use a different order. Because your Projects category is your "big picture, 30,000-foot" view, it makes sense for your Projects category to be at the top of your task list. To force your Projects category to the top of the view, prefix the name with two periods (that is, "..Projects"). Follow ..Projects with those categories you will likely use the most often: Next Actions, Talk To, and Waiting For. To maintain this location for those categories, prefix them with one period (for example, ".Next Actions," and so on). Follow these categories with those you will likely use a bit less often: Someday/Maybe, Future, and any location lists you have, such as Home and Errands. To maintain this order with these categories, begin them with an @ symbol (for example, "@Someday/Maybe," and so on). (See Figure 7-14.)

▶ This sorting method is called an ASCII sort (pronounced "ask-ee") in computer terminology.

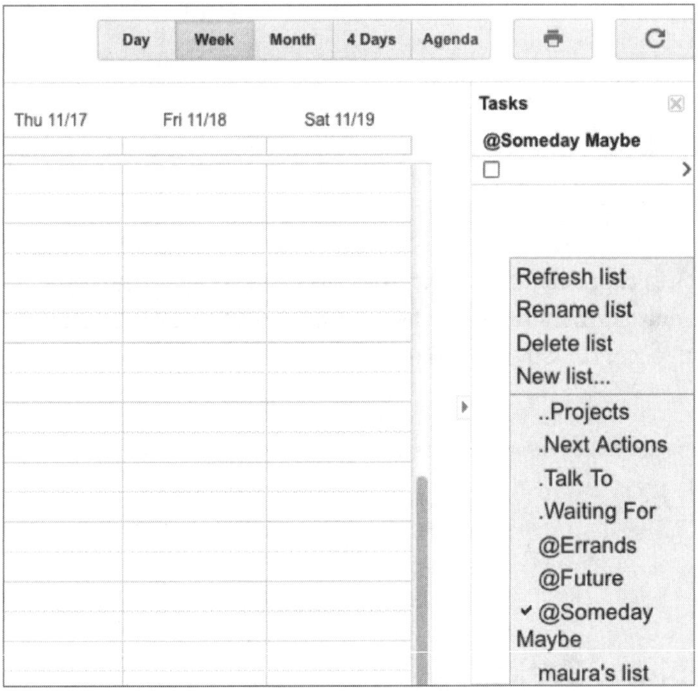

FIGURE 7-14

# Manipulating Your View

Google Tasks gives you very few options for manipulating your view. As I mentioned earlier, two significant drawbacks to Google Tasks are that it only allows you to view one task list at a time, so grouping or otherwise arranging isn't relevant. In order to view your tasks in each category by due date, click Actions in the bottom-right corner, and then select Sort by Due Date. (See Figure 7-15.)

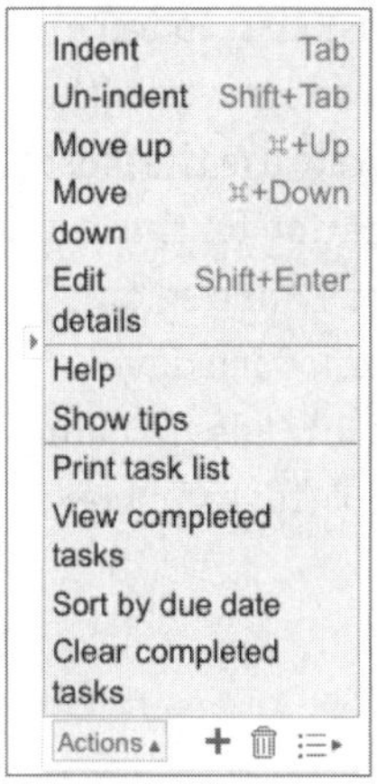

**FIGURE 7-15**

## Entering Tasks

In order to enter a task in your Google Task List, click the plus (+) key at the bottom of the list. To insert a due date or notes, click the black arrow (labeled Edit Details) at the end of the task subject or click the Shift+Enter keys. (See Figure 7-16.)

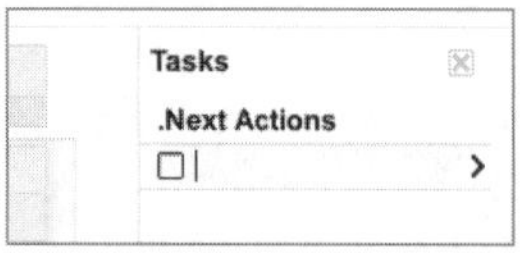

**FIGURE 7-16**

## Handling Completed Tasks

To remove completed tasks from your view, click Actions at the bottom of the screen and select Clear Completed Tasks. To view them later, select View Completed Tasks from the same Actions menu. (Refer to Figure 7-15.)

# SUMMARY

Of course, there are many other PIM options besides the three described in this chapter, but most other solutions require assembling your own set of tools—one app for your calendar, one for tasks, one for contacts, and so on. The three popular options covered in this chapter include most of the necessary components. Both Outlook and the Mac tools also offer a Notes option, but Chapter 13 covers another useful tool that I recommend for that purpose. Whatever tools you are considering, please evaluate them carefully based on the advantages and drawbacks described in this chapter.

# QUICK TIPS

The following are some important points from this chapter (also suitable for tweeting). For more information on Twitter, including relevant usernames and hashtags, please refer to the "Read This First" chapter.

▶ Don't delete those completed tasks! Save for job reviews or résumé updates to note accomplishments.

▶ If you're not sure you're using your software/apps to the max, a quick video search online turns up hundreds of short training videos.

▶ The secret to effective task list management is the right categories and custom views.

▶ Action-oriented to-do items prevent "speed bumps" when working from your list.

▶ Use an ASCII sort in category names so they show up in your task list in the most useful order.

## CHAPTER 8

# Clearing Your Space

Is there an area of your life that's a mess? Your desk, your bedroom, your car? Probably your email inbox? You are not alone. Most people are surrounded by physical or electronic clutter in some part of their lives. What many of us don't recognize is that cluttered environments cause tension and negative emotion. When a cluttered lifestyle becomes habitual, we fail to notice these stressful effects.

However, when I ask people with a cluttered office space how they feel about their work life, they respond with words like these:

▶ Stressed

▶ Overwhelmed

▶ Out of control

▶ Confused

▶ Drained

▶ Pressured

▶ Chaotic

Let's face it: People surrounded by clutter, whether physical or electronic, can't really make a convincing argument that they are on top of all those details. Some people with a cluttered desk tell me, "But I know where everything is." However, knowing (or thinking you know) where things are located isn't really the point. The "file by pile" method forces you to rely on your brain as a storage and organizational system, which is more mentally taxing than necessary. A clean and uncluttered environment is a much more peaceful and serene place to spend time; and a well-ordered file system is much more reliable than hoping you can remember which pile holds the item you're looking for.

# ELIMINATING THE THREE CAUSES OF CLUTTER

In this chapter I describe the three reasons for clutter, and how the Empowered Productivity™ System eliminates them. You don't need to be a naturally organized person, or even aspire to be a "neat and tidy" kind of person. Understanding these three causes of clutter will help you eliminate the mess and create an environment that supports your productivity and attention, rather than sabotages it; and it will eliminate some stress from your life as a result.

## Reason #1: "Out of Sight, Out of Mind" Syndrome

If you're like many people, you use your desktop or work space as a central location for all the things you need to do—all of your "work in progress." You might fear that if you put it away, you will forget to do it. This fear indicates the lack of a good methodology and support tools for managing information, such as the Empowered Productivity System and a good PIM (personal information manager). What you've learned of the Empowered Productivity System so far already eliminates this first reason for clutter. You don't have to fear putting it away because it won't be "out of sight, out of mind." Provided you are working the System, items will still be on your task list, so you will still see them and, if necessary, be reminded to act on them at the appropriate time.

## Reason #2: You Are Deferring Making a Decision

We often procrastinate when we are not ready to make a decision. You may be avoiding a decision about something because you suspect it's going to be complicated and take more time than you care to devote to it. You might not know yet what you need to do, or something might be happening too far in the future for you to decide right now. Whatever the reason, you feel like you need to leave it "out" until you get around to dealing with it.

In my work, one thing I have learned is that you usually do, in fact, know what to do with it, even if you have yourself convinced that you don't. If you push through that feeling of "I don't know" and give it your attention for a minute or two, I guarantee that you can come up with a solution. You can also decide whether you truly need to keep the item, and whether it requires action. As a result, you can process the various bits and pieces of information that enter your life more quickly and easily, thereby reducing or eliminating clutter. This reason for clutter will be eliminated after you read Chapter 10, which provides a tool to help you avoid procrastination and process your "stuff." It's designed for paper and email, but it works for just about any type of physical or electronic information that enters your world.

### Reason #3: It Doesn't Have a Home

Sometimes you can't put something away because you haven't designated a home for it. This is especially true for your work in progress, which you often need to access only temporarily. If you won't be keeping something after you've completed whatever action it requires it might seem to make sense to just leave an item out on your desk until you've finished it. However, in order to free yourself from the clutter caused by your work in progress, it's better to designate a home for this work. The next section on filing shows you exactly where that work should live.

If you recognize that there are things lying around your house in conspicuous places, find a spot in a drawer, a closet, a corner of the garage. . .anywhere you can designate a home for that item so you can put it away. This enables you to free your physical and mental space from clutter and the unconscious stress it causes.

## GETTING A GRIP ON PAPER BY FILING EFFECTIVELY

Filing: It seems simple enough, not something we need to be taught, right? Wrong! The truth is that most people don't know how to file, and they have drawers full of papers they never see. If you're like many people, most of what you file you probably don't need; but when you do need something, you can't find it. When you want to keep something, you don't know where it should go, so you either make a new file for it or stuff it into an existing file, where you never see it again.

Assuming you aren't yet completely paperless, effective filing is an important aspect of being in control of the details of your life. In order to be truly free of clutter, you need a filing system that is lean, clean, and effective. This means that you save only what you need, you can find anything in a matter of seconds, you know when to file something, and you know exactly where to put it. Very few people have files that work this well. If you are struggling with paper management, this section will help.

# LEARNING A STRATEGY

You've probably heard the adage "failing to plan is planning to fail." This advice also applies to filing. The first thing you need for effective files is a *strategy*—an overall plan that can accommodate any piece of paper that enters your life and needs to be kept. Your strategy dictates how many files you need and where each piece of paper belongs.

## Filing Categorically

You learned the benefits of categorical organization in Chapter 4, and you can bring these benefits to your paper filing as well. There are three types of files in this first level of organization:

- ▶ Action Files
- ▶ Handy Reference Files
- ▶ Archive Files

### ACTION FILES

*Action Files* are for those things that you are actively working on, and these files should mirror your task categories from Chapter 4. For example, let's say you have a "Fill out application" task on your Next Action list and you have printed a hard copy of that application. You can store it in a file labeled Next Actions, which contains any papers related to any of your Next Action tasks. Having a Next Actions file, especially combined with your task list, enables you to remove work in progress from your desk and give it a home.

Another type of Action File is for projects you are actively working on. Any papers associated with items in your task list with the category Projects can have a home in your Action Files. You may have multiple subfiles in this section, named for each of the active projects you're working on.

The next most helpful type of Action File is a Waiting For file. An example of something that should go in a Waiting For file is a printout of a web order. For example, if you're waiting for an order from Amazon.com to arrive, add a Waiting For item to your task list (for example, "Receive order from Amazon"), and put the printout in your Waiting For file until the package arrives. Here's another example: Perhaps you received a bill and had a question about it. You called the vendor but had to leave a message. Make a task in your task list that reads, "Hear back from the vendor," with the date and time of your call and assign it to the category Waiting For. Then put the bill in your Waiting For file until the vendor calls you back.

Many of the other categories of your task list—Talk To, Future, Someday/Maybe, and any Location categories you may have such as Home or Errands—typically do not have papers associated with them; they contain more thoughts and ideas. However, if you find yourself with papers related to these categories, you should certainly give them a home in your Action Files by creating a file for them.

## HANDY REFERENCE FILES

*Handy Reference Files* is the next category at this level. Items that go in these files do not require action, but they are things you would like to keep in a convenient location so that you can access them easily if necessary. Examples of items that would go in Handy Reference Files are insurance policies, medical records, pet information, education or professional information, your child's school records, important personal documents, manuals and warranties, professional or personal kudos, press coverage, and the like.

Another type of Handy Reference File, which I suggest you keep separate from your other Handy Reference Files, is financial files. These are a type of Handy Reference Files, but if you have several, it's more effective to group them together. Examples of information you might keep in your Handy Reference: Financial File include paid bills, bank and credit card statements, investment information, and so on. The need to keep these kinds of files is dwindling because most vendors store this information online now. However, in some scenarios it may be prudent to keep them, such as for any business or home-office expenses or any other expenses that are tax deductible. Or perhaps you plan to sell your home in the near future, in which case you may want to keep the household expense files on hand to share with the realtor. I provide some examples of Handy Reference: Financial Files later in this chapter.

## ARCHIVE FILES

The third category of files at this level is *Archive Files*, which are for documents that you will either rarely or never look at again, but that you can't discard for legal, historical, or sentimental reasons. Old tax returns and grade school report cards are examples of Archive Files. You should carefully consider what you keep in these files.

Archive Files should not take up space in your primary work area, otherwise they would only cause more clutter. If you won't access them often, then store them in a place where they won't distract you or make it more difficult to find what you do need. I show you some archive storage options later in the chapter.

## Filing by Location

The categories described earlier in this section can also be organized by location. Action Files and Handy Reference Files should be—you guessed it—handy! That means you should be able to reach them from your desk or workspace without having to get up. One drawer for Action Files, one drawer for Handy Reference, and (if necessary) one drawer for Handy Reference: Financial should suffice. If each of these sets of files can't fit in one drawer, you may be keeping too much. If your office setup doesn't include two drawers under your desk, you can also store Action Files and Handy Reference Files in the same drawer, using color to differentiate them (for example, green folders for Action, blue folders for Reference).

As mentioned earlier, Archive Files belong somewhere other than in your immediate work space. Organize and label these files as appropriate. Sometimes it's useful to organize Archive Files chronologically by year, rather than by category, but categorical organization works well too. Some categories you might use include Legal Documents, Tax Returns, and Memorabilia. Subcategories are also useful. For example, you could divide Memorabilia into subcategories such as Grade School, College, and Adulthood, or by age or decade. If you have moved a few times in your life, you could separate your memorabilia using subcategories that correspond to the cities in which you have lived. After the files are organized and labeled, put them in a box in a closet, attic, garage, storage room, or other out-of-the-way location. Remember, Archive Files contain things you rarely or never look at, so they don't need to be handy. The accordion-type file boxes shown in Figure 8-1 work well for Archive Files.

FIGURE 8-1

Another useful alternative is a regular file box. They come in cardboard (see Figure 8-2), which is an environmentally friendly option. I can often find these types of cardboard file boxes in overstock stores, or secondhand in Goodwill or other thrift shops.

FIGURE 8-2

# Further Categorization

Categorical organization is subjective. It requires some practice, and it might take you a little time to become proficient. The trick is to make your categories specific enough that you can find what you need, but not so specific that you only have one piece of paper in each file. If you make a category and later find that the file is very big and contains too much information for you to quickly find what you need, then the category is likely too broad, especially if it is a file you use frequently. If so, divide the main category into subsections. For example, a large file for "Insurance" would benefit from subfiles for "House," "Health," and "Car."

### ALPHABETIZING

Most people file alphabetically, but, as described earlier, I suggest you start by organizing each section by category, and use alphabetical filing for your second level of organization. For example, file your Action Files categorically by Next Action, Projects, and Waiting For, and also put them in this order (alphabetical) in the drawer. Earlier I also suggested starting with categorical organization for your Archive Files (Taxes, Memorabilia); and then use alphabetical or chronological order inside the drawer. The same structure also applies for your Handy Reference Files. There are two good reasons to file categorically first, instead of alphabetically:

▶ If you file alphabetically by specific name, you could theoretically have an infinite number of files, but only a finite number of categories apply to your life.

▶ Using this categorical strategy consistently minimizes the challenge of remembering a certain name.

For instance, your Handy Reference: Financial Files are where you put your paid invoices, bank statements, and so on. If you had your phone bills in a file called AT&T, for example, your files would have become confused when AT&T changed its name to Cingular, and again when it changed back to AT&T! A generic file name for the *category*, such as "Telephone," eliminates problems like this.

Here's another example: Let's say you need a plumber, and you call XYZ Plumbing. You pay the bill and file the invoice in a file you make called "XYZ Plumbing." A few weeks later, you are having the same problem and want to pull out the invoice to see what was fixed, how much it cost you, and when the company provided service; but you can't remember the name of the plumbing company you used, so you either spend the next 15 minutes hunting for the invoice or you give up and call ABC Plumbing, making a new file for the second plumbing bill. Now you have one single piece of paper in each file, both of which you can't easily find again unless you remember the name of the company. To avoid this frustrating scenario, instead create a file for the category, called "Repairs and Maintenance." You'll always know exactly where to look for any information related to those items; and unless you live in a "fixer-upper," you likely won't have too many papers to go through if you do have to pull out the file.

## ORGANIZING BY FOLDER TYPE

Anyone who has ever worked with or seen file folders knows that the tabs are cut differently: Some are left cut, some are center cut, and some are right cut (see Figure 8-3). Those differently placed tabs help you organize your files.

Some file folders are sold *uncut*, meaning the top edge runs the entire length of the file folder. Uncut files are not particularly useful if you are employing the Empowered Productivity System for filing.

Most people are under the impression that file folders with staggered tabs are cut that way so they are easily seen in the drawer. The actual reason is so that they can be used for categorical organization. The left-cut files are for main categories, the center-cut files are for subcategories, and the right-cut files are for sub-subcategories. For example, in your Handy Reference Files, you may have a main category (left-cut) called Insurance (which would be a placdholder), a subcategory (center-cut) called Medical Insurance (another placeholder), and two sub-subcategories (right-cuts) called Primary Medical and Secondary Medical. Perhaps you have your other insurance policies (subcategories, center-cut) in this section as well, such as Homeowners and Auto. Your drawer should be filed first categorically, then alphabetically. For example, these Handy Reference Files would look something like this:

Insurance (left-cut)

    Auto Insurance (center-cut)

    Homeowners Insurance (right-cut)

    Medical Insurance (left-cut)

        Primary Medical (center-cut)

        Secondary Medical (right-cut)

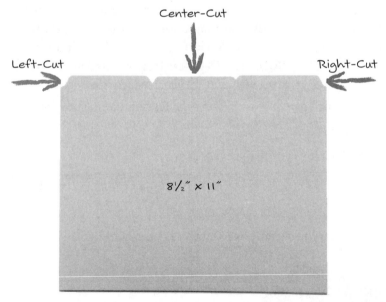

FIGURE 8-3

Remember my earlier caution to not let any single file get too big. For example, in your personal reference drawer, you may have a left-cut, main category file called "Insurance"; but if it contains large policies for auto insurance, hazard insurance, and medical insurance, plus all the other various information that you receive from the insurance companies, it may become too unwieldy to be useful, as it contains too much information for you to access any one piece easily. In this case, it would be more useful to have a left-cut, main category file called "Insurance," which is taped shut and just used as a placeholder, and then have center-cut files for "Auto," "Home/Personal," and "Medical" where you actually file the policies, making it easy to quickly locate each one and any other related information. You see examples at the end of the chapter of how this looks.

# GETTING THE RIGHT GEAR

The second part of the filing strategy is something else few people consider carefully: What's the best way to get your information in the drawer? File folders? Hanging files? Labels? No, it's not rocket science, but not all filing methods are equal; and making the wrong choice can mean the difference between having a system that serves you and having a clutter work space.

When you're setting up a filing system, you want to remove every possible obstacle to using your files. Drawers that don't easily open and close, file labels that aren't easy to read, and files that have uneven edges and don't smoothly slide in and out of the drawer are all obstacles to effective filing. Using the guidelines in this section removes all these obstacles, making it more likely that your files support your productivity.

I've found the following items to be the most useful for maintaining tidy files:

- ▶ Legal-size hanging files
- ▶ Letter-size file folders
- ▶ 3½" plastic tabs
- ▶ A label maker

These four items are shown in Figures 8-4 through 8-7, respectively.

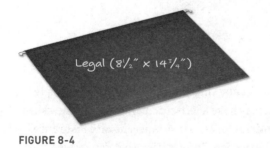

**FIGURE 8-4**

**FIGURE 8-5**

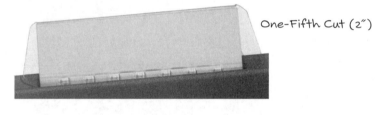

One-Fifth Cut (2")

One-Third Cut (3½")

**FIGURE 8-6**

**FIGURE 8-7**

## Inside the Drawer

When you set up your files, use only *one* file folder inside *one* hanging file, and use the exact same label in the exact same place for both. A main category file would have a left-cut tab, with its own hanging file and its own file folder. See Figure 8-8 for an example.

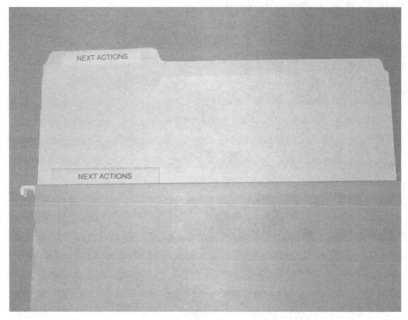

**FIGURE 8-8**

When you need to work with a file, take out only the inside file folder. Leave the hanging file in the drawer. This makes it easy to return the file you are using to its correct location, as they both have the same label. There is no question where a file belongs—every file has a clearly labeled "home" inside the drawer. Also, if you share your files with other people, it is immediately evident when someone has removed a file, because its hanging file is empty. This strategy also keeps the drawer looking clean and neat when you open it. Orderly files are easier to use; and when files are easier to use, you are less likely to create clutter.

I also suggest you put letter-size file folders inside legal-size hanging files for the following reasons:

> ▶ Letter-size files are 8½" × 11", the same size as standard documents. When you have many pieces of paper in a file and you put them into a folder of the same size, unless you are very, very neat, there will probably be some pieces hanging out from the sides. If you then attempt to put this bulging file folder into a hanging file that is exactly the same size, you'll end up tearing

or crumpling the papers in the file, resulting in messy files that are hard to remove and replace in the drawer. However, putting a letter-size file folder inside a legal-size hanging file avoids this problem, because the extra space can easily contain any pieces hanging over the edge of the file folder.

▶ Some people take their files with them on the road, and most briefcases are designed for letter-size files. Therefore, using letter-size file folders makes them easier to transport.

▶ If you archive your files into another drawer or box, they take up less room if they are letter-size. When it's time to archive, use the file folder only and reuse the hanging file for something else.

## Plastic Tabs

The next component I suggest is 3½" clear plastic tabs. Plastic tabs are available in two sizes: 2" (also referred to as ⅕ cut) and 3½" (also called ⅓ cut). Files are easiest to read when the labels are large and clearly worded (no abbreviations or acronyms). To ensure that you have enough room to fit long file names in a large font, use the larger tabs. You can't fit very many characters on the 2" tabs, whereas the 3½" tabs provide enough space to create meaningful labels, which in turn makes your files easy to see and read, thus making them more usable. Note that although colored tabs look pretty, they are harder to read than clear tabs.

## Label Makers

The last item necessary to making your files easy to read is a label maker. No matter how neat your handwriting is, your files will always look neater and cleaner if you make the labels with a label maker. Use a large font and be consistent. Don't switch between uppercase and lowercase letters. Don't set the label maker on "auto." This means that it will adjust the font to fit the label, which results in some labels having a small font and some having a large font. This disrupts the consistency of your file drawer, making it harder to quickly find what you need.

I recommend setting your label maker on the largest font and counting how many characters will fit on the tab. Select your label names to fit within that number of characters. The following are some other recommendations:

▶ Use label tape with a dark ink (black, blue, or purple) on white tape.

▶ Remember that you need two labels for most files (one for the file folder and one for the hanging folder).

▶ Use the paper inserts with the plastic tabs. Stick the label on the paper insert and slide the paper insert into the plastic tab. Using white tape ensures that you can reuse the file or tab. If you have clear tape, you can't put a new label over an old label. Putting the label on the paper insert ensures that it fits snugly inside the plastic tab. Otherwise, the label often slides out of the plastic tab.

▶ Always put the plastic tab on the *front* of the hanging file. That way, if the inside file, or something in it, sticks up a little higher than other files, it doesn't obstruct the plastic file label.

The next section demonstrates the difference this filing strategy can make in maintaining effective files.

## PUTTING THE PIECES TOGETHER

As shown in the following five figures, drawers without a filing strategy provide no relief from clutter—it's not clear where to find things, or where to put things. In Figure 8-9, labeling is the biggest problem. It's difficult to see what's in the drawer, which creates a problem both when filing and retrieving files.

**FIGURE 8-9**

In Figure 8-10, tabs are placed randomly instead of strategically, which contributes to the confusion of the files.

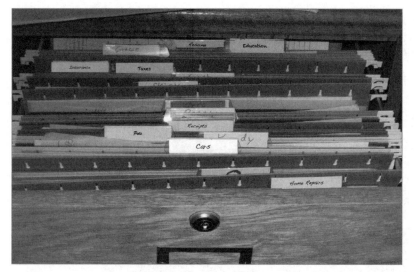

FIGURE 8-10

The folders in Figure 8-11 have letter-size paper inside letter-size files, so the papers stick up at the top and out from the sides of the folders, which impedes the opening and closing of the drawer and removal and replacement of the files.

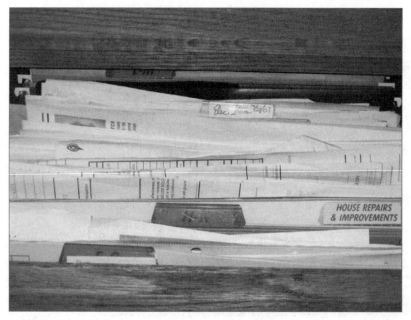

FIGURE 8-11

The files in Figure 8-12 are not categorized well, so the files are very large and different types are mixed together, making it hard to find and use the information.

FIGURE 8-12

The folders in Figure 8-13 have colored tabs instead of clear, some are alphabetical, some are categorical, and some are handwritten. The tabs are hard to read, the filing is inconsistent, and the drawer is confusing.

FIGURE 8-13

The following four figures also show drawers that lack a filing strategy. In these four examples, no hanging files are used, which makes the files difficult to move inside the drawer.

As you can see from Figure 8-14, without hanging files, the labels on folders are difficult to see. Even when the file labels are visible, however, they are still very difficult to read because they are handwritten, rather than created with a label maker.

FIGURE 8-14

In Figure 8-15, the files in the drawer appear to be filed alphabetically, but you can see that it's difficult, if not impossible, to understand the contents of the files.

FIGURE 8-15

The drawer in Figure 8-16 is crowded (letter inside letter) and poorly labeled, and the alphabetical organization still makes it difficult to determine what's in the files.

FIGURE 8-16

In Figure 8-17, the letter-size files that were used in place of legal-size hanging folders is just one problem contributing to the untidy condition of these drawers. Another issue is that without hanging files and tabs, you can't see the labels on the folders.

FIGURE 8-17

Now compare the preceding images to the examples in Figures 8-18 and 8-19. These drawers illustrate the benefits of letter files in legal-size hanging files, large and clear plastic tabs, a clear filing strategy, and the use of a label maker.

Figure 8-18 is an example of a Handy Reference: Financial drawer.

**FIGURE 8-18**

Figure 8-19 is an example of an Action drawer.

**FIGURE 8-19**

# ASSEMBLING YOUR FILE SYSTEM

This section contains some examples of each type of file. Bear in mind that financial files are a type of Handy Reference, but I think it's useful to keep your Handy Reference: Financial Files separate from your general Handy Reference Files.

## Action Files

The following list offers more detailed suggestions for your Action Files. As shown in the figures in the preceding section, the indent position in the following list corresponds to the cut of the file, which denotes the level of categorization.

Next Actions (put your general Next Actions paperwork in this file)

Bills to Be Paid

Contacts to Enter (in your PIM or your marketing database, for example)

Projects (you don't have any "general" project information, so this is just a hanging file, taped shut, that serves as a placeholder)

*Project Name* #1

*Project Name* #2

And so on (projects filed alphabetically by name)

Waiting For

## Handy Reference Files

The following is a list of suggested files for your Handy Reference Files. I have noticed that an increasing number of people deal with as much (or more) paper at home than at work, so these are suggestions for personal files.

Automobiles (put purchase and repair receipts here)

*Your Car* #1

*Your Car* #2

Credit Reports & Information

Education Records

Employment Records

Health (including copies of medical records, test results, and so on)

Medical

Dental (alternatively, instead of Medical, Dental, and so on, you could have a center-cut folder for each family member)

Home Ownership Info (appraisal, title, floor plan, and so on)

Important Personal Documents (catch-all for anything you consider important that isn't in your safe or safety deposit box, such as marriage license, jury duty information, passports, and so on)

Insurance Policies (but not insurance bills)

Jewelry & Valuables (for example, purchase receipts and appraisals)

Keepsakes/Mementos (such as pictures, cards, ticket stubs)

Kudos/Accomplishments (thank-you notes, press, recommendations, recognition, certificates)

Manuals & Warranties

Pets (vaccination and health records, licenses, pedigree information, etc.)

Tax Returns

# Handy Reference: Financial Files

This section provides a list of suggestions for your Handy Reference: Financial Files. As mentioned earlier, it is increasingly unnecessary to keep much of this information because you can access it online, so carefully consider whether these files are relevant. For example, some may be relevant if you are a business owner and the items are tax deductible. If you can justify why storing an item is helpful to you, then it is worth keeping. Don't save something because you *might* need it; in most cases, you can just contact the relevant vendor if you later need something.

Banking

Checks (if you print your checks, you can put the stack of blank ones in this file)

Statements

Expenses

Credit Card Statements

American Express

MasterCard

Visa

Debt Statements

    Home Equity Line

    Personal Loan

    School Loan

Health Expenses

Household Expenses

Insurance Expenses

Investment Expenses

    Rental Properties

    Retirement Accounts

    (Others?)

Repairs & Maintenance

Tax Deductible/Tax Related

Telephone

Utilities

Income (paycheck stubs or other income-related information)

## SUMMARY

Now that you know the secrets to an organized filing system, you should have everything you need at your fingertips, or at least within easy access. No more looking for important papers that seem to be "lost." No more torn papers and bulging folders. Organizing your files reduces clutter, helps you work more efficiently, and gives you greater peace of mind. With the right strategy and the right gear, you are on your way to eliminating paper clutter from your life!

# QUICK TIPS

The following are some important points from this chapter (also suitable for tweeting). For more information on Twitter, including relevant usernames and hashtags, please refer to the "Read This First" chapter.

- ▶ Productivity secret: "File by pile" is not only messy, it causes extra stress!

- ▶ Cause of clutter #1: Scared that "out-of-sight" means "out-of-mind" and forgotten.

- ▶ Cause of clutter #2: Can't decide what to do with it yet. Secret: Forcing yourself to spend 1 minute usually solves the problem.

- ▶ Cause of clutter #3: Item or paper doesn't have a home; consider your filing strategy.

- ▶ #Productivity secret: Match your paper files to the categories in your electronic task list to easily find what you need.

- ▶ Filing tip: Archive Files should NOT be in your workspace! Leave room for Action files & Handy Reference Files near your desk.

- ▶ Productivity Secret: Filing vendor files by name results in too many files. Organize by category instead.

- ▶ Filing tip: The cuts on manila folders aren't just for visibility; use them for categorical organization.

- ▶ #Productivity secret: When filing, most people keep more than they need, and can't find what they're looking for. Minimize!

## CHAPTER 9

# Emerging Concepts in Information Management

There are at least two ideas on the horizon that hold the possibility to affect the way you currently manage the details of your life. The first is the idea of "going paperless," which has been discussed as far back as the 1940s but still remains elusive.

The second is the newly emerging concept of *ambient information*—displaying information in a way that is neither intrusive nor distracting. This chapter takes a closer look at these concepts.

# CAN YOU GO PAPERLESS?

I explained in Chapter 5 why I believe that a paper-based PIM is not the most effective solution for managing the details of your life; but what about all the other paper in your world? Even if you're someone whose work-related paper use is declining, you might still deal with excessive amounts of paper in your personal life.

The idea of the "paperless office" has been around for decades, and the term seems to have been coined in a *Business Week* article in 1975. Not only a paperless office, but a paperless life, can be an appealing idea for several reasons.

## Environmental Appeal

Most people don't realize that close to 50 percent of the global wood harvest is used for paper production.[1]

Forest harvesting has a devastating effect on the environment, such as soil run-off and erosion, loss of wildlife habitat, and species extinction. Forests also regulate rainfall and regulate the temperature of the planet. Paper production consumes large quantities of water and electricity, and the industry creates thousands of ancillary by-products that affect the environment as well, such as chlorine, dyes, ink, and toner. These depressing side effects seem all the more worse when you consider how little of the paper we file is actually needed. Research shows that 80 percent of filed paper is never referenced again.[2]

## Productivity Appeal of Going Paperless

In addition to conserving valuable natural resources and protecting the environment, going paperless can have a huge effect on your overall productivity. As discussed in Chapter 8, effectively managing the paper in your life requires a structured and updated filing system.

Paper creates clutter that is time-consuming to organize and store. Imagine how much simpler your filing would be if you had much less paper to deal with! In the following sections I outline some of the challenges you may face in an effort to go paperless so that you can be prepared. I also provide some suggestions for overcoming them.

# Obstacles to Going Paperless

One development that was supposed to bring us closer to a paperless environment was the Electronic Signatures in Global & International Commerce Act (ESGICA), which states that electronic signatures are legal and enforceable. However, this law was passed more than a decade ago, in 2000, and signatures on paper documents are still the more common format. If it were easy to electronically sign soft copies of documents, this would significantly cut down on the need to print out documents, moving society closer to being paperless. However, two current barriers to electronic signature adoption, and to moving to a paperless life in general, are cost and technology challenges.

▶ Soft copies are typically electronic versions, whereas hard copies are printed versions of documents.

## COST

A significant obstacle to going paperless is cost: Technology that can replace paper is abundant, but consumer-level options just aren't always affordable for the average consumer. *Optical character recognition (OCR)*, which is the conversion of scanned documents into actual text that can be edited, holds promise, but most OCR devices that perform well are still prohibitively expensive for wide adoption. In addition, certain industries and the government have been slow to adopt OCR, leaving millions of people with no viable alternative to a paper copy.

## TECHNOLOGY CHALLENGES

In addition to the cost, there can be a steep learning curve as one adopts the new technology, and using electronic signatures requires some investment in education and administration. This has further hindered its adoption. The latest version of the Mac operating system, OS X Lion, makes it easier to insert signatures into PDF files using the computer's built-in camera, but Apple still has such a small market share that it remains to be seen whether this will help move electronic signatures into the mainstream. If you don't have a Mac and are interested in signing documents electronically, a quick Google search for "electronic signatures," "electronically sign documents," or "digital signatures" returns many free options.

## STORAGE

Electronic storage options pose another barrier. Many industries still insist on faxing or mailing physical pieces of paper, and scanning documents for digital storage is still time-consuming and tedious. Document scanning and electronic storage as an industry is growing, and it's easy to feel overwhelmed by the hype and jargon. As with electronic signature technology, scanning options change frequently, so I hesitate to recommend any specific tools, but the most basic setup is a scanner connected to ample electronic storage space, such as an external hard drive.

## Dealing with Business Cards

Electronic business card exchange is another area that, despite apparent popularity, has not yet eliminated the use of paper business cards and the clutter they often create. (Be honest: You have at least one stack of other people's cards on your desk, don't you?) Several technology solutions are available for exchanging contact information, including apps and services, although they all still have some drawbacks.

One major disadvantage is that most of these services automatically put the contact into your personal address book, which results in clutter and inefficiency. A question I suggest you ask yourself when receiving a business card is, "Did I make a connection with this person?" For example, if you simply shook someone's hand at an event, your personal address book (digital or otherwise) is probably not the best place to keep their contact information. Otherwise, after a short period of time, your address book would be cluttered with people you barely know.

If you have an action to follow up, storing a person's information in a Next Action in your task list ("Call to follow up with Joe regarding the meeting") may be a good temporary home until it is clear whether this person will be part of your life, professionally or otherwise. Conversely, people with whom you *do* make an immediate connection can be added to your personal contacts.

For all the other people whose contact information you collect, consider a marketing database, a separate contact manager from your PIM, or some other storage location, such as an Excel spreadsheet or even a traditional Rolodex. If the likelihood of calling or emailing a person in the near future is low, you probably don't need to save her contact information at all, as most people can be easily located again if necessary, via an Internet search or a search on LinkedIn.

## The Link Between Handwriting and Learning

There is one final concern regarding a paperless environment. Studies show an undeniable link between handwriting and learning, so how would a paperless society address that need? For example, a study done at the University of Washington showed that children in grades two, four, and six wrote more words, wrote them faster, and expressed more ideas when writing essays by hand versus with a keyboard.[3]

The current replacement seems to be *electronic paper*, such as writing with a stylus, or even your finger, on an iPad or other tablet computer. However, like the other solutions described earlier, these devices have not yet garnered widespread use, and they may prove to offer inferior results during the learning process when compared to handwriting on paper. I believe this is a compelling reason to delay completely eliminating paper, and therefore handwriting—at least from learning environments—until we understand the effect of going paperless on learning and creativity. However, as with many innovative technologies, these tools will likely be adopted—and the consequences dealt with in hindsight.

While a truly paperless environment may be at least a generation away, beginning to choose paperless options that fit your life can have exciting implications for protecting the environment, increasing efficiency, and reducing clutter, I believe the rate of change will accelerate when today's youth are old enough to be in positions of power, bringing a paperless life closer to a reality.

If any of these ideas interest you, I suggest that you choose one (electronic signatures, electronic business cards, a handwriting app on your tablet or smartphone, for example) and try it out. The ideas in this chapter and a quick Internet search on your topic of choice can get you started. Investing time to learn one or more of these solutions *can* pay dividends by increasing your productivity and efficiency.

# AMBIENT INFORMATION

We currently receive information in two ways: *push* and *pull*. *Push* means that the information is "pushed" to us—it automatically appears in our life via some sort of communication technology. As discussed in Chapter 2, this is often intrusive, unwanted, distracting, and a major impediment to controlling our attention. *Pull* refers to information we actively seek, which requires time and effort.

A third option for information consumption, known as *ambient information*, is on the horizon. It offers a delivery mechanism that isn't distracting and doesn't require effort. Ambient information technology enables information to be consumed in the background, and sometimes without even the individual's awareness.

An example can best demonstrate these three ways of receiving information. Suppose you want to determine the current weather. You could have pop-up alerts sent to your computer or smartphone (distracting push notifications). You could turn on the television or look it up on your computer (pulling the information, which requires time and effort). However, if you are inside a building with windows, then you are aware that it's foggy, raining, or bright and sunny. The windows provide you with *ambient* information; it doesn't distract you or require your effort. I believe the future of information delivery will capitalize on new technologies capable of delivering ambient information.

You may be able to increase your efficiency by considering how to make the information you consume more ambient. I show you specific ways to do this with your calendar in Chapter 13. One company currently offering products that provide information through ambient means is Ambient Devices, which you can find at www.ambientdevices.com.

You might have heard advice for achieving goals that capitalizes on the ambient aspects of information consumption, such as keeping your goals visible, using vision boards, or taping thoughts or images to your bathroom mirror. However, these techniques work only when used judiciously. For example, covering your bathroom mirror with all your goals would dilute the beneficial effect. As you implement tools and techniques for achieving your significant results, *focus* is a powerful tool in your arsenal.

# SUMMARY

A paperless environment and ambient information are two ideas that I predict will have increasing prominence in the field of productivity and effectiveness in the future. Being aware of the innovative technology in these areas may help you to capitalize on it through your journey to peak productivity and effectiveness.

The following are some important points from this chapter that are suitable for tweeting:

▶ #Productivity tip; Toss it! Vast majority of all filed paper is never referenced again. So much is available online now.

▶ Tell companies they don't need a hard copy original of your signature—digital versions became binding in 2000.

▶ #Productivity Tip: Don't add contact information to your address book until you've really connected—eliminates #clutter.

▶ Learning is connected to writing. Notes with paper & pen (or handwriting app!) are still a good idea—just *process* after.

▶ Ambient information neither distracts nor takes effort. Make your information ambient, such as color-coding your calendar.

# ENDNOTES

1. Janet N. Abramovitz and Ashley T. Mattoon, "Paper Cuts: Recovering the Paper Landscape," Worldwatch Institute (website), `http://www.worldwatch .org/system/files/EWP149.pdf`, Worldwatch Paper 149, 1999, p. 124.

2. Julie Morgenstern, quoted in "10 Solutions for Taming the Paper Tiger," by Lisa Skolnik, *Chicago Tribune*, July 14, 2002, `http://articles .chicagotribune.com/2002-07-14/features/0207140333_1_julie-morgenstern-organizing-paper`.

3. Gwendolyn Bounds, "How Handwriting Trains the Brain: Forming Letters is Key to Learning, Memory, Ideas," *The Wall Street Journal*, October 5, 2010, http://on.wsj.com/cqA4N6.

## CHAPTER 10

# The T.E.S.S.T.™ Process

**IN THIS CHAPTER**

▶ Making decisions effectively
▶ Dealing with procrastination
▶ Processing versus completing

As I mentioned in Chapter 8, one reason why clutter (both physical and electronic) might accumulate in your life is because you've deferred making a decision about what to do with it. Maybe you think making a decision is going to take more time than you have to devote, or you're afraid you might need it later, or perhaps you just don't feel like dealing with it.

In this chapter, I walk you through the T.E.S.S.T. decision process, which helps you efficiently process things such as paper and email so that they don't become stagnant and create clutter in your world. T.E.S.S.T. is an abbreviation for the following:

▶ Take immediate action
▶ Empower yourself and others
▶ Suspend it to your Next Actions
▶ Store it for future reference
▶ Trash or recycle it

T.E.S.S.T. gives you the tools you need to quickly and effectively make decisions about whether you need to keep something for action, keep it for reference, or trash it.

Papers and emails that haven't been "processed" contribute to stress and anxiety. (Read more about processing items in Chapter 11.) When you skim things without truly addressing them, you leave them as an unknown, discovering just enough about the item to know that you have to do *something* with it, but not deciding exactly what. Because you haven't really processed it and determined what further action to take, it sits in your subconscious and causes stress. When hundreds of emails per day plus reams of paper, documents, and unopened mail are left as unknowns, their effect compounds to create higher and higher stress levels. Therefore, timely processing of all the information and communication that enters your world is the secret to truly *controlling* your environment, and your stress levels.

▶ In this context, "process" means to examine something to decide if it needs to remain in your life. Processing doesn't require that you complete the task, only that you deal with it to the point that it is not hanging around as an "unknown."

## DECIDING ON ACTION

When you first start processing that pile of paper or your overflowing email inbox, a short series of questions can help you get started making effective decisions:

- ▶ Does this require action?
- ▶ If so, can someone else do this?
- ▶ Do I have all the information I need to complete this task?
- ▶ Can I do it quickly?

With each item you need to process, the first question to ask yourself is, "Does this require action? Is there anything I need to do, either now or in the future, related to this email or document?" The following paragraphs address the situation when an item does require action. Instructions for processing items that *don't* require action are ahead in the section "Storing or Trashing."

▶ If you're unsure whether to take action, consider if something will likely happen in the future that could help you make a better decision. If not, your indecision is probably just a form of procrastination, and you can overcome it by deciding now.

A natural response is to decide that you need to address it but to tell yourself you'll figure out the details later. Sometimes your next action is truly hard to decide, but in many cases indecision is simply the desire to procrastinate. Often nothing that will happen in the future will affect your ability to decide on the issue, so this is procrastination disguised as indecision. If so, now is as good a time as any to address this issue.

Sometimes there is a valid reason why you can't decide now. Perhaps you need to make a decision about an event that is happening quite far in the future. For example, suppose you receive a flyer in the mail for a conference that is happening next year.

In this case, you have plenty of time to decide, and other things may happen that will affect your decision. So the answer to the question, "Does this require action?" is yes. (The action required is to "Decide if I will attend.")

When you've determined that future action is required on the item in question, the next question to ask yourself is, "Can someone else do this for me?" There are several things to consider when answering this question. Are you the best person to do it? Do you have the skills required? Can you pay someone else to do it for less than your time is worth? Can you delegate it to a staff member, family member, or service provider? If you don't enjoy the task, aren't skilled at it, or don't consider it a good use of your time, then delegating it is probably the best course of action to maximize your productivity and effectiveness. That's shown in Figure 10-1, and you can read more about it in the "Delegating Is Empowering" section later in the chapter. For now, let's continue the process from the point when you've decided you are the best person to handle the task.

▶ For help answering this question, you might find it helpful to refer to Chapter 3, "Unloading the Shoulds."

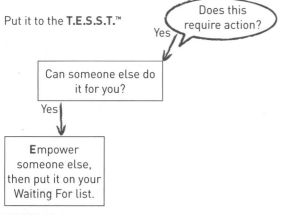

FIGURE 10-1

## The Two-Minute Rule

If you decide that an item requires action but it's not appropriate to empower someone else, then the next question to ask yourself is, "Do I have all of the information I need to complete this task?" In other words, is anything preventing you from taking action immediately? If you have everything you need, and the only thing standing in your way is the time or the opportunity, then your next question is, "Can I do it quickly, in a few minutes or less?" Some people call this the *two-minute rule* (see Figure 10-2).

Note one caution about the two-minute rule: Trying to apply it outside of the "processing" context can lead you astray. Think of processing as a single task—when you are processing documents on your desk or email in your inbox, your goal is to complete the processing task, not to complete each individual task. If you try to immediately take action on every item that you determine needs action, then you will never finish the processing. Therefore, only take action during processing time when *all* of the following are true: an item requires action, you are the person who should do it, you have all the information you need to complete that action, *and* you can do it in two minutes or less. You take the action now because adding it to your Next Actions list would take almost two minutes anyway, so if you could complete it in that time instead, then you should.

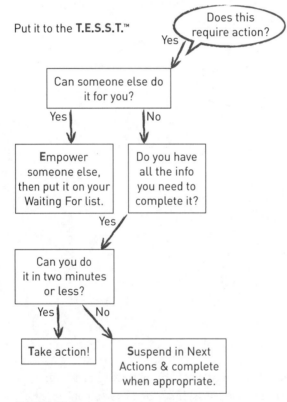

Put it to the **T.E.S.S.T.**™

Does this require action?

Yes

Can someone else do it for you?

Yes | No

**E**mpower someone else, then put it on your Waiting For list.

Do you have all the info you need to complete it?

Yes

Can you do it in two minutes or less?

Yes | No

**T**ake action!

**S**uspend in Next Actions & complete when appropriate.

**FIGURE 10-2**

If you determine that an item will take you more than two minutes to complete, then suspend (the first "S" in the T.E.S.S.T. process) it to your Next Actions list for completion later and get back to your processing.

## FIGHTING HABITS THAT SABOTAGE RATHER THAN SUPPORT

I'm often asked, "Why can't I just do things when I think of them, instead of taking the time to enter them into my task list?" The answer is that, unfortunately, your brain is not obedient; you don't control the thoughts that enter your mind. As discussed in Chapters 2 and 4, if you take action every time you think of something, you are stuck in a state of constant *reaction*; you're not in control because you're switching from task to task at the whim of whatever thought enters your mind. Thoughts arrive faster than you can act on them, so the items start to back up, forcing you to try to remember them. That's often the impetus to grab whatever is at hand—a random envelope, a sticky note, or whatever piece of paper happens to be lying around—and write down the thoughts that are beginning to pile up. This inefficient system takes you back to square one, lacking a central location where everything you need to do is captured, organized, and prioritized.

## Suspending to Next Actions

If you *don't* have all of the information you need, then your Next Action is obviously to get what you need. In most cases, finding or requesting what you need is a quick action to take, so you can complete it right then. If you get what you need right away then you are back to the question, "Do I have all the information I need to complete this task?" Now the answer is yes, so you can proceed from there (refer to Figure 10-2). If you don't get what you need right away then put the item on your Waiting For list until you receive it. The following scenario provides an example:

1. You open a piece of mail, which turns out to be a request from a customer. It requires action in the form of a response to the customer.

2. You determine that you are the best person to respond to the request.

3. You realize you can't respond to the customer until you confer with your co-worker, Joe.

4. You place a call to Joe to discuss but you get his voicemail.

5. You create a task, "Hear back from Joe regarding customer inquiry," with a category of Waiting For. You decide that if you don't hear back from Joe by

tomorrow, you will call him again, so you give your Waiting For task a due date of tomorrow.

6. You place the letter from the customer in your Waiting For file. You have now successfully processed that piece of paper.

7. When Joe calls you back, you mark the Waiting For task as complete, at which point you decide you can now respond to the customer because it can be done quickly in only a minute or two by phone. Therefore, you call the customer and either speak with the person or leave a voicemail with the answer. You can now remove the original request document from your Waiting For file and discard it. You've processed and completed the task successfully using the T.E.S.S.T. process.

Figure 10-3 shows the T.E.S.S.T. decision process for an item that *does* require action.

*▶ Look for more on "process" versus "do" in the next chapter.*

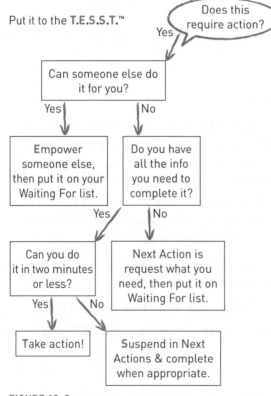

FIGURE 10-3

# DELEGATING IS EMPOWERING

I like to think of delegating as "empowering" (which represents the "E" in the T.E.S.S.T. process) yourself and others. When you delegate, it can empower others in several ways. If you delegate to an employee, it can empower them by providing an opportunity to learn more about the organization and how things are done. If you delegate to a child or teen, you empower them by offering a glimpse into the grown-up responsibilities they will soon face. If you delegate to a service provider, you empower them with the opportunity to earn ongoing business from you.

Also, delegating empowers *you*. It frees you up to do the things that you do best, the things that only you can do, and the things that have an impact on your life or work if they get done—your *significant results*. It can be empowering to find a source who can complete certain tasks for you.

For example, have you ever hired a cleaning person? The first visit or two is always a little awkward—getting acquainted, and explaining what you want done and how you like it done. After a while, however, you have a provider you can trust, one who understands exactly what you want done. Eventually, it almost seems like your house gets clean magically while you're gone—doing other things you enjoy. You find the contentment that comes from a clean house, combined with the relief that you didn't have to do it yourself. You've empowered yourself by relieving yourself from an onerous task, and you've empowered someone else by enabling a service provider to gain a new satisfied customer.

Here's a practical example of empowering someone to do something for you: You're at work on a Monday, and you receive an email request from someone outside the organization that requires a response—in other words, this email does require action. You could respond yourself, but you have a colleague who handles this type of request every day—there's someone else who can do it for you. Therefore, you forward the email to your colleague and ask if she would please respond to the request by the next business day (if she uses the Empowered Productivity™ System too, she creates a Next Action to answer the request). If follow-up is important, you add it to your task list with the category of Waiting For, with a due date of Wednesday, giving your colleague the rest of the day Monday and all day Tuesday to respond to the request. If you don't receive confirmation by Wednesday morning, prompted by the item on your Waiting For list, you check in with your colleague to ensure that the request has been handled. This is an example of successful processing using the T.E.S.S.T. process. So far we've gone through the different combinations of steps for when an item requires action. Next we look at the steps involved when it doesn't.

▶ If an item is important enough for you to follow up, then add it to your Waiting For list. Be sure you ask for an expected completion date so that you have a due date for your Waiting For task.

## STORING OR TRASHING

When you determine that an item does *not* require action, then your next processing task is to determine whether you should keep it (store) or trash the item. For many people, this is the point in the process that results in saving too many things. In my experience most people do keep more than they need.

Usually, the main reason you would keep something is the fear that in the future, you *might* need it; and because you can't predict the future, you would rather be "safe than sorry." Unfortunately, this habit results in keeping a great deal of information that you don't really need. If you have overflowing file cabinets in your office, or you receive messages from your IT department saying that you've exceeded your email storage limits, then you've experienced what I'm describing.

Fortunately, asking yourself two simple questions will enable you to avoid keeping things you don't need (see Figure 10-4). First, if you have determined that something doesn't require action and you're wondering if you need to keep it, consider whether you could get another copy later if it turns out that you do need it. Is the information you need readily available from your company's intranet? Would a Google search provide the information again? Could a co-worker or other department at your company provide it? If you can later retrieve an item you need from somewhere else without too much effort, then you do not need to keep that item (you should trash or recycle it).

The other question to help you decide whether to keep a piece of paper or an email is, "What's the worst thing that would happen if I later need this item but don't have it?" When I work with clients and ask this question, the answer is often a shrug of their shoulder. If you can't even think of a consequence, or the *worst* consequence might be a minor inconvenience, then you can feel safe trashing it.

Obviously, the converse of this process is also true: If obtaining the information later would be difficult or impossible, then keep it. Similarly, if thinking about the consequences of needing it but not having it causes you any level of anxiety, then keep it (see Figure 10-4).

▶ For more details about email folders and controlling your email, see Chapters 11 and 12.

You need to properly store any items that you decide to keep. Remember from Chapter 8 that there are only three kinds of files: Action, Handy Reference, and Archive. If the item is a physical document, you could file it in a reference or archive file, or you might choose to scan it and store it on your computer as an electronic file. If the item is an email, then move it from your email inbox to another folder in your email client. Figure 10-5 shows an example of an email folder setup.

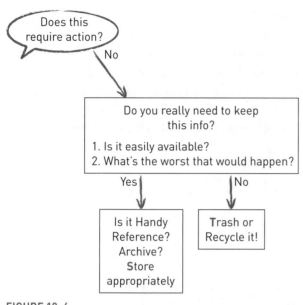

FIGURE 10-4

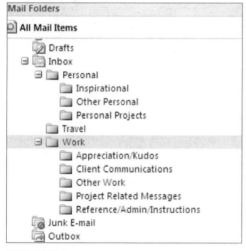

FIGURE 10-5

The point of *processing* your email inbox is to be in control of the items in it. You know the items are processed when they no longer appear in your inbox. Leaving processed messages in your email inbox creates clutter, and makes it difficult to identify the items that still need to be processed, which adds to your stress. Treat your email inbox and your desktop inbox the same way: as a storage container for *unprocessed* information. After an email has been processed, move it from your inbox to its "home." Regular processing of your inboxes gives you control over all the things for which you are responsible, and prevents the accumulation of clutter. Remember, clutter causes stress because you can't remember everything that's there, and as a result you always have some level of anxiety about things you may be forgetting to do. See Figure 10-6 for the complete T.E.S.S.T. process. You may find it useful to photocopy this page and hang it somewhere visible while you're still learning the process.

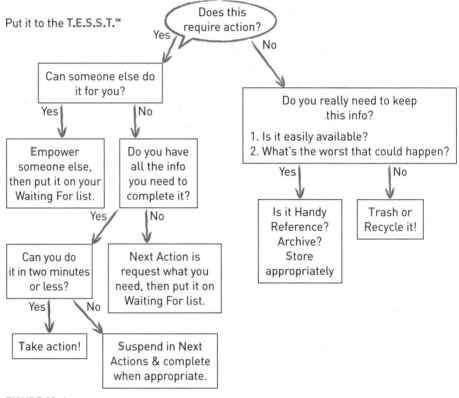

**FIGURE 10-6**

# SUMMARY

Using the T.E.S.S.T. process may seem like a lot of effort to go through for each email or paper that crosses your desk. However, after you've done it a few times, you begin to train your brain to think in *processing* terms, and it becomes intuitive. Pretty soon you'll be moving through the questions in the T.E.S.S.T. process in milliseconds, without even being aware that you are doing it. Mastering this process enables you to stay in control of the details, move through your work faster and more effectively, and operate at peak efficiency. It's another step in *empowering* your productivity.

# QUICK TIPS

The following are some important points from this chapter (also suitable for tweeting). For more information on Twitter, including relevant usernames and hashtags, please refer to the "Read This First" chapter.

- ▶ Notice if indecision is the source of your clutter. This is procrastination in disguise—solve it by deciding now!

- ▶ Five options when dealing with clutter: Take Action, Empower by Delegating, Suspend, Store, or Trash (T.E.S.S.T.).

- ▶ Simplify your processing—if an item doesn't require action, it's either reference or trash!

- ▶ Only apply the two-minute rule during processing time—otherwise you're at the mercy of your random thoughts.

- ▶ Think of delegating tasks as opportunities to empower others—to learn or to grow their business—and it empowers you too!

- ▶ When deciding what to keep for reference, ask, "Can I get another copy if I need it? If not, how big a deal would it be?"

## CHAPTER 11

# Controlling Your Email

Prior chapters covered the benefits of minimizing clutter, both physical and digital, and Chapter 10 introduced the difference between "processing" and "completing" as you work to reduce the clutter in your life. In this chapter and the next, I give you everything you need to take control of one of the biggest sources of digital clutter—your email inbox—and you even learn how to get it to zero immediately.

# THE ROLE OF EMAIL IN A MODERN LIFE

Two common perspectives on email are that it is something that is vitally important that must be attended to constantly, or that it's a nuisance to be ignored. Many of my clients have wistfully considered the idea of deleting all of their email messages and starting over, which is immediately followed by the realization that within a few days or a few weeks, they'd be back where they started, drowning in messages.

In order to implement a process for effective email management, it's important to consider the role it plays in your personal and professional life. How much a part of your work *is* email, really? On the one hand, many people feel that they could get much more done if they didn't have to deal with email, and I'm sure that is true. Has there ever been a time when your corporate email server was down, or you've been otherwise unable to access your messages? Did you feel relief? Were you more productive? You probably felt a sense of freedom, and got a lot more work done. Seen from this perspective, it probably seems like your life would be much easier to manage if you didn't have to deal with email, and you're probably right.

On the other hand, if you're reading this book, you're probably a *knowledge worker*. The work that most professionals do is driven by their knowledge about a particular subject or field in order to advance a common goal (such as the growth and profitability of a company). This requires using that knowledge for problem solving, creativity, and analysis; and for these tasks communication is critical. Because email is currently the most common form of business communication, dealing with your email is probably an important part of your work.

Similarly, if you have shared your personal email account with people in your life then you have an obligation to process those messages. If you instead ignore them, or only view them without dealing with them (or only deal with them infrequently), then two things will likely happen: The individuals in your personal life who are dedicated to reaching you will find a more reliable way to contact you, whereas those who are using email to stay casually connected will fall out of touch.

The early days of email offered a new, way to strengthen personal bonds with those who were not in close physical proximity. Although we have other similar tools now, email was the first electronic social network, and it revolutionized how we communicate. You could start a conversation in which others could participate at their convenience. You could include a virtually limitless number of people in that conversation, and the result was often an interesting and useful exchange, with everyone adding opinions and responses. In some cases, it was a more efficient way to collect and share information than meeting in person or using the phone.

In the early days of email, you hardly noticed or were bothered by the fact that a discussion could add potentially dozens of individual messages to your email inbox. It seemed a small price to pay for this novel way to have a "virtual conversation" with one or more people. However, now that email has been in wide use for a couple of decades, the novelty has worn off and the volume of mail has increased exponentially—I don't know anyone who wishes to receive *more* email. Considering the evolution of the medium offers insight into the way you approach your email. Reflecting on the example scenarios and the consequences of each for you can help you decide how important email is an should be in your life. Following are more specifics about how to manage it.

# THREE TYPES OF "CHECKING" EMAIL

You probably get so much email that it's difficult to keep your inbox from becoming overwhelming. The unrelenting deluge is the reason why most people have hundreds or even thousands of messages in their inboxes, including both those that are important and/or require some type of action, and those that are obviously trash—that is, unimportant. In order to deal with the ongoing avalanche, many people have decided that the only way to stay on top of it is to check it constantly. One study showed that office workers check their email up to 40 times per hour![1]

It isn't just the fear of getting behind that has us frequently checking our messages. It's also lack of focus. Checking email is *easy*—it has to be done and it typically doesn't require a lot of brainpower. In fact, working with email could be considered busywork. There is a certain comfort in the predictability of email; checking and responding to email provides a sense of accomplishment, however brief or false. It's like having a long list that you can check something off of every few minutes—an attraction that reinforces the already present lure of the dopamine squirt.

▶ Remember from Chapter 1 that research suggests that new experiences create a "dopamine squirt" that reinforces the behavior.[2]

My process for managing email begins with the Review, Process, Do strategy: You *review* as often as you feel is necessary, *process* to zero at least a couple times per week, and *do* what needs doing at the appropriate time. The following sections dive into each of these steps in a bit more detail.

## Review

*Reviewing* messages is just what it sounds like: skimming them quickly to determine those that are urgent, and therefore need a quick reply, and those that can be deleted immediately or handled completely with a quick phone call. The review process is quick and doesn't involve in-depth thought.

Unfortunately, reviewing is how some people deal with email all the time. Messages that don't fit into the categories of "truly urgent," "quick reply," or "immediately delete" are ignored or put off until "later." Then those messages are quickly buried by new messages; and pretty soon they are lost in the black hole of hundreds or thousands of messages that comprise most people's email inboxes. Therefore, "later" never arrives.

To regain control over your email inbox, understand that *reviewing* is only the first step; you also have to *process* and *do*. To prevent yourself from letting the review step become your default method for dealing with email, I suggest that you *only allow yourself to review email from your phone or other portable device*. When you review email from your computer, it is very easy to be distracted by it (browsing through old messages, dragging messages to folders, clicking links, and so on) and then you don't get anything else done. On your phone or other portable device it's easier to limit yourself to skimming because the experience isn't as user-friendly—reading a small screen and typing on a tiny keyboard are not as comfortable, so you are less likely to linger. Only review messages on your portable device, don't take the time to actually *process* them. Follow the rule that you only check email from your computer when you really have time to *process* the messages.

## Process

After a few days (or a few hours, depending on your situation) of only dealing with urgent, quick-reply, or quick-delete messages, you probably have items that need more attention. Perhaps these messages didn't start out as urgent, but after time they start to make you feel a little anxious and you know you need to address them soon.

At some points in your week, you have to set aside a stretch of time to *process* your inbox. Merlin Mann, of 43 Folders and Inbox Zero, describes *processing* as "more than checking, less than responding." David Allen, author of *Getting Things Done*, describes processing as "deciding what actions to take on stuff." As I explained in Chapter 10, to me *process* means dealing with every single message to decide whether to delete it or otherwise move it out of your inbox. It's not always important to begin or complete the task that each email contains, whether that's just to provide a thoughtful response or to complete some other request. But it is important to have a firm grasp on what all the items are that require some action from you. Unknown issues buried in your email inbox or unprocessed piles of paper on your desk create stress because you'll feel like something important might be hidden there.

The goal of *processing* your inbox is to empty it, but you can only accomplish this if you pause the messages from downloading into your inbox. Recall from Chapter 2 that an important step in taking control over your technology is controlling when you receive new messages. If your messages download automatically with no input from you, then your technology is in control. Those constantly downloading messages are distracting, and they reinforce your temptation to interrupt yourself to check every one. Consequently, you are constantly multitasking, constantly distracted, and therefore not working at your best.

Change your email client so that new messages arrive only when you press the Send/Receive button. During your processing time, press the Send/Receive button once, and then just move on down the list of messages, following the T.E.S.S.T.™ process. When you're done, your inbox will be empty; you'll know you are current on your communications (at least for the moment, because if you press that Send/Receive button, more messages will arrive), and your inbox will be at zero!

▶ You can find specific instructions for this in Chapter 12.

I know what you're thinking: You currently have thousands of messages in your inbox, so it will take you forever to process them all! Don't worry, I have a solution. Read the rest of this chapter for more information about processing and how to get to zero quickly so you can start fresh using the email management portion of the Empowered Productivity™ System.

## Do

Remember, processing all your messages doesn't mean you've taken action on all of them. As illustrated in the T.E.S.S.T. process, some things need to be done at a later date (Suspend to Next Actions) for one of the following reasons:

- ▶ You need more information.
- ▶ You need many minutes or hours to complete the task.
- ▶ You need someone else's help.

Process the email by putting the required action on your task list so that you can *do* it when you have the answers, time, and resources available.

Review, Process, Do: This is the methodology I recommend for dealing with the constant barrage of email most people are subjected to on a daily basis, and it's an important piece of my Empowered Productivity System.

In the rest of the chapter, I discuss the specific times I suggest that you perform the reviewing, processing, and doing. Before I get to that, I think it's helpful to outline the most common habits I see my clients using, and some more productive behaviors with which to replace them.

# REPLACING YOUR OLD TRICKS

To control communication, you need a good system, and by system I mean a real, step-by-step, I-could-explain-it-to-you-if-you-asked methodology, such as the email management methodology that is part of the Empowered Productivity System. However, most people's habits for managing email include some combination of the following:

- ► Skim and then skip to the next message.
- ► Mark emails that need action as "unread."
- ► "Flag" messages that need action.
- ► Assign categories to inbox messages.

► Processing is the most important component of staying in control of your email and eliminating the stress caused by the nagging fear that you are missing something important when you don't deal effectively with your messages.

If the "skim and skip" habit sounds familiar, you need to figure out why you are skipping over messages. This tactic is fine in the *review* part of the "Review, Process, Do" method described earlier, but remember that reviewing is only one piece of managing your email. You need to incorporate the process and do components as well.

The most common reason for "skimming and skipping" is that you are checking your messages when you don't really have time. As a result, you skip almost everything because of one or more of the following:

- ► You don't know the answer.
- ► You don't feel like dealing with it now.
- ► You think it will take too long.
- ► You are looking for only the "important" messages.

Read on for more details about how this habit and others you might have are sabotaging your productivity.

## The Pitfalls of the Skim and Skip Habit

There are several reasons why skimming and skipping messages, and using the techniques of marking as unread, flagging, and categorizing aren't very effective, and contribute to your stress:

- ► You don't really know how important a message is, what is required of you, what action(s) you might need to take, or how much time it will take you. You've *reviewed,* but you haven't *processed,* so the item is still an "unknown" that nags at you and causes anxiety.

- ▶ Because the tasks waiting in the emails are still relative unknowns, it's difficult or impossible to quantify your workload, or prioritize the tasks in email within the context of the rest of your work.

- ▶ As the deluge of messages continues to flow in, those that are flagged or unread are pushed farther and farther down the list in your email inbox, increasing the chance that one or more will slip through the cracks. The fear that something might fall by the wayside also elevates stress.

- ▶ The most important reason why these techniques aren't productive is because *you have more than one place to look for all the things you need to do*. This is a problem not just for email, but for all your communication channels. For example, some things you know need to be done because they are clearly your responsibility. These are the items that probably make it onto your to-do list. Your email also generates tasks for you to complete, and those tend to languish in your inbox, as described. Then there are items requiring action on your part that come up in meetings, via phone calls and voicemails, in casual conversation, and other communication channels. These items may be scribbled on one or more pieces of paper, or they may just be stored in your brain. Having so many different places to look for all the tasks that need doing prevents you from being able to organize and prioritize them, and to see each item in the context of everything else you need to do.

## The Result Is Worth the Effort

There is no question that dealing with email takes time, but if email is an unavoidable part of your work or personal life, as it is for most of us, then you need to plan for the time it takes to handle it. My work has shown me that it takes, on average, about two minutes to dispatch an average email message. For example, let's say you get about 100 emails per day, every day. That's 700 messages per week, or 1,400 minutes. That's almost 24 hours—one full day—every week just to process email!

If those numbers reinforce the reason why you avoid processing your email, don't despair—the operative words are "on average." After you become good at processing your messages, many will require less than two minutes to process. When you've mastered email processing, you might need only about three or four hours twice per week to effectively process your messages into your system. Starting to use an organized process is worth every minute you spend, in terms of both productivity and the control and peace of mind you get in return.

# DEVELOPING A BETTER SYSTEM

You already know that allowing your messages to download constantly interrupts you and sabotages your productivity, and that the solution is to shut off automatic downloading so that your messages arrive only when you click the Send/Receive button. However, you might still be wondering the following:

- How often you should *review* your messages?

- How many times should you *process* them?

- When is the best time to do both of these steps?

## Appropriate Timing

The answers to the first two questions depend on several things, including your calendar, or schedule, for the day, the nature of your job, and your dependence on communication with others to get your work done. Regarding how many times you should process messages, for most people the first number that comes to mind is too high. Nearly everyone overestimates how often they should at least *review* their messages. For many professions, I've found that reviewing messages two or three times per day is sufficient. That said, you are the only person who can determine this but make sure you the number of times per day you should review your messages factor in all the lessons from the Empowered Productivity System before you settle on a number. Also, that number can change.

Another critical question about managing email pertains to *when* you should check it: Should you check it first thing in the morning, or should you wait until later in the day? To make this decision, consider how you want to start your day. Remember that managing email is reactive; do you want to start your day by being reactive? Recall that doing so sets you on a path to potentially be in reactive mode for the rest of the day, and it can eliminate any chance of being proactive—and therefore productive in terms of making progress toward your significant results. The real question you need to ask yourself is whether checking (reviewing) email first thing in the morning *supports* your own focused attention or *sabotages* it. The answer to this question depends on several factors:

- **Do you have a handheld device for checking email?** The conventional wisdom is that you shouldn't review or process messages first thing in the morning, but I think this advice came about before email on a handheld device was possible or prevalent. I think it's OK to review your messages (following the "Review,

> ▶ This assumes you are using a client to manage your email, such as Microsoft Outlook or Apple Mail. If you are using Google or other web-based email, then simply close the email window in your browser to eliminate email as a source of distraction.

> ▶ When most people talk about "checking" email, they mean review in the context that we've described it here.

> ▶ Remember from the "Read This First" chapter that this entire book is based on the premise of productivity being defined as the ability to achieve your significant results.

Process, Do" guidelines) on your handheld device first thing in the morning. Skim for those messages that directly affect your plans for the day. In general, do not review your messages first thing in the morning on your computer because it's too tempting to get lost in the messages, decreasing your opportunity to be productive and achieve your significant results for the day. However, some exceptions to this rule follow.

▸ **Are you an independent professional (self-employed) or do you work in a large office?** If you work in an office and you decide to forego email and tackle your task list immediately, you are less likely to miss something while sitting at your desk, because someone will pop in to notify you about something that's going on, you'll overhear something, or someone will call you. Conversely, if you work independently, you have to make more of an effort to stay abreast of things.

▸ **Do you have time to be proactive, or do you have to rush off to a meeting?** The whole point of not reviewing email first thing in the morning is to have some time to be proactive and make progress on your significant results for the day. If you forego reviewing email on your computer as the first thing you do, you can spend some time being proactive, enabling you to cross items off your Next Actions list. If you need to rush off to a meeting, you would neither have time to be proactive nor be able to get bogged down by your email, so reviewing your email to confirm that the meeting hasn't been delayed or canceled is certainly prudent.

▸ **Do you work with people in another time zone?** If you work closely with people who are getting ready to leave work around the same time that you are arriving, then it makes sense to review your messages in case you need to deal with anything before the close of their business day.

▸ **How have you "trained" the people with whom you regularly interact?** In this case, "training" is not something you did intentionally; it's more about the expectations other people have based on your usual behavior. For example, real estate agents ask me, "How do I get my clients to stop calling me at 9:00 at night?" My response: "Stop answering." People who need to communicate with you *will do what works*. If you have trained them that you will respond to an email immediately, then they will feel comfortable using email for emergencies. Conversely, if emailing you about something important fails to elicit a response, they will have to try reaching you some other way. Whatever is effective is the method they will use for the *next* urgent communication. You can't control the way other people behave, but you *can* create circumstances that support your own productivity, rather than sabotage it.

NOTE Regarding this issue of "training" others, it's also critical that you make a distinction about "important/urgent." Is "urgent" to someone else also urgent to you? If not, that might affect your response time. Consider whether you might have inaccurate assumptions about the appropriate response time. I've worked with companies whose employees felt that delivering anything less than an immediate response meant that they weren't providing good customer service. However, when they actually asked their customers, they discovered that a response within one business day was considered good service (meaning that an immediate response was *not* necessary).

As I mentioned, if you have a handheld device, *and* you have the self-discipline to avoid being distracted, then reviewing your messages on your handheld device several times a day, including first thing in the morning, is certainly a valid option (I do it myself). Be careful, however, because the temptation to review messages on your phone and then rush to your computer to "just respond to this one" is strong; and it's all downhill from there!

Now that you know how to determine how often you should review, the next logical question is, "How often should you process?" This also depends on a few factors, including the following:

- **The nature of your email communications**—How much of your important work comes to you via email?

- **The results of your reviewing**—Did you find a lot that needs attention, or could most of it wait a bit?

- **Your schedule for the day or week**—If you are booked up one or more days, you need to plan for the fact that you likely won't have time to process email on those days and therefore need to work the time for processing into your schedule later in that week.

Achieving peace of mind with respect to your email is a balance only you can find. You might need to process email daily; or with effective reviewing you may only need to process it once per week; or something in between. Keep in mind that the important point here is whether you are sabotaging or supporting your productivity and attention with your email habits. Consider all the factors from this chapter carefully and frequently, knowing there isn't an exact formula that works in every situation.

# Implementing the 60-Second Rule

To *process* your email, use the T.E.S.S.T. Decision Chart (see Figure 11-1). You'll find that there are really only five possible combinations of actions you can take:

- ▶ Read and delete
- ▶ Read, respond, and delete
- ▶ Read and file for later reference
- ▶ Read, respond, and file
- ▶ Move the item out of your inbox and into your task list if dealing with the message will take longer than a few minutes

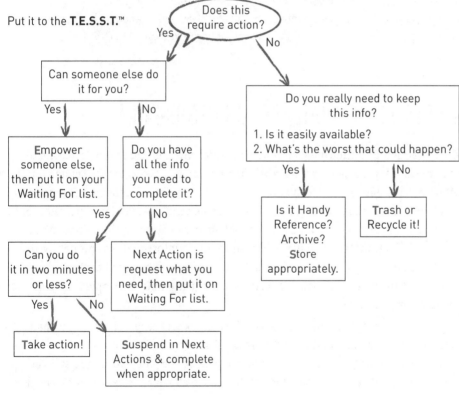

**FIGURE 11-1**

▶ Incidentally, the same is true for your Twitter, LinkedIn, and Facebook accounts and other communication tools.

During processing, commit to spending one full minute thinking about each message, unless you can process it in less time. This will help you to break the "skim and skip" habit. If you can read a message in 10 seconds, use the extra 50 seconds (rather than skip to the next one) to apply the T.E.S.S.T. process—figuring out what to do with the message (not leave it in your inbox!). Allowing this time to stop to think is the biggest barrier to get over. You won't actually need an entire minute to process each of your messages, and some might require a bit more than a minute; but knowing that you have allowed yourself an entire minute for each message can help you break the habit of checking your email when you don't really have time.

> **WARNING** Avoid assuming that a message's length has anything to do with the effort it will take to review or process it. For example, don't assume that because a message is long that you don't have the time to read it. If you do use the full minute you've allotted for a message, you can often gather enough information to fully process it, rather than leave it in your inbox to be dealt with later.

## TO GET LESS EMAIL, SEND LESS EMAIL

When practicing controlling your inbox, consider whether *you* are contributing to the unnecessary messages you receive. Email is quick and easy for the sender, but it often inconveniences the receiver if email is not the most efficient communication tool to use for that specific situation. Many people send an email for issues that could be handled much more quickly by phone, but email seems faster than a phone call; and some people prefer to avoid the human contact. Unfortunately, this habit can greatly undermine your control. One message can, and often does, result in a long thread of many messages back and forth, whereas the phone call would have resolved the issue immediately.

Similarly, because sending a message is so quick and easy, often we send many more than is necessary, and we add more details than the situation actually requires. Here's a good rule of thumb: If you would not pick up the phone to share a specific piece of information, then consider whether you really need to send it as an email.

Earlier in this chapter I suggested that email was probably the first electronic social network we had; and because of that we may have some lingering habits that no longer serve us.

In the past 10 years, a dozen or more types of new social networks and other tools have been developed that improve upon the process for a "virtual conversation."

Internet applications have provided us with many alternatives for collecting input from large groups of people. Some examples of online tools you can use to conduct a virtual conversation include the following:

- ► Online survey tools
- ► Message boards such as Yahoo! and Google Groups
- ► Shared documents
- ► Evite and other planning and invitation tools
- ► Online scheduling tools such as TimeBridge and When Is Good?
- ► Blogging platforms and "wikis" with comment and correction capabilities
- ► Video- and image-sharing sites with commenting capabilities
- ► Social networking platforms such as Facebook, Google+, LinkedIn, and Twitter

Of course, there are still more "old-fashioned" ways to conduct group discussions: in-person meetings or remote meetings by video or phone or both.

All the Internet applications mentioned in the preceding list can "pull" a participant (meaning that you have to visit the site to participate in a conversation), which takes time and effort, or "push" the information (a notification is sent to the participant, usually via email, alerting them about a continuation of a discussion or inviting them into a new discussion), which is often intrusive and distracting. Neither is a great solution, but it's the price we pay for the capability to converse immediately and simultaneously with virtually any person, anywhere in the world, who has an Internet connection.

The somewhat Faustian bargain we make for this capability of easier, more inclusive, and more convenient communication is either the crushing weight of endless email messages that are seemingly impossible to stay on top of, or the time and effort it takes to seek out these connections and communications on our own. Personally, I prefer the latter and believe it's more efficient, because it offers the necessary ingredient for surviving—with our sanity intact—the information and technology revolution we are living in: the ability to control the information we receive, and consequently to control the resulting demands on our attention.

Capitalizing on these other options for group conversation means that if you want a piece of information, if you care to participate in a conversation, it's available, but otherwise you remain undisturbed, undistracted, and free from all the clutter caused by jokes, videos, articles, and conversations you didn't ask for and may prefer not to receive.

# THREE THINGS YOU SHOULDN'T DO

Do you work at a company where everyone is copied on everything? My work has shown me that much of the email a company generates is unnecessary, ineffective, and primarily unread. Many messages are sent as a "cc," a "bcc," or a "reply to all." The fact that "cc" stands for "carbon copy" and "bcc" stands for "blind carbon copy" should give you a hint that their time has passed. Who even remembers what a carbon copy is?

Following are some of the reasons you might be using "cc," "bcc," or "reply all," and some ideas for improving your effectiveness with email.

> **NOTE** The title of this section suggests that you should *never* use these features. However, my intent is only to suggest that you should consider whether they offer the most effective option in a given situation.

## Carbon Copy

The rampant use of cc on emails is one of the major contributors to decreased productivity due to email, especially in large companies. Following are some of the most common reasons for using cc on emails and an alternative perspective on each that will help you to be more effective.

### CC FOR FYI

*Bad idea:* Sometimes a cc is used to "keep people in the loop." This is not the best way to keep your co-workers informed. First, the people copied have to read the message to determine whether it's even relevant to them. Second, they may not glean from it what you want them to know. Third, unless a message is addressed to them, recipients of a cc are unlikely to read it. Co-workers who are not using the Empowered Productivity System will probably use one of the ineffective techniques mentioned earlier in the chapter: delete it without reading it, move it to a reference folder, or mark it as unread but leave it in their inbox. When you cc messages to co-workers, you create this extra work for them and if they aren't reading your messages, you have not met your objective of keeping them updated on the topic of your email. This is one of the most frequent causes of communication breakdown in an organization.

*Better:* If you want to inform someone about *part* of a message you have sent to someone else, cut and paste the information from the first message into a separate email that you send directly to the person. This ensures that the person knows exactly what you want them to know, and there is no chance for misinterpretation and less of a chance that your co-worker will overlook the message. Alternatively, put the co-worker in the "to" line and *address* the co-worker *directly in the original message, near the top.* For example, "Hi Jane—I'm writing to summarize our meeting. Joe—I'm copying you because I wanted you to know what we agreed upon yesterday."

### CC TO COVER YOURSELF

*Bad idea:* Maybe you're not really sure if you're on the right track, so you copy your boss, figuring that this will give her an opportunity to correct you if she doesn't agree with your course of action. You translate her lack of response as approval. However, when you cc her, she probably doesn't read the message, and the fact that you copied her does not absolve you of responsibility anyway. This is another source of communication breakdown within an organization, sometimes with damaging results.

*Better:* Run your intentions by your boss prior to the communication. Or, if you prefer, this is another case in which you can add your boss to the "to" line and address her directly in the message and invite her input. For example: "Joe, I think we should go with the 5×7 flyer. Mary, please let me know if you disagree."

## Blind Carbon Copy

A good use of bcc is when you are emailing many people and you don't want any of the recipients to see the email addresses of the other recipients. However, the common use of bcc that's described here is not efficient.

*Bad idea:* You've probably heard at least one horror story about a bcc gone embarrassingly awry. A common use for bcc is to share a message with someone when you don't want the actual recipient to know. Ethics aside, there is simply too much potential for unintended consequences with a bcc.

*Better:* If you want to privately copy someone on a message, send it to the primary recipient and then go into your Sent folder and forward the message to another recipient, explaining to the "private" recipient why he or she is receiving it. For example, "Mary, below is the message I sent to Jane to call attention to her frequent tardiness."

## Reply All

I'm not a big fan of "reply all." Sometimes it seems a little narcissistic: Does everyone *really* need to see your response? Using reply all is probably a leftover habit from when email was the only electronic social network and therefore the only method we had for virtual group communication.

For the sake of overburdened email inboxes everywhere, I suggest that you think twice before you send an email encouraging a reply all, or responding to one with a reply all. It's not the most efficient way to collect group feedback. When I work with large companies, I often see huge labor and talent costs because people send group messages using reply all, instantly creating dozens of messages for their fellow colleagues to deal with.

Busy employees in these organizations are receiving hundreds of messages per day. If it optimistically takes just one minute to deal with every email message, and the typical employee receives 200 or more messages per day, then more than one-third of salary overhead is spent paying staff to do nothing but read and respond to email messages, most of which are internal communications. How many of these messages really contribute to corporate productivity? Recall from earlier chapters that reacting to email robs employees of the opportunity to be *proactive*, and it's only during proactive times that we can achieve significant results.

As with cc, I suggest that you refrain from unnecessarily replying to all when extra people are on a message. As a result, others might not be tempted to use reply all.

Changing the way you use email enables you to set an example for communication within your organization, minimize communication breakdowns, reduce email clutter, and save everyone some time.

# THREE THINGS YOU SHOULD DO

Some of the most efficient techniques for using email are often overlooked, even though they seem obvious once they are pointed out. The following sections describe three email best practices you can employ to increase your productivity.

## Use Descriptive Subjects

Many people access their email on handheld devices, where space is limited and opening and closing messages requires extra hand gestures that waste time. However, you can offer the recipients of your messages the opportunity to save some time by placing the most useful part of the message right in the subject line. Consider the following email message:

*Subject*: Important information regarding today's meeting!

*Body*: The meeting has been canceled.

In this case, putting the relevant information (the meeting has been canceled) in the subject line would have been the most effective way to compose the email. Some people take this a step further, by ending the subject line with "EOM," which stands for "end of message," so that the recipient knows it's not necessary to open the message. However, my experience has indicated that acronyms such as this are not yet common enough to be widely used; and rather than save time, they result in extra email responses asking what EOM means! Therefore, unless you can be sure that everyone with whom you communicate already knows these types of acronyms, using them will not be effective.

> **TIP** If you receive an email message (or text message, or other communication) that contains an acronym or word that you don't understand, avoid asking the sender. Instead, take the initiative and do an Internet search on the unknown term. Usually you can get the answer in seconds, without burdening the sender with the need to educate you.

In addition to being as informative as possible in the subject line, also be mindful that the subject line of an email viewed on a handheld device is limited, so strive to be both informative and brief.

## Keep the Thread Intact

The phrase "jump the thread" is an idiom that warns against replying to a message about one topic with a response about a second topic, without changing the subject line. For example:

*Initial message subject*: Action steps from the meeting

*Initial message body*: We agreed in the meeting that the following people would take the following actions. . .

*Response message subject*: RE: Action steps from the meeting

*Response message body*: Thank you. I also wanted to let you know that I spoke with the customer regarding that issue we discussed last week. . .

This responder has "jumped the thread," bringing up an issue totally unrelated to the one indicated by the subject line of the initial message. It is very easy to overlook or automatically delete messages like this, especially if the recipient assumes that the original issue is resolved. Instead, start a new message with an appropriate subject line. Some people use the old message(s) with a new subject line, but a new message is a lot "cleaner" than a set of old messages that can confuse the recipient with unrelated information in the message history.

## Use Other Tools When Appropriate

Elaborating on the suggestions made earlier regarding what to do when you send an email, don't take the "lazy" option if it's not the most efficient one for the situation. Because most people spend so much time in their email, it often seems like using email is the fastest and most convenient option to communicate any piece of information or request; but sometimes it isn't. Consider whether a phone call might solve the issue more efficiently, keeping in mind that the phone call can be ignored if it's not convenient for the recipient to answer it. Similarly, although it may seem like finding a convenient time for a phone call, video conference, or meeting will take longer than a group email, that isn't always true. Sometimes other tools save more time in the long run if they reduce the number of messages everyone has to process.

# ASSESSING THE COSTS OF YOUR CURRENT EMAIL HABITS

It's important to recognize that there are costs associated with not processing your email in terms of the stress and anxiety it adds to your life. If you get tens or hundreds of messages daily, trying to stay on top of them (by allowing automatic downloading and trying to review every message as soon as it hits your inbox) is not only virtually impossible and unsustainable; it also guarantees that you are always distracted. This constant distraction prevents flow, forces constant multitasking, and results in increased stress and poor performance. The benefits reaped from taking the time to process your email properly using the methodology from the Empowered Productivity System far outweigh these costs.

There is also a cost to keeping every message instead of applying the two questions from the T.E.S.S.T. process and giving yourself permission to trash or recycle. The costs of keeping everything include the following:

▶ The clutter it adds to your physical and/or electronic space.

▶ The wasted time it takes to look through everything you *don't* need when searching for what you actually *do* need.

*▶ 1. Is it easily available somewhere else? 2. What's the worst that would happen if you thought you needed it, but didn't have it?*

- ▶ The slowdown of your system caused by maxing out your storage space.

- ▶ The slowdown of your programs because the data stored in them is too big. (If you've ever seen the hourglass in Microsoft Outlook, or the spinning pinwheel on a Mac when trying to switch functions, then you have experienced this.)

Although there will be scenarios in which the cost of keeping something is worth bearing, it's important to recognize these costs and weigh them during your processing in order to prevent excess clutter and the problems it causes.

# GETTING TO ZERO

You can use the ideas in this chapter to control your email going forward, but I know that many of you are already buried in messages, and trying to process the backlog can prevent you from starting fresh.

To start with an empty inbox *today*, immediately shut off automatic downloading of messages in your email client if you haven't already. Next, create a subfolder under your email folder called Old Emails to Process, and move everything before yesterday or the last few days into that folder. How far back you go is up to you; the point is to leave only a manageable number of messages in your inbox that you can process right away. This will enable you to start fresh with your new process the next time you access your email.

▶ I explain specifically how to do this in the most common email clients in the next chapter.

Process all of your remaining messages using the T.E.S.S.T. flow chart and the system for *processing* that you learned in this chapter, until you have zero messages in your inbox. You can process the messages in the Old Email to Process folder when you have some time, or wait until something comes up (someone says, "Did you get the email I sent you last week?"). It's not as drastic as deleting everything and starting over, but it achieves the same result of getting your inbox to zero.

# SUMMARY

When you get to zero, *resist* the urge to check your mail again! Go do something else! Work off your Next Actions list for a while, or otherwise be proactive. It's impossible to imagine the relief you will feel from an empty inbox until you have one. Bask in it.

# QUICK TIPS

The following are some important points from this chapter (also suitable for tweeting). For more information on Twitter, including relevant usernames and hashtags, please refer to the "Read This First" chapter.

▶ The RIGHT way to check email: Review, Process, Do with appropriate timing

▶ Tip: Only allow yourself to check email on your smartphone unless you're in "email processing" mode.

▶ The goal of processing email is to move it out of the inbox (file or trash) and move any action item onto your to-do list.

▶ Is your email management habit to "Skim & Skip?" This creates more stress worrying about things falling through the cracks.

▶ Break the "Skim & Skip" email habit by committing one full minute to processing each message—saves time in the long run.

▶ If it takes about two minutes to process an email, 100 emails a day is almost 24 hours a week to process—are you leaving enough time?

▶ Train the people you email regularly to support your productivity by not expecting an immediate response.

▶ Tip: To get less email, send less email messages!

▶ When collecting input from a large group, consider if a survey tool or shared document would be better than email.

▶ Using cc to keep people in the loop usually backfires— emails go unnoticed and inbox clutter.

▶ Productivity tip: Use brief but descriptive subjects to make email processing easier for your recipients.

# ENDNOTES

1. Steve Bird, "Study: Most Office Workers Feel 'E-Mail Stress'," August 17, 2007, FoxNews website, www.foxnews.com/printer_friendly_story/ 0,3566,293491,00.html.

2. Matt Richtel, "The Lure of Data: Is It Addictive?," July 6, 2003, *The New York Times* website, www.nytimes.com/2003/07/06/business/the-lure-of-data-is-it-addictive.html?src=pm%E2%80%9D.

## CHAPTER 12

# Defending Your Attention Using Technology

Managing email is a challenge for most busy professionals. In addition to applying the techniques from the last chapter, it's helpful to ensure that you are making the most of the technology, or tools, available and using them in the most efficient way.

In Chapter 11, I address some techniques for managing email that are common, but actually ineffective, such as flagging, categorizing, or marking messages left in the inbox as unread. *Processing* those messages, as explained in the "Review, Process, Do" section of Chapter 11, eliminates the need for these unproductive habits and provides a more effective alternative for managing emails that require some action. This chapter addresses some other common but ineffective techniques, discusses some useful technology for staying in control of your communications, and provides more specific instructions for using the most popular email clients (Microsoft Outlook, Apple Mail, and Gmail) to support the efficient behaviors of the Empowered Productivity™ System.

# BREAKING BAD HABITS

Setting up rules in your email client or program can sometimes reduce the number of messages waiting to be processed in your inbox. Also, because electronic storage is relatively inexpensive and takes up little physical space, many people have adopted the habit of keeping every message. In this section I explain why I believe these to be ineffective habits, and I offer some alternatives later in the chapter.

One common habit for controlling email is setting up *rules* in an email client, so that specified types of email messages go into designated folders. Although you might think that this helps to keep your inbox manageable by diverting some messages into other folders, in my opinion rules don't truly help because they merely add to the number of folders you need to process! Some email clients, such as Microsoft Outlook, display a number beside the email folder to indicate how many unread/messages are contained in the folder. I find that rather than being helpful, this number contributes to stress; it's a constant reminder of unknown items that may need your attention. And instead of having just one folder with this number, rules results in many folders taunting you with the count of unread messages. Rules and filters give you the illusion of control. In reality, they cause your focus to be scattered and might actually increase the amount of time it takes you to manage your messages.

Another similar habit I see is people keeping every message as they process their email, moving them to one of many email folders they have created. The T.E.S.S.T™ process described in Chapter 10 helps you determine what actually needs to be kept and what can be deleted; but when you *do* need to keep a message, it's inefficient to have to scroll through dozens of folders, or more, to locate the appropriate place in which to file it.

As with your paper files, I suggest you file email messages categorically, separating items into the major areas of your life. For example, you might choose to sort by business-related email and personal email, and then perhaps one more level of categorization, such as "internal," "clients," and "project-related" for your business email. Keep in mind that the more folders you have, the harder it is to find things, and the longer it takes you to file what you choose to keep, so keep the number of folders you have to a minimum. Taking advantage of your client's search and sort features can help you quickly find a particular message, and minimizes the need for an extensive and detailed list of email reference folders.

▶ The sort feature in Microsoft Outlook works as well as other clients, but the search is slower. If you are an Outlook user, consider using a few more folders than just the handful mentioned here.

Many people don't realize that the search and sort features in email clients are very good. In addition to running a search, you usually have the capability to sort by date, sender, subject, and a host of other options. I suggest that you rely on these rather than spend a lot of time creating folders and subfolders. With just a few folders, a sort feature, and a search feature, you should be able to find any email you need in a matter of seconds.

**TIP** If you respond to a message you need to keep, delete the one in your inbox and file the one from your Sent folder. This ensures that you have a complete record—both the initial message and your response.

The following sections describe other online tools and processes that will make it easier for you to control your email.

# REDUCING "NOISE" AND EXERTING MORE CONTROL

Social networking applications such as Twitter, Facebook, MySpace, LinkedIn, YouTube, and others give us unprecedented opportunities to connect with, and attract the attention of, people who in the past were much farther removed: long-lost friends, celebrities, politicians, corporate executives, and so on.

These tools encourage users to share personal information and details that in the past were kept private, or were not readily accessible. Social networks are reshaping the concept of privacy and ushering in a generation that has a vastly different perspective on personal information than the one that preceded it. Fortunately, we also have the technology to keep others at arm's length if we choose. The following sections describe three excellent tools for protecting your contact information, such as your email address and your phone number. This enables you to exert some control over who can contact you, as well as when and how you can be reached—or not.

## Otherinbox

First, I recommend a two-step process that starts with obtaining a *secondary* email address from a free provider such as Yahoo! or Google. Your primary email address could be your work address or a personal address you give to co-workers, friends, and family. Having a secondary email address enables you to reap all the advantages that you get from providing an email address to vendors and service providers (for example, notifications from shippers, financial institutions, utility companies, social networking sites, discount coupons, and contest entries) without seeing all the spam that often accompanies such exposure. This is often called a *junk mailbox*.

Setting up a secondary email address for junk mail is only the first step, though. Many people with a junk mailbox don't process it frequently enough to be effective because they don't give the email address to anyone deemed "important." Consequently, the junk mailbox is often ignored, and any important or useful notifications are missed.

Therefore, the second step I suggest is to sign up for a free account at Otherinbox .com. Otherinbox has a feature called *Organizer* (for Gmail and Yahoo!) that keeps your secondary inbox manageable. Using a list of known marketers and retailers, Otherinbox scans this inbox for messages from these senders. It automatically categorizes these messages and sorts them into folders for you. Recall from the first section of this chapter that I don't recommend using rules that sort your incoming messages into multiple folders, because then you have many places to look for the email you need to process. Otherinbox solves this problem by sending you a *Daily Digest* message (which you can have sent to your primary address) that summarizes all the messages it organized for you. This digest enables you to process all those messages almost instantly, with a quick scan, so you are alerted if anything needs your attention. In addition, Otherinbox has an automatic spam filter, so you don't even see the spam. It also has a great unsubscribe feature that makes it fast and painless to unsubscribe from messages you don't want and automatically filters those messages out of your inbox for you.

> **NOTE** In addition to the sorting, filtering, and organizing benefits that Otherinbox provides, Gmail and Yahoo! also allow you to create rules that automatically forward specific messages to your primary address, so you still get the messages instantly without having to divulge your primary email address to a broad audience.

Gmail recently introduced a feature called *Priority Inbox* that determines which of your messages are the most important and moves those to the top. Using Priority Inbox in conjunction with Gmail Organizer from Otherinbox provides a powerful combination for controlling your email, especially those messages often known as *robomail*, which are not messages from actual individuals whom you know but are also not spam. They are the "in-between messages" such as notifications, coupons, and newsletters that you want or need, but that can usually be dealt with at your convenience.

Otherinbox is a great example of a way that you can use technology to exert more control over the extent to which your email distracts you.

> **NOTE** Otherinbox is a startup in Austin, Texas, and I've been using it since before its official launch in 2008. It has saved me hours of time, while also enabling me to "protect" my primary email address. Remember that a junk mailbox or secondary email alone is not enough, and it can cause as many problems as it solves. Conversely, a secondary email address combined with a free Otherinbox account significantly lessens your email burden and helps you to control your technology instead of allowing it to control you.

## Google Voice

Another tool I recommend for helping you to achieve control over your communications is Google Voice. This service offers many of the benefits for a phone number that Otherinbox offers for email.

Google Voice provides you with a phone number and a voicemail account in any area code you select. You can program it to forward calls to one or more phone numbers, such as a home phone or cell phone, or simply to take messages for you. You can receive transcribed messages as text in your email along with a link to the original recording, if you choose. You can also receive text messages that are sent to your Google Voice number. In addition, using the website or a smartphone app, you can make calls from your Google Voice number, so that's the number displayed on the caller ID of your recipient. Google Voice gives you the control to take calls, block calls, let them roll into voicemail without ringing you (a "do not disturb" setting), and even listen in as the caller's message is being recorded. Giving others your Google Voice number protects your "real" phone number, prevents corporations and marketers from reaching you directly if you don't want them to, and adds a whole new dimension to the capability to screen your calls.

Here's an example of how Google Voice can help you: Perhaps you have a demanding job that sometimes requires you to be accessible when you are away from the office. If you can't conveniently forward your office phone calls, you might have to provide your personal mobile number(s) to work contacts, which often results in unwanted calls arriving during personal time. Instead, you can provide a Google Voice number as your work phone number, forwarding it to the appropriate phone or to a colleague, giving you the flexibility to take calls while out of the office only when you choose, while still protecting your personal numbers and your personal time.

## Spam Filters

My last recommendation is a great spam filter. If you receive more than a few email messages daily that are clearly spam, then you should consider investigating some options to prevent this.

If you have a corporate email account, your IT department probably provides a spam filter for you, so consulting the staff if you're getting spam is a good first step. If you have email on a personal domain, hosted by a service, their technical support department can probably advise you on minimizing the spam you receive, and many allow you to customize your settings.

If you get the majority of your email through a Yahoo! or Google account, Otherinbox can act as your spam filter. If you use another free email service, such as Hotmail or MSN, or if you have found that your work spam filter or Otherinbox is still letting too much spam come through, then consider purchasing spam filter software. A quick Internet search yields many options, so include the word "reviews" in your search, such as "spam blocker software reviews."

There are also companies that provide subscription services for spam blocking, and these offer the benefit of continual updates. Some services, such as SpamArrest, use challenge-response technology: Users must respond to a verification message before the sender's original message is sent to your inbox, which virtually eliminates the possibility of receiving spam email.

One often hears the lament that privacy is dead because of twenty-first-century technology; but you can be a savvy productivity student, harnessing technology such as Otherinbox, Google Voice, and spam filters to your advantage in order to protect your privacy and exert more control over your incoming communication.

## PICKING THE RIGHT EMAIL CLIENT

Technically, you have two choices for interacting with email. The first is to use a *client*, which usually implies downloading your messages to your personal computer and managing them through a software program such as Microsoft Outlook or Apple Mail. The other option is *webmail*, which means accessing your messages on a server. To interface with the server, you access it by using a web browser to log on to a website. This is also known as email "in the cloud." An example of webmail is getting your messages by opening your web browser and going to Yahoo! or Google, signing in, and clicking Mail.

A program's interface is one of the most important factors in choosing an email program. For example, one thing to consider is how easy it is to create a task from an email. If you work for a company, you're probably accessing your work email through a program such as Microsoft Outlook. Consequently, you can very easily create a task from an email, and you have access to many other convenient features that will help support your productivity.

How you handle your personal messages is up to you, but you'll have the same considerations here that you had in the "Manage One Life, Not Two" section of Chapter 6: Do you want to receive personal messages in your work email? And if those personal messages require the creation of a task, are you going to keep your personal tasks and your work tasks together? The issue of merging your personal life and your professional life requires some careful consideration—you can be most effective and efficient if you have everything you need to manage in one place. However, storing personal information in a tool that does not belong to you, and could even be taken away without notice, is a big concern. Note that some companies allow departing employees to purchase their company laptops and smartphones at a depreciated rate. If your company offers this, it may ease some of your concerns.

If you don't yet have an answer to this problem that you are comfortable with, it may help to review Chapter 6, understand your company policies, and ask others at your organization how they handle this issue.

If you've already chosen your task list tool, you might have already decided which email interface to use. For example, if you are using the task list in Microsoft Outlook, then also receiving your messages in Outlook makes sense. If you are using the to-do list in iCal and/or the Reminders app on your iPhone, then it makes sense to use Apple Mail.

As I discussed in Chapter 7, there are some productivity drawbacks to using Google, such as not being able to set a reminder on your tasks or only being able to see one task list at a time. If you have a Gmail, Yahoo!, or other free email account, I suggest you program a client, such as Apple Mail or Microsoft Outlook, to receive your messages from that account into your client, so that you don't have to access them from the website. Using webmail makes it difficult for each of your PIM components to work well together, which poses a barrier to effectively controlling your commitments, communication, and information.

As mentioned previously, most email clients have similar features, but what is critical to your productivity and to your ability to use the Empowered Productivity System to manage details is how easy it is for you to create a task or calendar appointment from an email message. Because many of your tasks are likely to appear via email, the ability to easily create a task from a message will enhance your productivity.

The next section covers the two most useful email-processing techniques (creating a task or calendar appointment from an email, and creating email folders for storing reference or archive messages). It also describes specifically how to shut off the automatic message download in the three most common email interfaces: Microsoft Outlook, Apple Mail, and Gmail.

# CREATING TASKS FROM EMAIL

For most of us, the days zoom past in a blur of activity. How quickly and easily you can get things done and make progress on your goals has a direct effect on your productivity—your ability to *achieve your significant results*. Because of this, you want to eliminate anything that might stand in your way of moving forward—things I call *speed bumps*. One example of a speed bump that slows you down is an item on your Next Actions list about which you were not specific. As you read an item on your list if you have to stop to think about the specific action you need to take in order to mark that task as complete, then you didn't give it enough thought when you entered it.

Often the actions we need to take are typically received via email—a customer request for a proposal, instructions from your boss, or a spouse's request for a document filed at home. In order to stay in control and successfully manage all these various commitments, the required actions need to make it into your task list tool. Therefore, another type of speed bump is a difficult or unnecessarily time-consuming method for creating a task from an email message. The instructions below illustrate how to do this as quickly as possible in three common email programs: Microsoft Outlook, Apple Mail, and Gmail.

## Microsoft Outlook

To create a task from email in Microsoft Outlook, right-click and hold on a message as you drag it to hover over the Tasks icon. A dialog box with three options will appear (see Figure 12-1):

- ▶ Copy Here as Task with Text
- ▶ Copy Here as Task with Attachment
- ▶ Move Here as Task with Attachment

The first and second options, for copying, put one copy of the email in a task and leave a copy of the email in your inbox. The Move option takes the message out of your inbox. Because the goal is to empty your inbox, I suggest that you choose to *move* the message. However, if you want to archive the email for reference, *copy* it into the task and then file the original message from your inbox into a folder. Don't leave the message in your inbox after you've processed it! That just creates clutter.

This method also works for creating calendar appointments from an email. Just drag and hover over the Calendar icon instead of the Task icon.

The Copy Here as Task with Text option inserts the body of the email and all relevant details into the body of the task. Note that this option removes all email functionality (Reply, Forward, and so on). After creating the task, its subject line will initially contain the subject of the email. Be sure to change this to whatever action you need to take with regard to the message. Be as specific as possible and start with an action verb. Figure 12-2 shows a newly created task whose subject has not yet been changed.

Selecting Copy Here as Task with Attachment inserts the email itself as an icon into the body of the task, as shown in Figure 12-3.

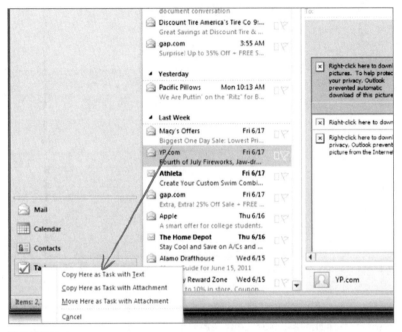

FIGURE 12-1

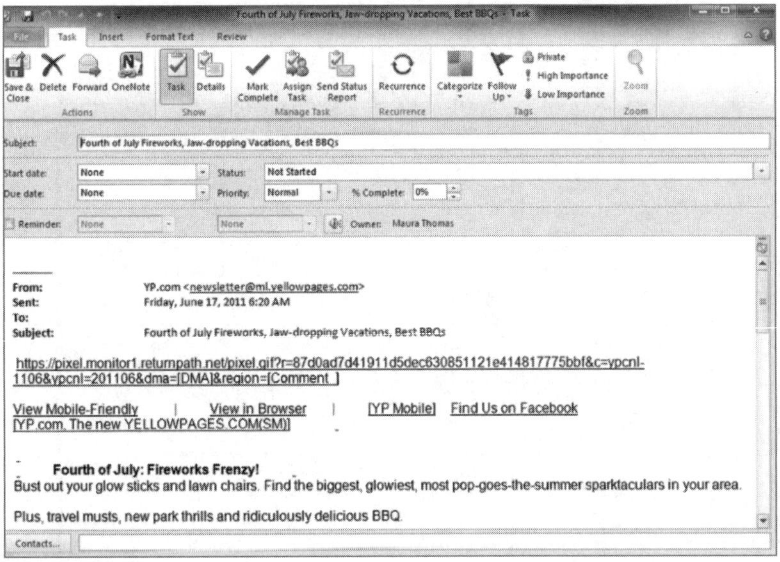

FIGURE 12-2

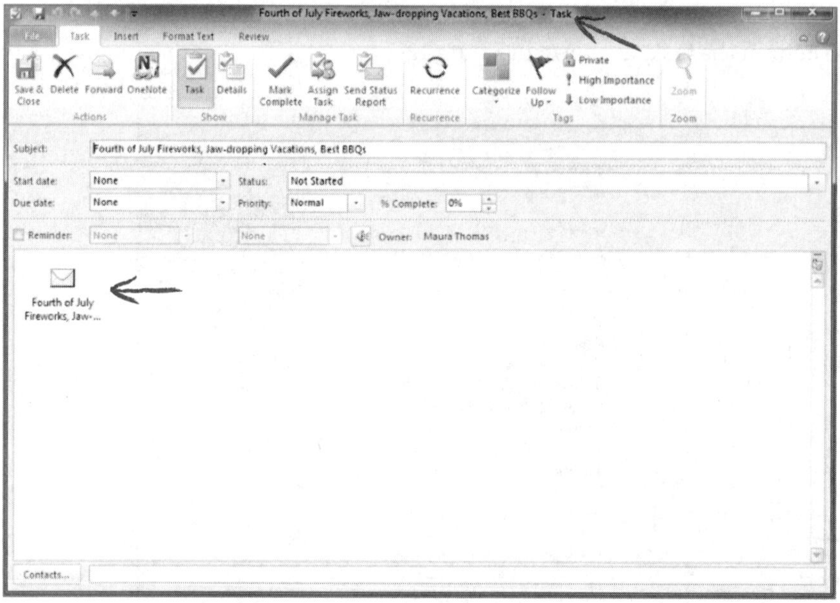

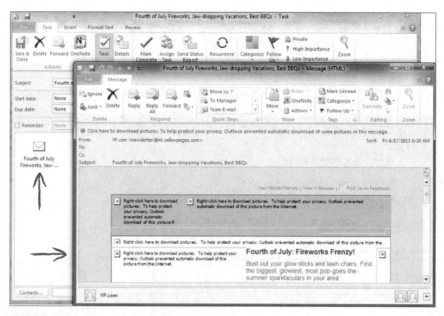

FIGURE 12-3

This option preserves all the email properties of the original message, enabling you to open it from inside the task (see Figure 12-4) by clicking it. When it's open, you can reply or forward as desired.

FIGURE 12-4

If you want to create an email folder for storing reference or archive messages simply right-click Inbox in your folder list and then select New Folder. Remember that it's better to have fewer, more general folders (and to rely on your sort and search features) than to have dozens of nested folders, which create an extra burden for filing and later retrieval. Outlook sorts the folders alphabetically.

## Apple Mail and iCal

Apple Mail and iCal are part of the Apple operating system. As of version 10.7.2, the easiest way to create a task from an email is with help from third-party software called MailTags, by indev (http://indev.ca). Luckily, this software makes it quick, easy, and seamless to create a task from email. MailTags has a free trial version; as of this writing you can purchase and download it for $29.95 from the indev website. I believe it is a good investment in your productivity if you are using the Mac-native tools (Apple Mail, iCal, and Address Book) as your PIM (personal information manager).

▶ Refer to Chapter 5 for a refresher on the components of a good PIM.

After you download and install MailTags (either the free trial or the purchased version), beside every message in any of your mailboxes you will see a tag image with a plus sign on the far right (see Figure 12-5).

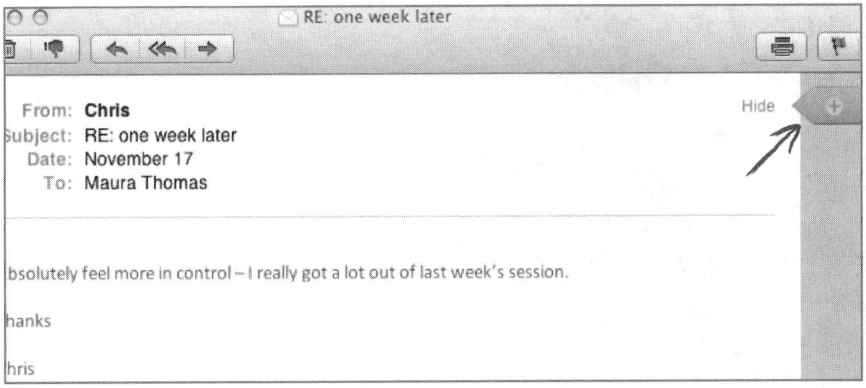

FIGURE 12-5

Clicking this tag opens the dialog box shown in Figure 12-6. Fill in the appropriate fields to create a task or event (appointment) from the message.

For example, clicking +Task expands the window so you can enter the relevant details for a task (see Figure 12-7). You can then copy and paste or otherwise transfer whatever information you need from the email in order to complete the task.

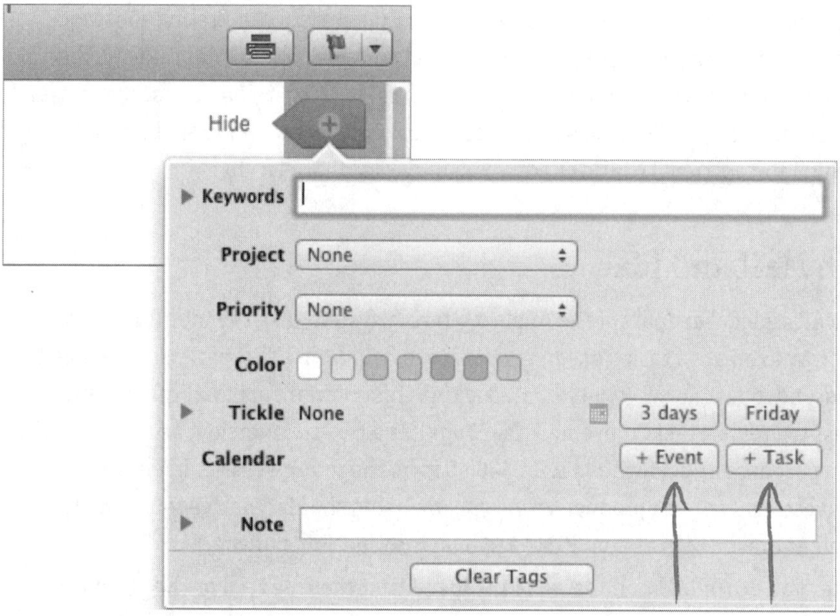

Hide

► Keywords

Project   None

Priority   None

Color

► Tickle   None   [ 3 days ] [ Friday ]

Calendar   [ + Event ] [ + Task ]

► Note

[ Clear Tags ]

**FIGURE 12-6**

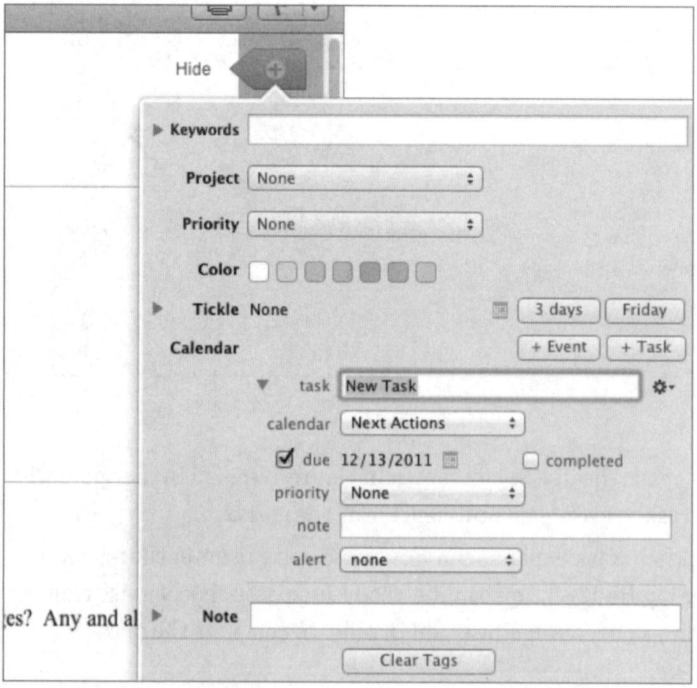

Hide

► Keywords

Project   None

Priority   None

Color

► Tickle   None   [ 3 days ] [ Friday ]

Calendar   [ + Event ] [ + Task ]

▼   task   New Task

calendar   Next Actions

☑ due   12/13/2011   ☐ completed

priority   None

note

alert   none

es? Any and al   ► Note

[ Clear Tags ]

**FIGURE 12-7**

Apple Mail refers to email folders as "Mailboxes," so to create new email folders for storing reference or archive messages in Apple Mail simply click the Mailbox menu at the top and select New Mailbox (see Figure 12-8). You can then arrange the mailboxes in your folder list however you like by simply dragging them.

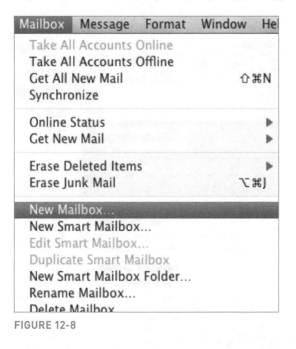

FIGURE 12-8

## Google

In Chapter 7 I mentioned some drawbacks to using Google as your PIM, such as the lack of reminders. An additional drawback of using Google as your PIM, or at least for your task list, is that you can't view your complete task list; you can only view one category at a time. Also, you can't view your calendar and your email simultaneously without opening multiple browser windows.

If you prefer to use Google tools, following are the instructions for creating a task from an email message in Gmail.

First, click an email message to open it, or put a check in the box at the far left of the message item. Click the More button and select Add to Tasks (see Figure 12-9).

A small task window will appear at the bottom-right corner of the screen, as shown in Figure 12-10. You can edit the pertinent information for the task or you can select the arrow and maximize the window, as shown in Figure 12-11.

▶ Remember that some of these problems are solved by using Remember the Milk. Read more in Chapter 16.

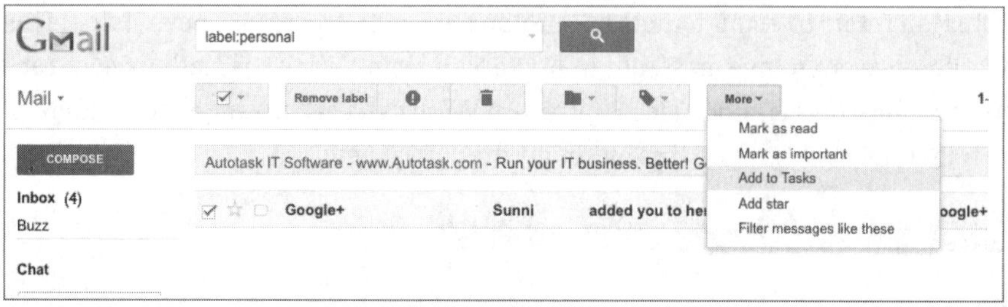

FIGURE 12-9

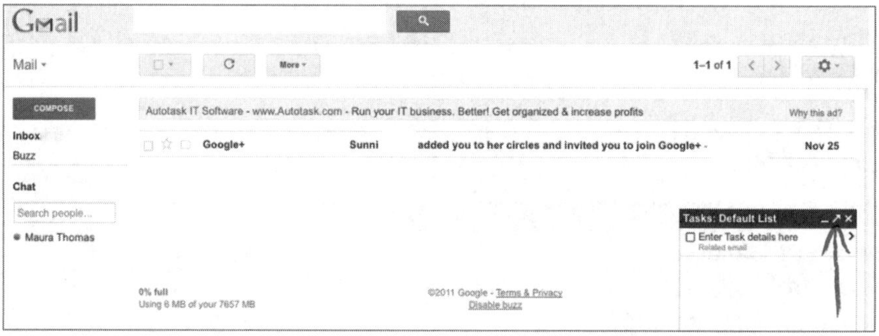

FIGURE 12-10

FIGURE 12-11

Gmail doesn't use email folders exactly; instead it enables you to assign labels to your messages and then filter the messages by label; but in fact, they all remain in your inbox unless you archive or delete them. To add a label to an email in Gmail, simply select it and click the label icon at the top of your inbox. (If you hold your cursor over the icon, the word "Labels" appears.)

With minor differences, you can apply these instructions to other email clients. A quick Internet search will usually provide you with written or video instructions about using the various features of an application. What's most important is the methodology behind the instructions. The techniques for processing your email covered in Chapters 10 and 11 are the most useful concepts with regard to staying in control of your email communication.

# CONTROL YOUR EMAIL: SHUT OFF THE AUTOMATIC DOWNLOAD

I mentioned in several chapters that one way to control your technology (rather than letting it control you) is to shut off the automatic downloading of your email messages so they only come in when you are ready to receive them. Without this, you are constantly distracted by endless new messages when your email program is open. In the following sections I provide step-by-step instructions for exerting this control in Microsoft Outlook and in Apple Mail. If you are using Gmail, as of this writing, you don't have control over when the messages download—they appear automatically as they arrive. So the only way to avoid being distracted by new messages is to log out of Gmail or close the browser window. If you're using Microsoft Outlook or Apple Mail, after using the following instructions, your email messages will no longer download until you click on the Send/Receive button (Outlook) or the Envelope image button (Apple Mail).

## Microsoft Outlook

To turn off automatic download in Outlook, go to File ➜ Options ➜ Advanced. Scroll down to Send and Receive and select the Send/Receive button on the right, as shown in Figure 12-12.

In the Send/Receive Groups dialog box, uncheck the box beside Schedule an Automatic Send/Receive Every 30 Minutes. (See Figure 12-13.)

Click Close or OK until all of the option windows are closed.

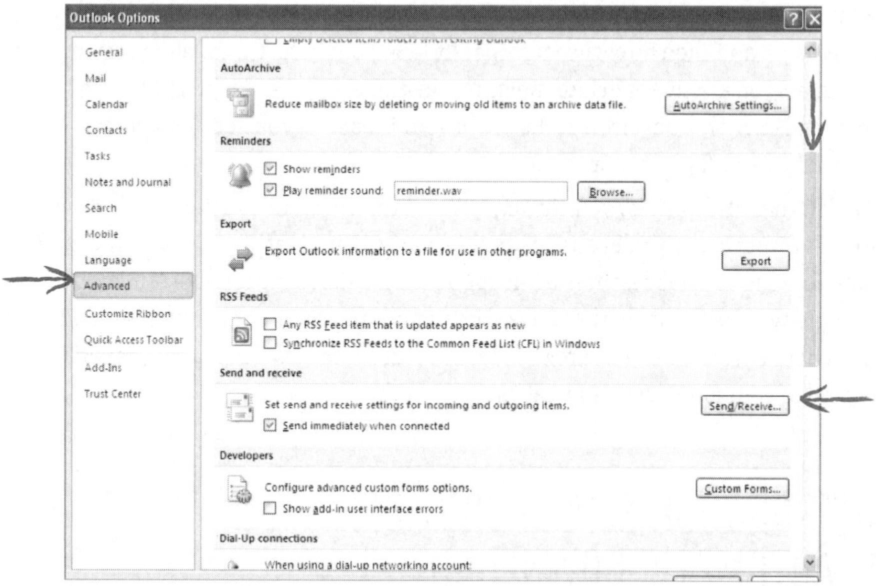


FIGURE 12-12

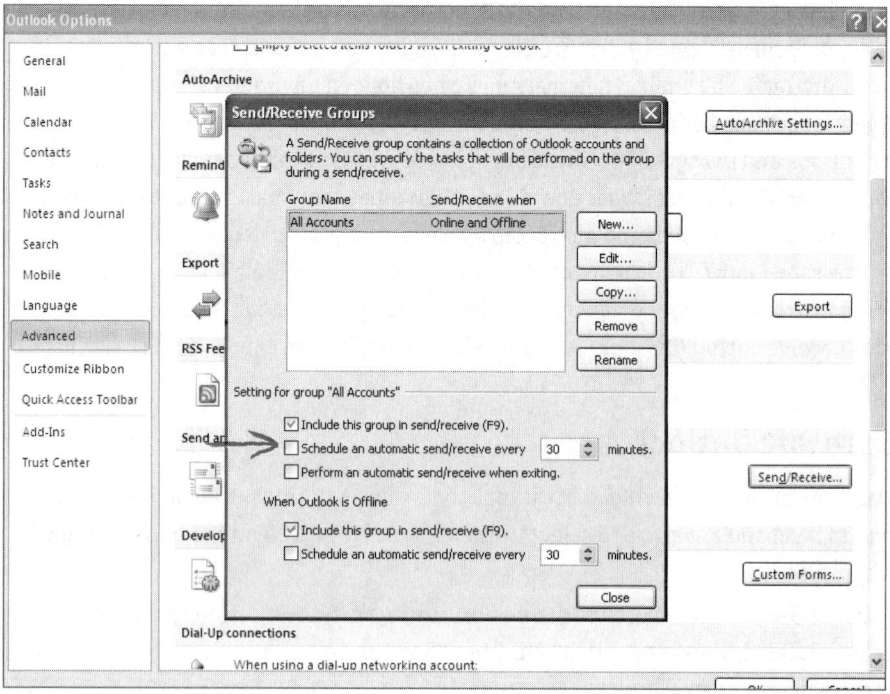


FIGURE 12-13

## Apple Mail

In Apple Mail, select Mail ➜ Preferences. On the General tab, select Manually from the drop-down next to Check for New Messages, as shown in Figure 12-14.

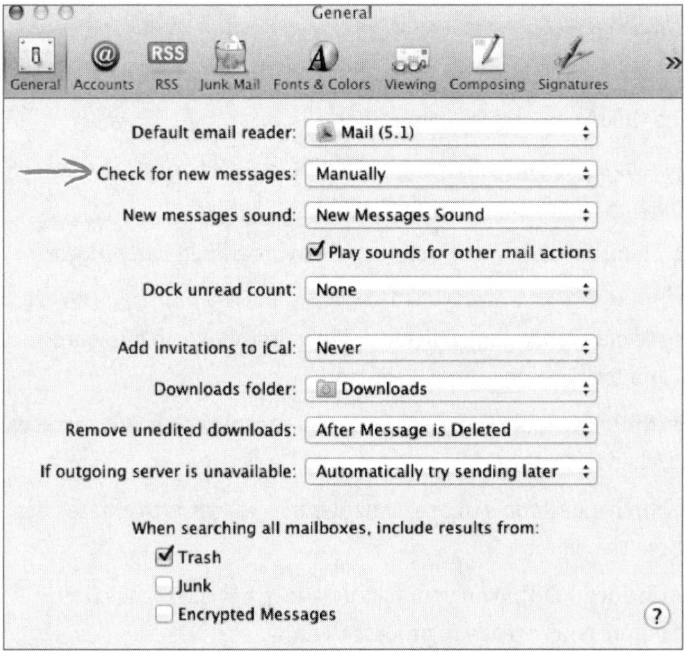

FIGURE 12-14

Click the red circle at the top left of the Preferences window to close.

# SUMMARY

The instructions in this and prior chapters provide you with the understanding of not only *how* to use certain features of your email clients, but also *why* to use them. For example, a Microsoft Outlook class might teach you how to create a task from an email, but that information is less useful when you don't understand why to process your messages or how to process them using the Review, Process, Do method. It's why a methodology like the Empowered Productivity System adds more to your productivity than just software training. The methodology is the secret to using any electronic tools successfully.

# QUICK TIPS

The following are some important points from this chapter (also suitable for tweeting). For more information on Twitter, including relevant usernames and hashtags, please refer to the "Read This First" chapter.

▶ Flagging, categorizing, or marking email as unread in your inbox is inefficient. Instead, set aside time to process your messages.

▶ When you respond to a message you want to archive, delete the one in your inbox and file the one from your Sent folder instead.

▶ Make your Junk Email inbox more effective with an organized Daily Digest from Otherinbox.

▶ Use Google Voice to get transcribed voicemails in your inbox and customize Do-Not-Disturb and forwarding for more control.

▶ A desktop client (Outlook, Apple Mail) makes it easier to process email messages and create tasks when necessary.

▶ When deciding which email tools to use, consider how easy it is to create new tasks straight from the email.

▶ Shut off automatic downloading on your email to keep new messages from distracting you before you're ready to process them.

# PART III

# TOOLS FOR SUCCESS

# Mastering Your Technology

The technology of the twenty-first century—even common devices we use every day—is in some ways more advanced and complicated than we could have imagined a few decades ago. I call those of us who are adults over age 35 the "transition generation" because we remember what it was like in the days before widespread email use, before smartphones, before social media. . . the days when the word "friend" meant something completely different than what it does today!

New technology offers a host of benefits, advantages, and conveniences, but the cost of these is the time it takes to stay current with the latest gadgets, apps, and tools. Some learning curves pose a serious challenge, and it's hard to predict how much benefit the process will bring. After all, it's easy to assume that if you've lived without something this long, then maybe you don't need it. However, "need" is a relative term. Do you *need* the latest gadgets and apps? Perhaps not—but if they can make your life easier and save you time, do you *want* them? It's hard to answer that question ahead of time, because you don't know in advance how much time investment will be required to learn to use a new device relative to how much convenience it will provide. Also, how do you know when you have enough?

At the very least, you may as well take full advantage of the tools you're *already* using. In this chapter, I show you the useful but somewhat hidden features of the tools I've recommended thus far, and describe some additional tools that I believe are necessary to truly maximize your productivity.

# MAKING BETTER USE OF YOUR CALENDAR

In Chapter 9 I discussed the concept of "ambient information." Doing what you can to make the information you need more peripherally available, or ambient, minimizes both your distractions and the effort it could otherwise take to actively seek that information. There are a couple of ways to make it easier to get the information you need from your calendar at a glance—in other words, a couple of ways to make your relevant information more ambient.

## Block versus Linear

First, if your default view of your calendar is a *block* view, I would suggest that you could glean more information at a glance by switching to a *linear* view. In most electronic calendars, a month view is block, and a week view is linear.

A block calendar (see Figure 13-1) can display the appointments you have on a given day, but without clicking on each appointment it's difficult or impossible to know exactly how much of your day is booked.

A *linear* view of your calendar (see Figure 13-2) gives you much more information—you can tell exactly how much of your time is committed and how much is free with just a glance—each vertical block represents a whole day, and the empty spaces give you a quick sense of your unscheduled time for that day.

To set a linear (or weekly) view in most electronic calendars, look for the weekly option at the top of the calendar screen.

## Color-coding

Another way to make your calendar information more consumable, or ambient, is to color-code your appointments. If you glance at a week or month view of your calendar and all the appointments you see are white (refer to Figure 13-2), that glance does not give you any sense of what kind of week or month you should expect in terms of types of appointments. Without reading every appointment, it's difficult to tell what you should expect for a particular week.

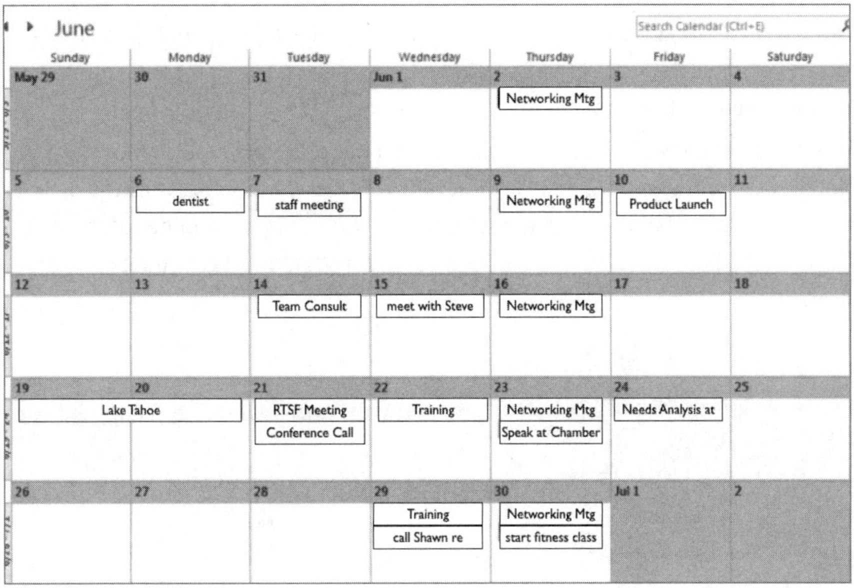

**June**

Search Calendar (Ctrl+E)

| Sunday | Monday | Tuesday | Wednesday | Thursday | Friday | Saturday |
|---|---|---|---|---|---|---|
| May 29 | 30 | 31 | Jun 1 | 2 Networking Mtg | 3 | 4 |
| 5 | 6 dentist | 7 staff meeting | 8 | 9 Networking Mtg | 10 Product Launch | 11 |
| 12 | 13 | 14 Team Consult | 15 meet with Steve | 16 Networking Mtg | 17 | 18 |
| 19 | 20 Lake Tahoe | 21 RTSF Meeting / Conference Call | 22 Training | 23 Networking Mtg / Speak at Chamber | 24 Needs Analysis at | 25 |
| 26 | 27 | 28 | 29 Training / call Shawn re | 30 Networking Mtg / start fitness class | Jul 1 | 2 |

FIGURE 13-1

**June 19 - 25**

Search Calendar (Ctrl+E)

| 19 Sunday | 20 Monday | 21 Tuesday | 22 Wednesday | 23 Thursday | 24 Friday | 25 Saturday |
|---|---|---|---|---|---|---|
| Lake Tahoe | | | | | | |
| | | | | Networking | needs analysis at ABC client | |
| | | speak at Chamber | | | | |
| | | lunch with Kerrin | training | training | | |

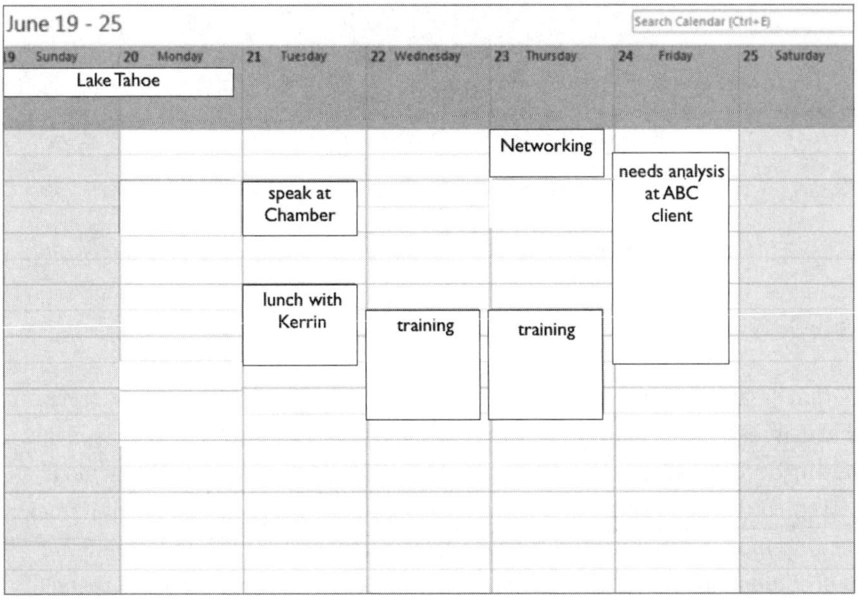

FIGURE 13-2

Think about the information that is relevant to you about an appointment. Perhaps you want to know whether a specific appointment is a meeting you requested or a meeting requested by someone else. Perhaps you'd like to know whether the meeting will be in the office or at a location to which you'll have to travel. Maybe you like to track your sales activities versus your marketing activities, or which appointments are with clients, or which are business-related and which are personal. After determining which categories are important for you, select a color for each one and then assign the correct category color every time you make an appointment.

In the calendar shown in Figure 13-3, one color denotes personal activities, one color denotes billable time with a client, and another denotes networking or marketing activities. Using a system like this, one glance at the calendar gives you an indication of what to expect for the week without requiring that you read each appointment.

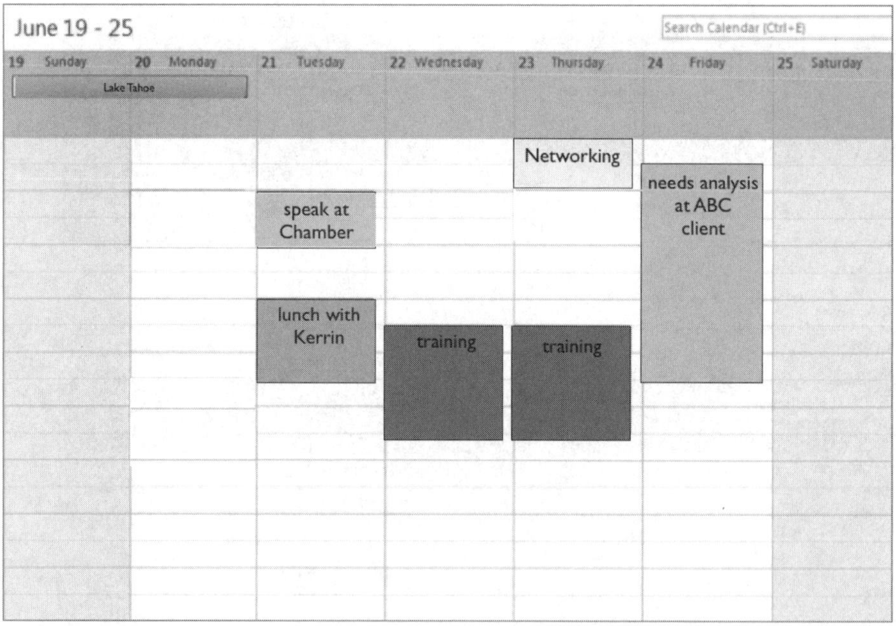

| June 19 - 25 | | | | | | Search Calendar (Ctrl+E) |
|---|---|---|---|---|---|---|
| 19 Sunday | 20 Monday | 21 Tuesday | 22 Wednesday | 23 Thursday | 24 Friday | 25 Saturday |
| | Lake Tahoe | | | | | |
| | | | | Networking | needs analysis at ABC client | |
| | | speak at Chamber | | | | |
| | | lunch with Kerrin | training | training | | |

FIGURE 13-3

Another great reason to color-code your calendar is that it creates a time-use report card that can serve to pat you on the back or get you back on track. For example, if you have outlined some goals for yourself, such as how many hours you'd like to spend in a week doing "x" (volunteering, exercising, working on billable hours, and so on), then color-coding your calendar items is a great way to quickly see, at a glance, where you are out of alignment with your goals. For instance, let's say you've decided to spend four hours each week volunteering, and you've coded the volunteer time on your calendar as blue; a quick glance at a weekly or monthly view for all the blue appointments gives you a sense of whether or not you're reaching your goals in that area.

In Microsoft Outlook, you can assign categories for your calendar the same way you do for tasks, which is why I suggest in Chapter 7 that you make all your task categories the same "non" color, such as gray or white, reserving the colors for your calendar categories. If you forget how to create categories in Outlook, refer to Chapter 7.

▶ Hint: Look for the colored square at the top of a task or appointment window, and select "all categories."

In Apple's iCal, categories are called calendars, and you create new ones by choosing File ➜ New Calendar. Press Command+I to choose a color for the new calendar (see Figure 13-4).

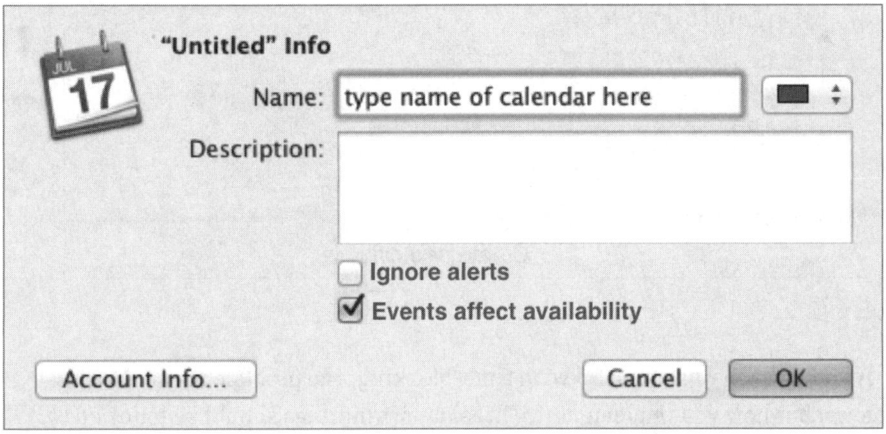

**FIGURE 13-4**

Categories are also called calendars in Google Calendar. To create new ones, select the drop-down arrow beside My Calendars on the left side, and select Create New Calendar (see Figure 13-5). Google assigns a different color automatically, but you can change it by clicking the down arrow on the right of the new calendar name in the My Calendars list, where a color-picker displays.

## Time-Blocking

I'm often asked about time-blocking (making an appointment with yourself) to accomplish tasks. This can be an important tool to combat procrastination, but I suggest that in most cases you don't assign a specific task to an appointment you make with yourself. Instead, just block off the time to be proactive. You then have the flexibility to work from your Next Actions list and tackle whatever task seems the most appropriate at that moment. I suggest that you be very selective with your time-blocking. *You* are the first person you'll cancel an appointment with, so sometimes time-blocking can be tricky.

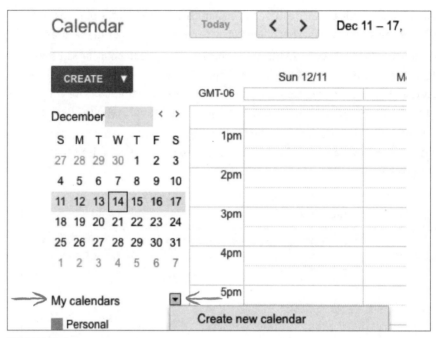

FIGURE 13-5

If you've been unsuccessful with time-blocking, the problem may not be the behavior but how you implement it. Three important rules should be followed to make this technique effective:

▶ **Rule #1:** Don't block your time too far in the future; it's too uncertain. To get important things done, block time on your calendar today or tomorrow. If you schedule too far in advance and your priorities change, you'll end up breaking those appointments with yourself. There's one exception to this: If you have an important deadline in the future, it's helpful to block some time a day or so before that deadline in order to finish up the project, add final thoughts, or give it one last once-over (or actually do it, if you're a deadline junkie!).

▶ **Rule #2:** Use time-blocking very selectively—only for very important things, and only once in a while. If you do it too often, you'll start breaking those appointments with yourself, and the technique will lose its effectiveness.

▶ **Rule #3:** Don't make your time-blocks too long. It's very difficult to block out a whole day, for example. Focus waxes and wanes, things such as hunger cause distractions, and the desire to check on things (voicemail, email, Twitter stream, and so on) become too tempting. I find time-blocking works best in blocks of two hours or less.

Here's one final tip about time-blocking: If you set aside time to do something but you just can't seem to get focused, grab a piece of paper and a pen and try "stream of consciousness" writing—a brain dump. This helps to eliminate mental clutter and uncover those intellectual gems you know are in there somewhere. Don't censor yourself, and don't try to organize as you write. Just write whatever comes to you, and chances are good that before too long your brain will find its way back to that important thing you're trying to get done. Even if you don't get back on track with your original goal, in the worst case you'll likely end up with some other pearl of wisdom or great idea. Your brain is much better at creative, strategic thinking and problem solving than at remembering details, and if you clear your mind of the minutiae (mental clutter), the "good stuff" often appears.

# KNOWING THE SECRETS

This section highlights some often overlooked features of the three common tools (Microsoft Outlook, the Apple suite, and Google Apps) that are useful for increasing your productivity.

## Post in This Folder

The Post in This Folder function of Microsoft Outlook offers the capability to document and capture a real-life discussion with a time and date stamp, which you can then store, search for, and sort—just as you can with email. To capture a conversation or other "live" experience, first select the email folder in which you would like to store the information. Then select New Items ➜ More Items ➜ Post in This Folder (see Figure 13-6).

In the dialog that appears (see Figure 13-7), you can add any relevant details about the conversation or experience. When you click Post, the item displays in your email list as if it were an email, but you see a post icon instead of an email icon (see Figure 13-8). If you've ever emailed yourself simply to capture some information into your email for filing, then you'll find this feature helpful.

## Easily Track Birthdays

You can amaze your friends, family, and clients with how well you "remember" their birthdays (even if you don't see them on Facebook!). You may not be aware that most comprehensive PIMs have a feature that automatically coordinates dates in the contacts section with the calendar.

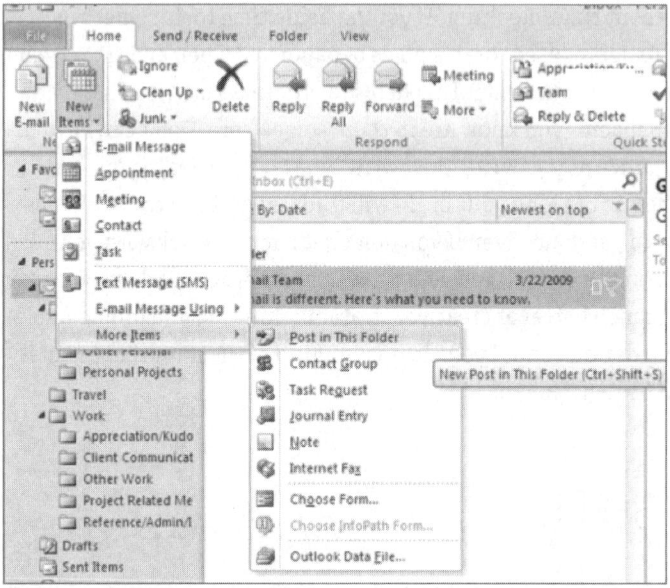

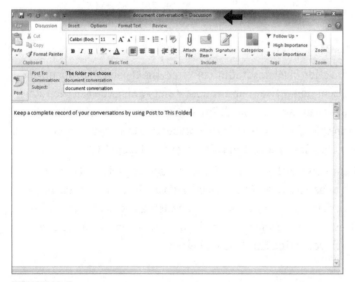

FIGURE 13-6

FIGURE 13-7

If you are using the Birthday field in Outlook Contacts or Apple Address Book, this field can be used to automatically populate your calendar with important dates every year without you having to do anything further. If you're using Microsoft Outlook, look for the Show tab at the top of a contact and select Details. Here you can see fields for birthdays and anniversaries (see Figure 13-9). If you enter a date in these fields, it is automatically displayed on your calendar every year as an event. You can also open this recurring event and add a reminder a few days ahead of time if you need to send a card or purchase a gift.

▶ An event (a day-specific but not time-specific item) is displayed at the top of a specific day on your calendar. An appointment is displayed on a particular day at a particular time. To make an event, use the All-day check box when you create the appointment.

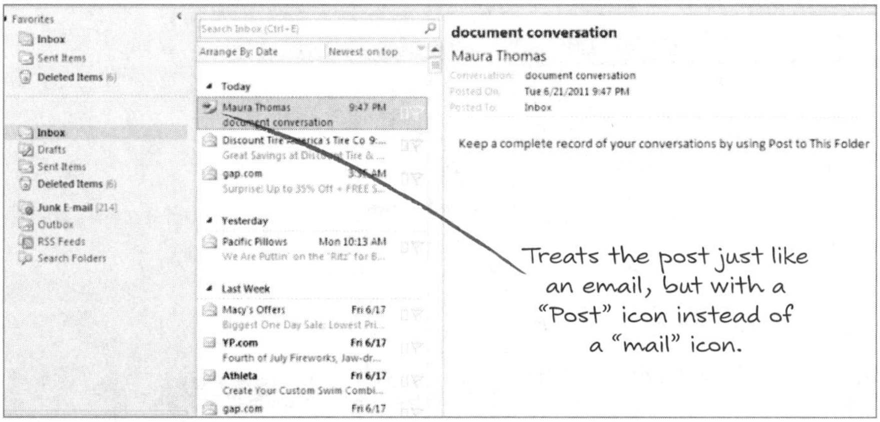

Treats the post just like an email, but with a "Post" icon instead of a "mail" icon.

FIGURE 13-8

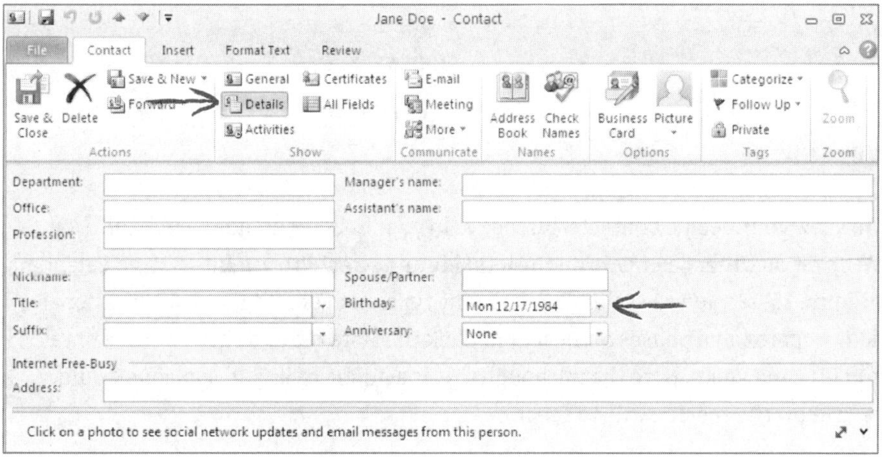

FIGURE 13-9

In Apple's Address Book, open a contact and select Card ➜ Add Field ➜ Birthday (see Figure 13-10).

Then open iCal, click on the iCal menu, and select Preferences. In the General tab, select Show Birthdays Calendar (see Figure 13-11).

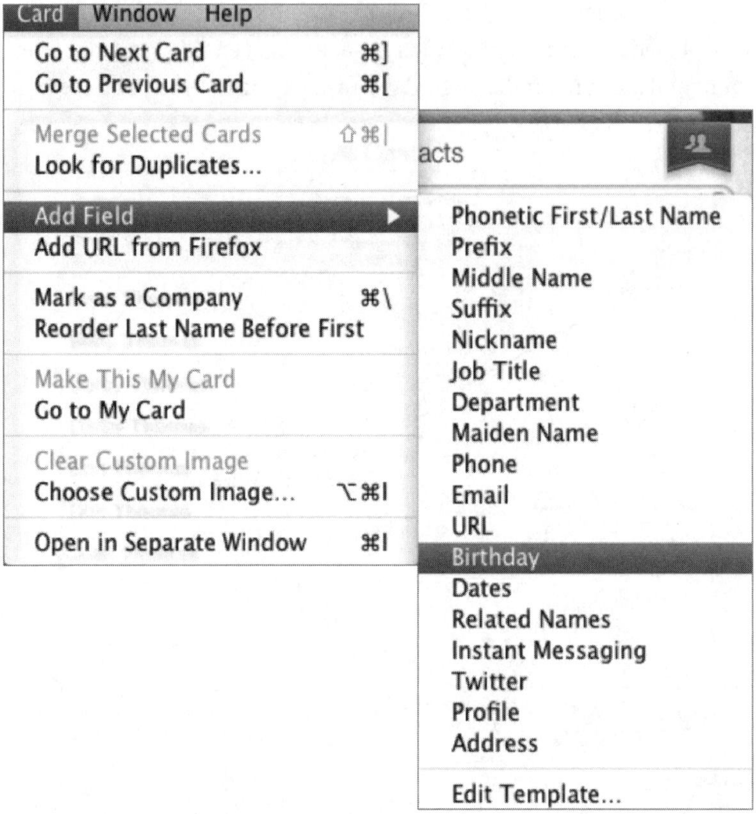

**FIGURE 13-10**

To show your Google Contacts' birthdays in your Google Calendar, click the drop-down arrow on Other Calendars on the left side and select Browse Interesting Calendars (see Figure 13-12). You see calendars for many types of events, such as international holidays, sports, and phases of the moon. Click the More tab and then choose Contacts' Birthdays and Events. Note that although this is a public calendar, someone would have to know the specific URL to see it.

> **NOTE** All of these instructions pull the birthday data from information you've put into the associated contact application. For example, if you are using Google Calendar and you don't insert birthdays into your Google Contacts, nothing will appear in your calendar even when you've selected to view the Contacts' Birthdays and Events calendar.

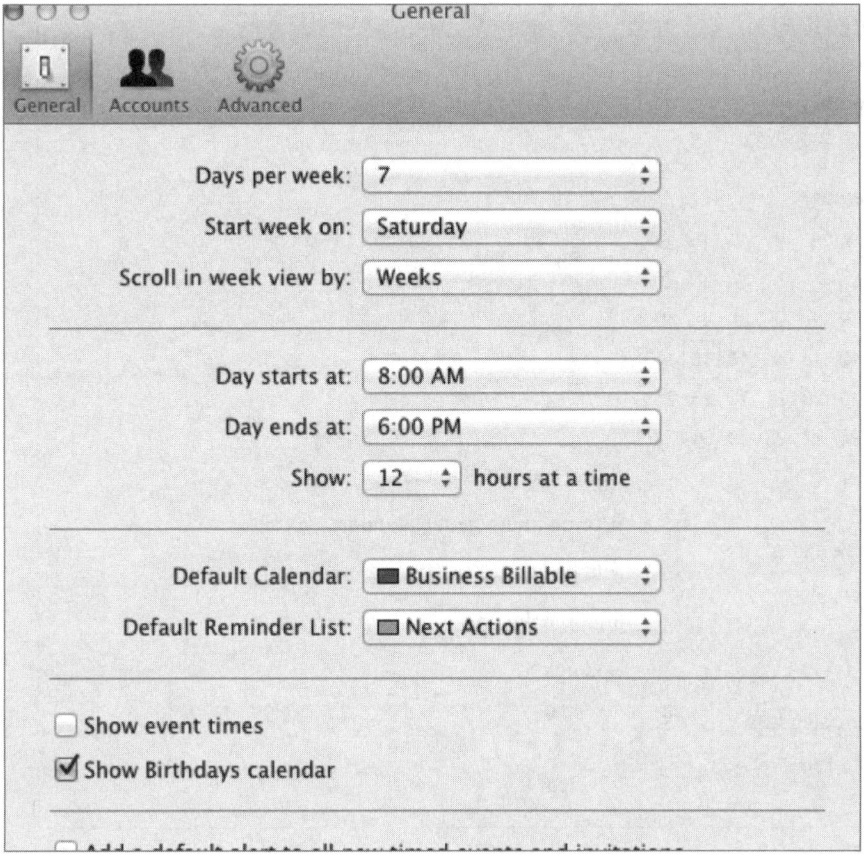

FIGURE 13-11

## Other Ways to Master Your Address Book

If your productivity tools of choice include Microsoft Outlook or the Apple suite, following are some tips for getting useful information from your Address Book. There isn't much to say about Google Contacts, as it's pretty standard. Also, Google is changing every day, integrating existing Google apps such as Calendar, Gmail, and Contacts with its latest social network, Google+, which has advantages and disadvantages. A discussion of Google+ and other social networks is outside the scope of this book (although there is some information about *managing* and *controlling* these newer communication options in the next chapter).

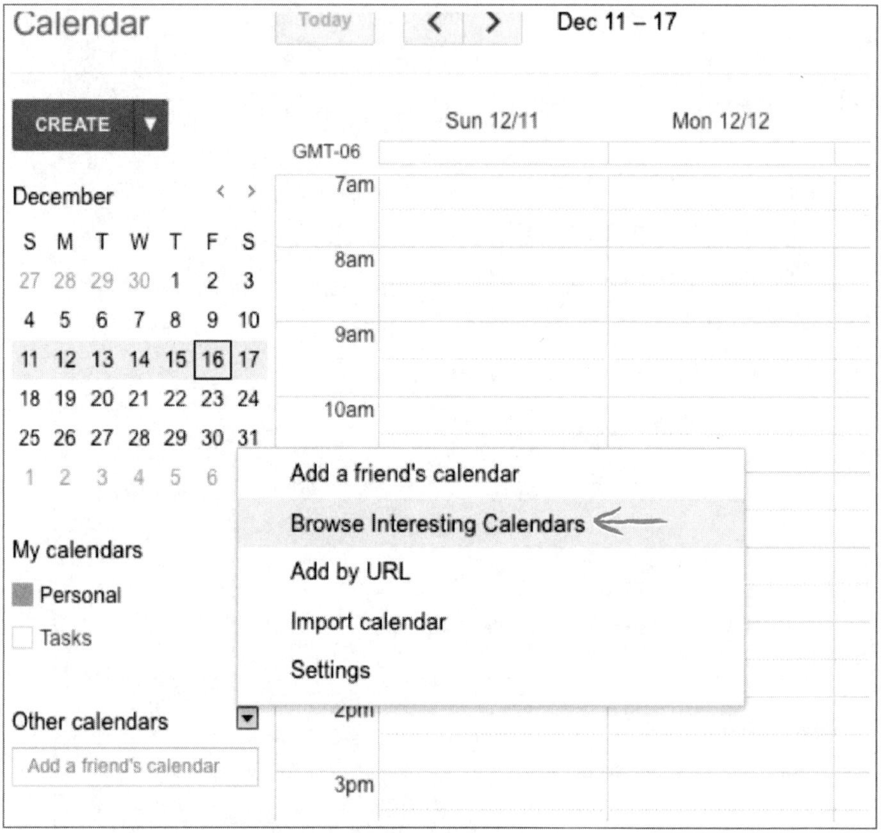

FIGURE 13-12

## MICROSOFT OUTLOOK CONTACTS

In Microsoft Outlook Contacts, when you click on the Details tab to add birthdays, be sure to check out the other fields available to you there in case there is anything you think may be useful to you. For example, you might enjoy using the Picture field, which displays the photo of a contact you add every time that person emails you. If you are syncing Contacts with some smartphones, you also see that picture when the person calls you. Just click the picture of the head in the contact (see Figure 13-13) and you can browse your computer for the image. If it's someone you've newly met, you may find it useful to look for a picture of the person on the Web (try www.google.com/images) because that may help you remember that person better.

Outlook also enables you to associate any task or appointment with a particular contact, and then in that person's contact profile you can see all the tasks, appointments, and emails that you have associated with that person. In order to take advantage of this feature, which is called *Activities,* select File ➔ Options ➔ Contacts. In the Linking section, check the box beside Show Contacts Linked to the Current Item (see Figure 13-14).

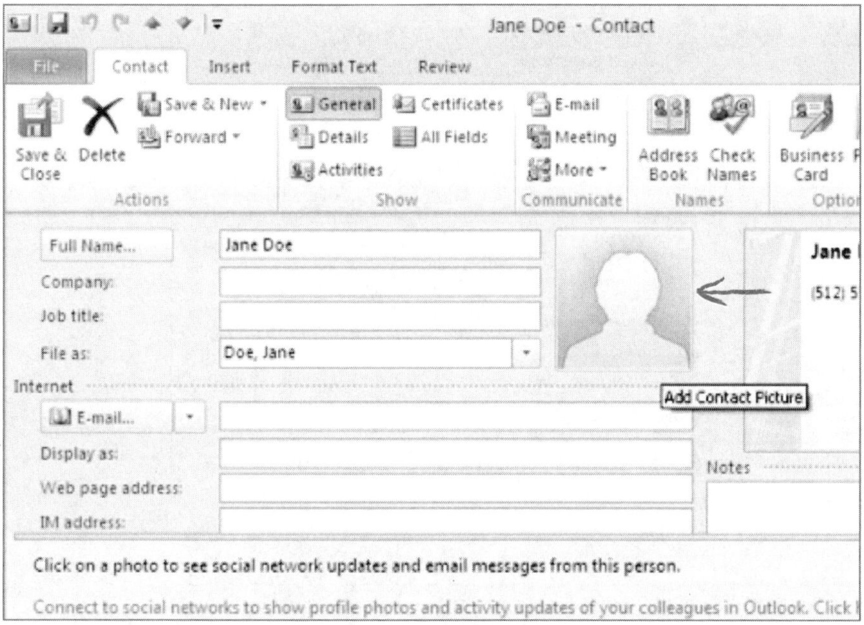

FIGURE 13-13

For example, create an appointment for a meeting with someone in your Address Book. In the Contacts field at the bottom, choose the person you'll be meeting with from your contacts (see Figure 13-15).

Then, open the contact, select Activities, and make sure All Items is showing in the drop-down menu at the top (see Figure 13-16). The first time you do this, Outlook searches for a bit, during which time you may see the hourglass. When Outlook is done searching, every email containing that person, and every task or calendar item you've associated with that person, appears in that window to be saved.

Visit the book's companion website at www.personal-productivity-secrets.com for a video of the Outlook Contacts feature in action.

## APPLE ADDRESS BOOK

Apple's Address Book offers similar functionality, with a little less effort. You don't have to associate any items with a contact in order for Apple to show you all the items related to that contact; Address Book does it automatically. Simply find the contact in your Address Book, then right-click (or Control+click) and select Spotlight (see Figure 13-17).

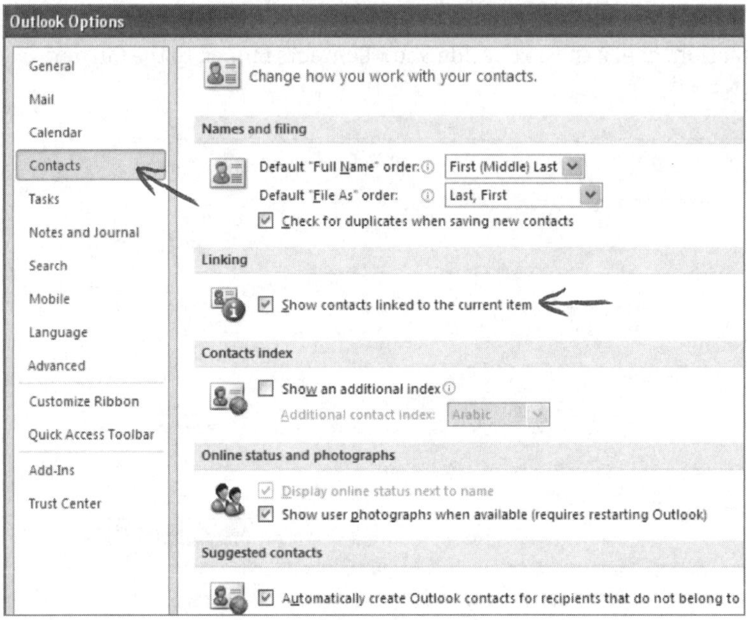

**FIGURE 13-14**

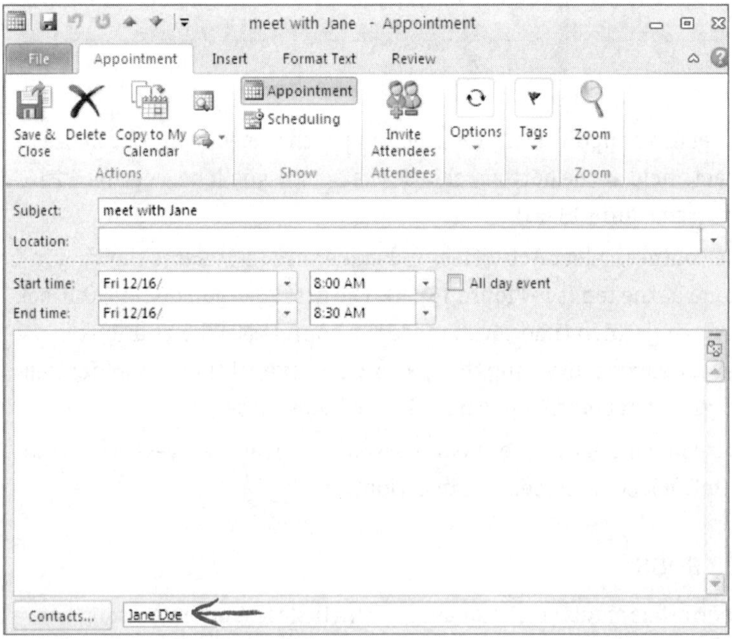

**FIGURE 13-15**

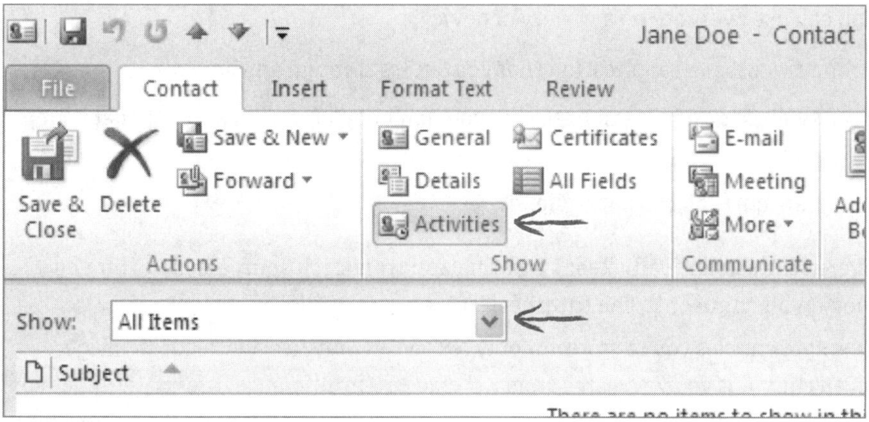

FIGURE 13-16

FIGURE 13-17

The Finder window that appears will contain any items anywhere on your computer that contain a reference to this person.

# A GREAT ADD-ON

As I mentioned in Chapter 5, the Notes feature of a PIM is a good place to keep reference information, such as holiday presents you've already bought, or gifts you gave everyone last year so that you don't repeat anything, or ideas for your next blog post. You might also save instructions for tasks you occasionally need to perform, such as troubleshooting the photocopier or forwarding your phone. Microsoft Office has a Notes section, as does Apple Mail, where you can store this type of reference information, but my recommendation is to pass on both of these options and use a free third-party application called Evernote. Evernote is more feature-rich than the Notes sections included with other PIMs, and it is easier to keep synchronized across multiple devices.

▶ See the "Recommended Resources" appendix to learn where to get Evernote and for a complete listing of every site, app, and software recommended in this book.

You can use Evernote on a variety of devices:

▶ As a web-based application that you access through any browser

▶ As a desktop application, so that you don't need Internet access to get your notes

▶ As an app for most smartphones

Evernote automatically keeps information from each source in sync for you whenever you connect to the Internet.

Evernote enables you to store not only text notes, but also audio notes, images, and even clippings you've created from web pages. Any reference information that you need readily available to you can be stored for easy access in Evernote. Notes are an important component of any comprehensive set of productivity tools, and Evernote does the job nicely.

# BEING PREPARED AND FLEXIBLE ON THE GO

Recent technology has brought many conveniences, such as the ability to work remotely. Some companies even have a completely "virtual" staff with no central office location at all. This has made many jobs much more independent and portable.

This convenience can have a downside, however, if you don't control it. For example, many people lament that this ever-present technology means that they have to be "always on." This complaint reflects someone who is not in control of his or her technology. My grandmother used to say, "Just because the phone rings, doesn't mean you have to answer it." Portable device or not, you can disconnect when you want to. Remember that any technology you choose to use is for *your* convenience only. The conveniences you can gain for yourself by having easy, organized access to all those details you're managing is worth the effort it takes to learn to exert control.

Control means having at your fingertips, at any time, all the details about where you are supposed to be and when (your calendar), all the things you're committed to doing (your to-do list), all information for your contacts, reference information, and the ability to *initiate* communication if you so choose. Being prepared with these things makes you effective, gives you the ability to be proactive, and provides the antidote to a particular kind of stress—that nagging but vague feeling that you're supposed to be doing something or you're forgetting something. This low-level anxiety is a type of internal distraction that is quieted when you can consult your System to view all the things that you aren't doing, and then rest assured that you aren't forgetting anything, or remedy the situation if you are. The unknown causes much of our stress, so the antidote is to know what you are responsible for at any moment, regardless of where you are.

On the other hand, if you're not careful, having all your details and responsibilities at your fingertips can rob you of any time for idle thought. Most busy people take fewer and fewer opportunities to just think. It's nice, and perhaps even important, to have those idle minutes to take a couple of deep breaths, look around, take in the scenery, and let your mind wander. It's helpful to allow time in your day for this, but it's even better if you can carve out some real thinking time in your day. Thirty minutes? Fifteen? Many people struggle to find even 10 minutes to sit someplace quiet, without a phone or computer, and see where their minds take them.

As long as you maintain control over your technology, it won't prevent you from taking this "thinking" time. One way to take advantage of technology that gives you the flexibility to manage your life from anywhere is to invest in a smartphone, if you don't already have one. If you do have one, are you using it most effectively? I come across many people in my work who have the latest handheld device but are making poor use of it.

## Using a Smartphone Effectively

Consider that your handheld device (smartphone) is not really intended to be your primary data entry tool. It's still more convenient to manage the details of your life on a larger screen with a larger keyboard, so use one of the computer-based PIMs I discuss throughout the book as the central location where you manage your calendar, contacts, task list, notes, and so on.

However, you should take advantage of the opportunity to take that information with you on your smartphone so that you can consult it, refer to it, use it as your capture tool, and even enter information into it when necessary. Keeping all your information current among your various computers and devices means that you can virtually always have what you need, and synchronizing them is easier than ever.

## Deciding on a Smartphone

Which smartphone to purchase or upgrade to can be a challenging question. Frankly, however, they are becoming more and more alike, so much of the decision now comes down to personal preference. Because a smartphone is more like a handheld computer that happens to make phone calls than it is like a standard cell phone, I think the three most important questions to ask yourself before a smartphone purchase are the following:

1. What, exactly, would you like to be able to do with your smartphone?

2. Which platform (Google, Windows, Mac) do you currently use the most, and do you plan to continue in this direction?

3. How tech savvy are you?

Question 1 is relevant because if there are specific categories of applications, or apps, you'd like to use on your device, some smartphones offer many more options than others. The App Store for iPhone, for example, currently has many options in hundreds of categories, such as calculators, entertainment and games, news, productivity, web searching, social networking, sports, travel, and on and on. A smartphone can also offer you the benefits of other technology; for example, you can watch movies or television shows, get GPS driving directions, listen to music or podcasts with an mp3 player, take photos with a camera, and record videos with a video recorder—all built into the smartphone.

Here's why Question 2 is important to consider: If you are a big fan of Google, and you use Gmail, Google Calendar, Docs, Voice, and so on, then a phone on the Google platform (an Android device) is likely the best fit for you. If you're a heavy Microsoft user, favoring Live and SharePoint for collaborating, and running your life via Outlook, then a Windows Mobile device is probably your best option. Similarly, if you are a Mac user, an iPhone is the obvious choice.

Question 3 is relevant because if you are, for example, mostly a Windows user, some adjustments and tweaking will be necessary to get an iPhone to sync with your Windows applications. It's always more difficult to enable different operating systems to "talk" to each other, so if you're not very tech savvy you might find it easier to pick one platform and stick with it for all your devices.

▶ For example, use your favorite browser to try searching for something such as "sync iPhone 4 iOS 5 with Microsoft Outlook 2010 on Windows 7."

There are many possible combinations for syncing smartphones with computers, but luckily information abounds about how to do this. If you choose Mac tools, simply make an appointment at your local Apple store and the staff will get you set up. If you choose Windows or Google devices, or you are cross-platform syncing, just do an Internet search, using your specific devices, software, and operating system; you can find both text and video instructions available free on the Web, including on my website at www.RegainYourTime.com.

Now that you have information about choosing the right set of tools, the methodology with which to use the tools, and advice for managing the details on the go, it's time to outline the habits you need to help keep you on track.

## THE BENEFITS OF APPLE

As of this writing, I use and recommend Apple devices, including an iPhone. I believe that Apple could significantly improve on its OS-native productivity suite (iCal, Apple Mail, and Address Book), but as you've learned by now, I have found relatively easy ways to compensate for its shortcomings. I do think that aside from productivity, an Apple computer is better at almost everything else. It's more intuitive to learn and use, it's generally less susceptible to viruses and hacking, it's more stable than Windows (freezing and crashing less), you can make an appointment and meet with an expert without charge if you are having a problem with it, and it's better for creating and managing pictures, audio recordings, and video. It's true that it's easiest to use the iPhone if you are an Apple user anyway, but the iPhone does integrate relatively well with other platforms.

# STAYING ON TRACK

You may have gathered by now that any productivity methodology, including the Empowered Productivity™ System, requires some effort to manage. It's like anything else: If you make the effort to keep your house clean, then you will enjoy the benefits of having a clean house. If you make the effort to maintain your car, then you will reap the benefits of minimal downtime and inconvenience caused by a car that is unreliable and always in need of repair.

If you have a full and busy life, it's unrealistic to think that it should not take you any time to manage that life. The effort you put in to "work your System" provides dividends to your time, your peace of mind, your quality of output, and how well and frequently you achieve *your* "significant results."

The Weekly Update, described in the next section, is the specific set of habits that keeps your new System running smoothly and helps you manage your life and responsibilities with less stress.

## The Weekly Update

If you decide to follow the instructions in this book and implement the Empowered Productivity System to manage the details of your life, there is one factor that determines your long-term success over all others. It's called the *Weekly Update*. Creating a habit of the Weekly Update keep you "at zero"—that is, all your commitments, communication, and information are out of your head and in your System, and your email and paper inboxes are clean and processed. The Weekly Update takes a minimal amount of time and provides you with peace of mind and an unshakable sense of control. The better you get at the whole Empowered Productivity System process, the faster your Weekly Updates will go.

Following are the instructions to help you make a habit of doing your Weekly Update. I suggest that you create a recurring event on your calendar (Fridays are best) for a Weekly Update, and copy these instructions into that event, so that you always have a reminder to do the process and have the instructions handy. If you register for the follow-up email program at www.personal-productivity-secrets.com, you'll receive these instructions in an email and can then copy and paste them into your event.

▶ Reminder:
An event is day specific, whereas an appointment is day and time specific. An event is displayed at the top of the day in the daily and weekly view to let you know something should happen on that day, but no specific time is indicated.

1. Scan all tasks, and update/adjust as necessary for the following:

   ▷ Completed tasks that you forgot to mark as complete

   ▷ The Next Action (or appointment, or Waiting For) for every Project on your list, to ensure that each Project is moving forward

   ▷ Overdue items, which probably show up red or with an exclamation mark beside them. When prioritizing by due date as explained in Chapter 5, it's important to keep your list current.

   ▷ Waiting For tasks, to ensure that nothing is falling through the cracks; follow up as necessary

   ▷ Approximately once per quarter, scan your Future and Someday/Maybe lists to see if anything should be moved to Next Actions or Projects.

2. Do a brain dump—empty your brain of anything you are carrying in your mind and process each item into your System. Try it first without the brain dump prompts referenced in Chapter 6, and then review them to ensure that you have truly captured everything.

▶ Remember the "Review, Process, Do.

3. Process your inboxes (paper and email) using the T.E.S.S.T.™ process. This should be done at other times of the week as well, but certainly during your Weekly Update.

4. Review your calendar for the week that's ending. Check for any action items; ensure you've "closed all the loops."

5. Review your upcoming calendar, to ensure that you have no surprises in the coming week and are prepared, or plan to be prepared, for every event.

6. Flip through your Next Action and Waiting For paper files and clean them out as necessary.

7. Ensure that your electronic files, including your PIM, are backed up thoroughly (see "Don't Take Chances with Your System" later in this chapter).

## Self-Checks

After you've had a week or more to implement the Empowered Productivity System, some things should be starting to feel more familiar. Two of the earliest habits you develop should be "keeping things out of your head" and being proactive—relying on your task list to *choose* what gets your attention. If a day or more goes by and you haven't looked at your task list, it means that you are still always working in *reactive* mode. You are relinquishing control over your own attention too often; your *significant results* won't be achieved unless you carve out the time to be *proactive*.

The following are some other self-checks:

▶ Are you carrying details in your head? What are you working hard to "not forget"? Any tasks that need to go on your list?

▶ How often are you checking your email? Constantly? If so, remember that this means that you are always multitasking at best (and at worst doing nothing but email), which means you're probably not getting to the important things, or it's probably taking you longer than necessary to complete them when you do (and likely at a lower quality).

▶ Are you still skimming and skipping your email, leaving the messages in your inbox? Process your messages when you have time and devote up to a full minute to each one until you've decided to respond, delete, file, or move to tasks.

▶ Is there still paper clutter on your desk? Have you designated a home for it? Are you deferring making a decision? The T.E.S.S.T. flowchart will help with those issues.

# DON'T TAKE CHANCES WITH YOUR SYSTEM

If you have fully or even partly implemented the Empowered Productivity System, then your electronic tools are serving as the "command center" of your life. Don't take any chances of losing this important information: Back up your System! If you are syncing with a handheld device and/or tablet, do that first to ensure that everything from the device is also stored in your computer. If you're using Windows and Microsoft Outlook on a personal computer, then I recommend using a service that backs up all your files to the Internet, such as Carbonite, or do an Internet search for "backup services." There are many to choose from.

Ensure that any backup program that you run includes your PST file, which is the file that contains all the information you have entered in Outlook. For instructions on finding and backing up your specific version of Outlook, with your specific backup system, try another Internet search, as these details are updated frequently.

If your PIM is on your work computer, then it may be best to consult your IT department to ensure that your Outlook PST file is included in routine backups. If you are syncing with an Exchange Server, all your data lives on the server, which your IT staff probably backs up, but it wouldn't hurt to confirm this.

If you are using Mac products, Apple has fantastic software that is part of the operating system called Time Machine. Visit www.apple.com/findouthow to learn how to use Time Machine, or make a Genius Bar appointment at your local Apple store.

If you're using Google, the very nature of having your data "in the cloud" implies that it is backed up on the Internet. It's up to you to determine whether you feel safe relying on that. There are services that claim to help you copy it from Google and back up a copy somewhere else. An Internet search of "back up Google data" should yield the most current results you need.

# SUMMARY

This chapter provided information to help you make better use of the tools you have available to you, such as your software programs and smartphone. It also provided advice to help you implement the Empowered Productivity System and make a habit of the new, more effective behaviors that will support your productivity and attention rather than sabotage them. Remember that reading about these behaviors won't be nearly as helpful as actually trying them, and trying them won't be as helpful as sticking with them. Also, don't miss the opportunity to receive implementation and ongoing support via email by registering for the free follow-up program at www.personal-productivity-secrets.com.

# QUICK TIPS

The following are some important points from this chapter (also suitable for tweeting). For more information on Twitter, including relevant usernames and hashtags, please refer to the "Read This First" chapter.

- ▶ Switch from block view (month) to linear view (week) in your calendar for more info at a glance.

- ▶ Color-code calendar appointments by type to get a quick sense of the upcoming day or week and help track goals.

- ▶ Rule #1 for useful time blocking: Don't block time with yourself too far in advance—things change.

- ▶ Rule #2 for useful time blocking: Be discerning with appointments with yourself—too often and you'll ignore them.

- ▶ Rule #3 for useful time blocking: Keep blocks under 2 hours for maximum focus.

- ▶ Trouble focusing on the task at hand? Do a quick brain dump—stream of consciousness writing—to clear your head.

- ▶ Outlook users can capture in-person or phone conversation details by using Post in This Folder

- ▶ Select Contact/Show Details or Preferences/Show Birthdays in Outlook/iCal to add contacts' birthdays to your calendar.

- ▶ Emails and appointments in iCal and Outlook can link to contacts in your address book.

- ▶ Use Evernote instead of the built-in Notes feature of your PIM for more robust notes that easily sync across devices.

- ▶ Choosing a smartphone? Consider what your needs are, which platform do you already use, and how tech-savvy you are.

- ▶ Self-check your productivity habits: What are you working hard to "not forget"? Are there any tasks that need to go on your list?

- ▶ Save time in the long run: Don't close an email without taking an action of some kind: delete, reply, move to your task list, or file.

## CHAPTER 14

# Managing New Communication— Social Media

One of the biggest challenges of our technology-driven lives is determining which products and services add real value, rather than becoming an added distraction. For social platforms and virtual places, such as Facebook and Google+, a large part of the value is whether the people you associate with are using it, too, and how they use it. For example, a webcam is only useful or fun if the other party has one.

Similarly, I hated Twitter when everyone used it to share what they were having for lunch, but I now find exceptional value in following, for example, politicians as they send updates from the floor of Congress and NASA astronauts as they share details from their lives in space. As more and more users have adopted social media, its value has steadily grown so that not only has it allowed us access to information that we never had before, but it's also become a routine part of the way we keep up with the people in our lives.

# "SOCIALIZING" COMMUNICATION

Social media is becoming more popular than email for communication, especially among younger Internet users. As the younger generation enters the workforce, we might like to think that they will trade social media for email, but what I predict will happen instead is that they will convert the workplace from email-centric to social media–centric communications. The specific social platforms adopted will matter less than the fact that the environment of business communication will change. In fact, more progressive companies are already beginning to incorporate social media into their daily communication—with customers, with partners, and internally among employees. I know of one global company that recently banned the use of internal email for its 80,000 employees in favor of social media. In other words, if you find yourself avoiding social media because you don't have time for "one more thing," then you may soon find yourself at a disadvantage at work, especially if you work in a progressive company or a company that employs many younger workers. Social media is not a passing fad, so the longer you avoid at least learning about it in general, the more difficult it will be for you to join in later.

I define social media as any tool or platform that enables the following kind of communication:

- ▶ One-to-many or many-to-many
- ▶ Two-way
- ▶ Primarily public (offering some privacy settings in some instances)

▶ Social media is even creating opportunities for historically "broadcast" media to become interactive. TV and radio shows invite viewers/listeners to send comments and questions via social media platforms, which are then addressed live during the show.

Facebook, LinkedIn, and Twitter often come to mind first when we think of social media, but using my definition, we can also include blogs that allow comments, image-sharing sites such as Flickr and Picasa, video-sharing sites such as YouTube and Vimeo, location-based services such as Foursquare and Yelp, and a host of others currently in existence or rapidly coming to market.

If you're new to social media, it might help to think about it as a huge virtual party where many interesting people in different parts of the world are discussing many potentially interesting things. This party is ongoing and it's a great place to connect with people who share your interests, find out what's going on in the world in real time, and learn about things that interest you. However, you eventually need to leave any party—even the best one you've ever attended—to do other things.

The lure of social media, and one of the things that makes it such a challenge to controlling your attention, is the fear of what you might be missing when you're not engaging in it. In order to be productive you have to accept that you *will* miss things, but they will probably be waiting for you when you "get back to the party." Because social media has a real-time component and therefore provides a constant stream of information, it can feed your fear of not being able to keep up with "one more thing," and the fear that your time and attention are being "swallowed up," both of which are valid concerns. However, you don't need to avoid social media completely. They are communication tools just like any other, and the secret to using them effectively is to ensure that *you* control your social media channels, if and when you choose to engage in them, rather than allowing them to control you.

One way to control your social media channels is to recognize that they do not require or demand constant monitoring or instant feedback. There are tools that can "push" your social media communications to you in real time (via text or email), but using these tools is an example of sabotaging your own attention and productivity instead of supporting it because you're receiving a constant stream of information instead of choosing when you want to receive it. With very few exceptions, it just isn't necessary; do you really need to know immediately if someone commented on your YouTube video or tweeted at you or updated her status on LinkedIn? Feeling like you need to know all these things as they happen creates urgency from the unimportant, if you remember Eisenhower's advice from Chapter 3.

▶ The secret to controlling social media? Don't mistake "immediate" for "important."

## CONTROL OR BE CONTROLLED

In order to decide if you should engage in a particular social media technology, and control it effectively, consider the following questions:

- ▶ Why? What's the purpose that would be served if you participated?
- ▶ When will you engage, and are those opportunities feasible and realistic?
- ▶ How will you interact with these social media tools?

The following sections discuss these questions in more detail.

### Why?

Ask yourself what social media might offer you that would be useful. What are your reasons for considering it? The answers to that question will help you decide which types of social media to use and how often it makes sense to engage.

When it comes to new technology, people generally fall into one of two groups: the early adopters and everyone else. The former enjoy diving into new technologies and checking things out. At the other end of the spectrum in the "everyone else" category are people who have what I call *One More Thing Syndrome*. When people in this group encounter new technologies, such as Twitter, they are likely to respond with, "Oh, no! It's *one more thing* I have to manage, and I'm already drowning in what I have!"

Whether you're an early adopter, suffer from One More Thing Syndrome, or fall somewhere in between, you are faced with decisions regarding how new technologies will be incorporated into your life. Learning new tools takes time and effort. If you're an early adopter you probably relish the thought of digging into something new, but you still need to stay in control of your attention. Because early adopters actually enjoy the time and effort associated with learning new technologies, it is easy for them to lose part of their day as they "play," experiment, and learn. That's not necessarily a bad thing, as long as it is balanced with other priorities.

If you're not an early adopter, I suggest you wait until you have a compelling reason to adopt a new technology. For example, if you realize that you can save some time if you own a smartphone, or if you're connected in real life to people who use Google+ to communicate online, these are compelling reasons to invest some time in those tools. Otherwise, look for quick and easy opportunities to learn about new technologies that come to your attention so you can make an educated decision about whether to use them. Video tutorials on YouTube or other video sites are a great way to learn the basics of a new technology you're considering.

> ▶ How often do you go to a video-sharing site to learn something new? This is a great way to learn everything from how to fix a household appliance to mastering the hidden features of technology you use every day, such as email clients and smartphones.

For example, if you decide that you want to use Twitter to expand the reach of your business, you'll probably need to be tweeting pretty regularly to meet that objective. Conversely, if you decide to get a Facebook account to keep up with what your friends are doing, then it probably doesn't matter much how often you log in. New tools and platforms launch frequently, so it's important to be selective about what you participate in, and how often, to prevent social media from eclipsing your personal productivity. This is especially true for early adopters.

## When?

The next factor to consider is when you will participate in social media. If you work at a computer all day but social media is not part of your work, then you have to be aware of its potential to constantly distract you, and control it in order to get your work done. If you avoid or are prevented from using social media entirely when at work, then you might be limited to evenings and weekends to engage, so it's important to consider if that fits with your lifestyle.

# How?

How you plan to engage with social media is another important consideration. Do you work at a desk? Can you access those sites from the computer on your desk? Does it make sense for you to do so? If you're frequently on the go, then you'll likely have more opportunities to engage from a smartphone, if you have one. If you don't have a smartphone and accessing social media is important to you, you might consider investing in one.

> **NOTE** Is your organization missing opportunities to capitalize on social media? Social media can have disadvantages, but some companies are completely un-aware of the benefits it can provide. Implemented with key business objectives in mind, social media can help companies attract the attention of new customers, connect with and solicit feedback from current customers, and create new ways to deliver customer support. Perhaps these ideas and the others in this section can help you bring a fresh perspective to your workplace.

Some businesses have policies that assume that social media sites are nothing but opportunities for employees to waste time socializing. However, a wholesale ban of all social media might be an overlooked business opportunity. Because social media gives individuals a platform and a voice that was much more difficult to achieve before this technology existed, management often fears that employees could damage a company's reputation if it isn't banned from the workplace, and this concern is not without merit. However, consider that a workplace ban by itself doesn't eliminate the potential for an employee to damage a company's reputation, so a more general HR policy is probably more effective than a total ban on social media in the workplace.

The advantage of using social media in a business setting is that sometimes a "celebrity" emerges, and that person's reputation can *benefit* the business for as long as the employee works there. It can also add a "face" to the corporation. For example, Richard Binhammer, Director of Social Media and Community at Dell, has become famous on social media as @RichardAtDell and has helped transform the computer company's brand from "Dell Hell" to that of a social media leader.

If you are responsible for the social media policies at your organization, be sure to consider both the potential risks *and* the potential advantages to the company posed by your staff and the new communication technologies that exist.

# KNOW WHAT YOU'RE DOING

▶ A hashtag is a word or phrase preceded by the pound sign (#) in Twitter in order to highlight a keyword or topic and used to categorize tweets.

Another way to stay in control of the technology you choose is to learn about all the features and tools it offers, so you can receive the most value for your time and attention invested. For example, Twitter has a *lists* feature that enables you to group the people you follow by topic or industry or other relevant category. Hashtags are another feature that provides context. Google+ offers *circles* so that you can group your connections by their relationship to you. All of these are examples of features that can save you time and help you quickly get what you need from a particular service.

If you end up feeling that the time you spent engaging in a particular social media tool was wasted, it could be that you are not using it well (go back to your answer to the question of "why" from earlier in the chapter). For example, if you're questioning the value of Twitter, perhaps you are following the wrong people. In the case of LinkedIn, perhaps you are not taking advantage of the groups and discussions that the platform provides. Be sure to match your reasons for engaging with your knowledge of the features to provide the best return for your investment in time and attention.

If you're going to engage in a technology, it can provide value more quickly when you learn how to use it *well*.

# SUMMARY

Social media provide communication tools just like email and the telephone, and they are quickly becoming just as integral a part of both socializing and business correspondence. Like anything, these tools have advantages and disadvantages, fans and critics. As with the advent of most new technologies, there are those who predict they will "be the death" of personal productivity. With the ideas and techniques outlined in this chapter, I'm confident you'll be able to use social media *and* keep your personal productivity humming along.

# QUICK TIPS

The following are some important points from this chapter (also suitable for tweeting). For more information on Twitter, including relevant usernames and hashtags, please refer to the "Read This First" chapter.

▶ Manage social media by reducing your "fear of missing out"—it's not an urgent medium, so engage when it makes sense for you.

▶ A secret to controlling social media: Don't mistake "immediate" for "important."

▶ Tip: Turn off any push notifications from social media—just because it's new doesn't make it worth the distraction!

▶ If you're new to social media, search for how-to videos to quickly learn to use it effectively.

▶ Managers: Reconsider policies that ban social media altogether—they often end up preventing benefits from social media, too.

▶ Secret to productivity on social media: Make sure you know why you're there and that you're connected to the right people!

## CHAPTER 15

# Implications for Groups and Teams

**IN THIS CHAPTER**

▶ Affecting company culture
▶ Avoiding communication breakdowns
▶ Evaluating tools

Personal productivity is not only important to an individual; its effects are magnified throughout an organization. The ways in which individuals manage their commitments and communications can have staggering implications for a company's bottom line. For example, when employees don't manage email properly, the internal communications skyrocket, and staff members spend hours simply managing email from one another. The CEO of Atos, the multi-billion-dollar technology company mentioned in Chapter 14, implemented a "zero-email" policy within the firm when he realized the negative effect it was having on productivity.

> "We are producing data on a massive scale that is fast polluting our working environments and also encroaching into our personal lives," CEO Thierry Breton said in a statement when announcing the policy. "At [Atos] we are taking action now to reverse this trend, just as organizations took measures to reduce environmental pollution after the industrial revolution."[1]

Simply trading one communication tool for another, or for several others, doesn't work without a carefully considered strategy and management's dedication to training the staff. It's difficult to effect widespread behavioral change within a workplace, and I think we'll look back on these initial efforts and find much to learn.

This chapter illustrates the effect that personal productivity has on company culture, staff relationships, and the bottom line, and offers suggestions for improving business communication, regardless of your position within the company.

# PRODUCTIVITY AND COMPANY CULTURE

Personal productivity and workload management habits that sabotage individual productivity lead to corporate cultures that sabotage the results of the company as a whole. This results in ineffective staff and an unpleasant work environment. Some factors that contribute to this environment include

- ▶ The way email is used within a company
- ▶ The other ways staff communicate with each other
- ▶ The relative effectiveness of company meetings
- ▶ The electronic tools used by the staff

The following sections discuss each of these items in detail.

## Chained to Email

Many successful, fast-paced businesses have become very email-centric, relying almost exclusively on email for internal communications. In addition to the hours of time spent on this, there is another, more insidious consequence: When email is the default mode of operation within a company, employees end up on email all day, responding immediately to messages received. This reinforces the expectation that messages will *always* be met with an immediate response, so email becomes an acceptable form of communication for even urgent or time-sensitive information.

As a result, employees have no choice but to be vigilant about staying on top of their email messages by checking them constantly. Focusing so much attention on email leaves little opportunity to get anything *else* done; employees are effectively chained to their email. Therefore, because there are certainly other things that must be done, those other things (less "urgent" but probably more important) end up victims of multitasking. As discussed in Chapter 1, studies have proven for more than a decade that multitasking requires more time per task and lowers the quality of what is achieved. Therefore, in a workplace with an excessive focus on email, it's likely that employees are both taking too long to complete their work *and* producing lower-quality output.

## Productivity and Business Relationships

In addition to the email-centric culture, personal productivity styles can also cause interpersonal issues. Employees with a heavy workload have different ways of handling it. Some produce competent work and meet deadlines, but they may be unhappy, seem constantly stressed, and work long hours to get their work done. They are prized for their successes, but these employees are the most likely to suffer burnout and leave the company.

Other employees seem to be continuously busy but it's difficult to identify exactly what they produce. Indeed, many business cultures mistake activity for productivity. This problem is often caused by unclear objectives and an inability to prioritize effectively.

"In some cases," In some cases, employees serve as company bottlenecks. This is a problem often caused by unrealistic expectations—not only those of management, but also the employees themselves—about what can reasonably be accomplished in a given time frame. Without a comprehensive workflow management process for capturing all commitments, communication, and information, employees manage their responsibilities by relying on their memories. The result is a muddied understanding of the true magnitude of their workloads, a tendency to substitute activity for productivity, and impractical predictions about task and project achievement.

▶ Remember the lesson from Chapter 4 that you can only manage what you can see, and you can only see what is outside your head.

Accountability also plays a role. When a company has employees who don't produce or who consistently miss deadlines, but there are no consequences, the productivity of the whole organization suffers. In many cases, poorly performing employees aren't held accountable because of the poor workload-management skills of the individuals delegating the work. These situations have the potential to lead to animosity, individual rivalries, territorialism, and resentment. These complex interpersonal issues within a company reflect the different work habits and abilities of the employees.

Some people are naturally better at managing full and hectic workloads. Others aren't, but this doesn't mean they can't learn. Most people are ill-equipped to handle the demands on their attention caused by the information and technology avalanche of the twenty-first century. You (or your employees) could be losing hours of each day simply because information isn't being managed well or at all, and usually people don't manage information well because they have never been taught how to do so.

▶ Many people consider "being organized" an inherent talent that someone either has or doesn't have, but organization and productivity are skills like any other; they can be learned and practiced.

If you recognize among your staff or co-workers interpersonal challenges, stress issues, excessive work hours, or any combination of these issues, personal productivity skills could be lacking. Improving your own productivity with the techniques in this book will affect your workplace, but sharing the skills throughout the organization can have an exponential impact on the company's bottom line—as well as on employee satisfaction, teamwork, and effectiveness.

## Ineffective Communication

In addition to poor email management skills, many companies suffer from ineffective communication in general. Excessive and unproductive meetings are a symptom. Another is an increasing number of communication tools (such as instant messaging and corporate social media sites) with decreasing effectiveness. This results in more time spent looking for things and trying to keep up with all the different channels of communication rather than actually getting work done. Following are some tips for effective communication in general, and specifically for conducting and attending effective meetings.

It's important to recognize that information sharing is a two-way street, with responsibility falling on both the receiver *and* the giver. Everyone scrambles to keep up with the deluge of information they *receive*. However, if you pay more attention to your responsibility as the giver of information, everyone's load could be lightened.

### STANDARD QUESTIONS APPLY

To be a responsible giver of information, there are four questions you need to consider. First, *who* is the appropriate person to receive the information? For example, email is often sent to a large number of people simply because the sender didn't know the correct person to target. A little legwork by the sender on the front end can save time for recipients who don't truly need to receive the message.

> *CROSSREF* Also relevant to this topic is the "Three Things You Shouldn't Do" section in Chapter 11.

Second, remember that in the fast-paced, short-attention-span, time-starved environment that many professionals work within, brevity is welcome. Consider *what* you are sharing; whether you are being as concise as possible, and how to quickly get to your point. Sometimes background information is helpful, but understand that most readers choose to read a short email over a long one, saving a long message to review later—but often later never comes.

Third, because technology enables us to be connected virtually anywhere we are, it's more important than ever to consider *when* you are conveying information, and whether it is the best time. For example, relaying detailed information that needs to be written down is best not delivered when the recipient is taking the call from the car while driving. Similarly, important information is best not delivered with a shout as the recipient is rushing off to an appointment. Don't treat information like a "hot potato," believing that as long as you have "tossed it" to the recipient, you have fulfilled your obligation. Irresponsible "giving" is a common reason for communication breakdown in an organization.

Lastly, there are so many ways to communicate that we often choose what is easiest for us in the moment, instead of what would be most effective. Consider whether the type of information you're delivering is suited to the channel you're using: delegation of tasks or requests for favors are well suited to traditional channels such as voicemail or email, enabling easy addition to a task list. Asking someone to do something at a later date is best not delivered via tools such as text or social media, as these lend themselves to shorter, more immediate, and current types of correspondence. Sometimes people are guilty of "hiding behind" their email or other technologies to distance themselves from a difficult situation, which often makes it worse. Here's another example: Posting a question to a message board when the answer is already available on the website wastes everyone's time. *How* you choose to communicate is a key component of the message's effective communication.

## DEATH BY MEETING

A complaint I hear often from my clients and the staff at my client companies is that they spend too much time in meetings with dubious results. Implementing the following techniques will make the meetings you attend more effective.

First, be clear about the purpose for the meeting. For example, fill in this blank: At the end of the meeting we will have/know/do _____. Share this goal when you invite people to your meeting, and be clear about the desired outcome of every meeting to which you are invited.

Second, establish an agenda if you are the meeting planner, or ask for one if you are an attendee. Even better, assign time limits, or at least guidelines, for each topic on the agenda, and appoint a timekeeper and minute-taker at the meeting. After the meeting, the minutes should be published, preferably in the body of an email, not as an attachment. (Including the notes in the body of the message increases the likelihood that they will be read, or at least skimmed). An agenda with time limits and published minutes shows respect for everyone's time, collects all the ideas and comments that come out of the meeting provides an opportunity to take a discussion offline if necessary, and keeps everyone on track. It also provides insight into whether the desired agenda is reasonable for the time allotted.

The expectations of the participants are important to identify at the outset of any meeting. If you are a participant, can you identify exactly why you are being invited to a meeting, and what is expected of you? Are you the best person to meet that expectation? Is there redundancy in the invite list? As the meeting planner, consider these questions in relation to everyone you invite. Ensuring that an entire team is not attending when one spokesperson would suffice, and that each attendee can, in fact, provide what is expected of them, increases the effectiveness of any meeting.

If you are a leader in your company, consider whether the company culture allows people to opt out of a meeting, or is it expected that everyone who is invited will always attend? Making meetings optional gives employees control over their workday, which is an essential factor in job satisfaction. As an attendee, make sure you understand what part you will be expected to play in the meeting, and whether or not it is useful to your current objectives. Invitations to meetings that have no agenda and haven't specified a goal should be reconsidered carefully. These can be opportunities to regain more time in your day to be *proactive*.

Third, the effectiveness of every meeting depends on three critical questions posed at the end of the meeting and recorded with their answers in the minutes:

1. What's the next action?
2. Who is responsible?
3. When is the due date?

The first question is important because although there will be much discussion, the goal is often not met if required follow-up actions are not clearly identified. The second question matters because unless a specific person is tasked with a specific responsibility, the follow-up actions are unlikely to get done. Answering the third question ensures that the priorities of the group mesh with the priorities of the individual, but this can only be known if it is negotiated up front.

Having these questions and answers recorded in minutes that are distributed creates accountability through publicity. When no one knows you have a deadline, it's much easier to miss it. A public deadline is much harder to avoid.

# IS A PIM ENOUGH?

When personal productivity intersects with corporate goals, sometimes other tools are necessary to combine the two effectively. However, most people don't adequately evaluate the need for these other tools in the context of their productivity as a whole. When managing contacts becomes challenging, for example, many individuals opt for a CRM (customer relationship management) tool, without realizing that the contact features of their PIM might suffice.

▶ Reminder: PIM = Personal Information Manager

Similarly, when managing projects becomes a challenge to a business, sometimes an investment is made in some sort of global project management tool without considering that this has the potential to create a duplication of effort for the employees involved. The following sections offer ideas to address these problems.

## Do You Need a CRM?

People who have jobs that are heavily focused around human interaction, such as sales roles, often want a tool that is written specifically for this purpose, without considering the effect it will have on the rest of their productivity process. Contacts and contact management is just one part of the entire workflow management system, as outlined in Chapter 5. It's ineffective to try to solve problems of managing customer relationships with only a complex CRM solution without also having a complementary system for calendaring, email, and to-do lists.

▶ An example of a CRM tool is Act! or Salesforce.

To properly evaluate whether you need a CRM, I suggest that you look at it within the context of your overall productivity. Although it might provide the features you're looking for—to manage a sales pipeline, for example—does it also have the other necessary features important to your productivity: a comprehensive calendar, task list, email, and notes? If it doesn't, how will your productivity be affected if you need to use other tools for those purposes? How will your CRM integrate with your task list, for example, or your email? In the context of your overall productivity, will those extra contact management features still be valuable if they cause you to work harder in other parts of your system?

The most common PIMs have many contact management features that the average user isn't aware of. Review the "Master Your Address Book" section of Chapter 13 to make full use of the tools you're already using. This may prevent you from making the mistake of overcomplicating your system with excessive features you don't even need.

## PIMs and Project Management

It's always a balancing act to successfully and efficiently manage an individual's workload within the context of group projects. Individuals need to manage their own workloads, and some of what they do has nothing to do with group projects, but the leadership team needs to manage all the projects. This often results in employees grumbling about spending more time *tracking* work than actually *doing* work. This is not insignificant; it does take time away from getting work done. It's completely valid and necessary, however, for the leadership team to maintain a handle on what's going on, and for everyone to be able to see a project's status.

The ideal solution would be a project management tool that allows for seamless syncing of tasks related to a group project with a *personal* information management tool. Tasks could then be manipulated as the individual sees fit (alarms, categories or context, personal due dates, notes, and so on), and then sync with the group collaboration tool when they are completed. In my opinion, the absence of such a solution represents a huge hole in the market of project management tools. It suggests that the management/staff conflict between "What's the status of the project?" and "Go away and let me *do* the project" will continue because the only option seems to be duplicate task tracking by employees—once for their own personal workload in their PIM, and once for the benefit of the team in the corporate project management tool.

With my clients, sometimes this conflict does not come up right away because at the beginning of our work together, individuals don't typically have a good workflow management process or tool in place. Either they aren't tracking their tasks because they don't have a solid handle on all of their responsibilities, or they spend most of their time in reactive mode (reacting to whatever is in their email inbox, in their team collaboration tool, on their desk, in their voicemail, or on paper as notes from meetings). After they have been trained on a workflow methodology such as the Empowered Productivity™ System, and they have regained control over all those details, they are able to be much more proactive. It is then that they discover the double entry that is required to manage their personal workload *and* what is required for the company as a whole. In other words, stress levels decrease and productivity increases exponentially, but there is still inefficiency.

I've been researching project management products for years, looking for a tool that effectively combines collaborative project management and personal workflow management, but as of this writing I haven't discovered any that suit my vision. Therefore, if you need to share projects with team, my best advice is to evaluate the available tools in the context of this issue, and be mindful of the ways to eliminate, or at least minimize, any residual inefficiency.

In the absence of a "perfect" solution, double-entry of your project-related tasks—once in your PIM and once in any group project management tool that your company may require—is the most efficient option. It does require a little extra time, but the minute or two of copying and pasting required pays dividends in the efficiency and peace of mind you receive by having all of your responsibilities in one place.

## SUMMARY

If you run a business, have staff, or manage a team, the information in this chapter should be particularly relevant. However, anyone who works with other people, at least some of the time, can benefit from productivity gains by creating habits of the behaviors described in this chapter. Even just changing the way you send email or schedule meetings will set an example of effectiveness and peak personal productivity that can affect the way those around you behave.

## QUICK TIPS

The following are some important points from this chapter (also suitable for tweeting). For more information on Twitter, including relevant usernames and hashtags, please refer to the "Read This First" chapter.

▶ Companies without good email policies spend hours just managing internal communications. Are ineffective habits taking a toll at your company?

▶ Responding to email immediately reinforces the expectation that emails will always be answered immediately.

▶ Email should be avoided for urgent or time-sensitive information because it's more productive for employees to be off email some of the time.

▶ People who attend to email vigilantly and respond immediately are probably also delivering lower-quality output on their "real" work.

▶ Employees who rely on memory to manage their workloads often suffer from unrealistic predictions about what they can achieve.

▶ Some people consider "organization" a talent you're born with, but, in fact, it can be learned & practiced.

▶ Frequent and unproductive meetings are a symptom of poor communication skills.

- ▶ Consider whether all the recipients of your email really need the message—help reduce email clutter for others!

- ▶ Brevity can get your message read first! Recipients sometimes save long emails to read later. . . often never!

- ▶ Don't treat information as a hot potato—that is, not your problem after you've tossed it to someone else.

- ▶ Tip: Start each meeting with a goal—"At the end of this session we will have/know/do _____."

- ▶ Create meeting agendas with time limits per item to keep on track and respect attendees' time.

- ▶ End each meeting with defined next actions: Who is responsible and when is it due?

- ▶ Email a summary of meeting minutes with the next actions—public deadlines are more likely to be met.

- ▶ Before implementing a CRM or project management tool, evaluate whether benefits outweigh the possible disruption to your productivity flow.

# ENDNOTES

**1.** Susanna Kim, *Tech Firm Implements Employee 'Zero Email' Policy*, ABC News, November 29, 2011, Web, http://abcnews.go.com/blogs/business/2011/11/tech-company-implements-employee-zero-email-policy/.

## CHAPTER 16

# Modern Conveniences— Reviews and Recommendations

**IN THIS CHAPTER**

- ▶ Apps, software, and hardware
- ▶ The smartphone lifestyle

One of my favorite things to learn is new apps, gadgets, and services that can make my life easier or less complicated, or save me time. In this last chapter of the book, I share my favorites and give you some ideas for ways to use them to improve your productivity and your effectiveness.

Providing a list like this is challenging because the number of tools available is huge and the tools change rapidly. Also, the same product can vary slightly or completely, depending on your platform and your device and sometimes on your location. However, most combinations of devices (computers and smartphones) offer enough selection that if you can't find the exact item I reference, a quick Internet or app store search will likely provide something similar.

These recommendations fall into three categories: hardware, apps and software, and services. Hardware includes the devices themselves—for example smartphones and tablets; products built into these devices, such as a camera and mp3 player; and peripheral devices or accessories, such as a speaker or special cable.

The apps and software category includes programs for your computer, smartphone, or tablet that are available for download onto your device from a website or from an online store for apps. You can purchase apps online (or download free apps) for Mac computers, iOS devices such as iPhone, iPad, and iPod touch, Android handheld devices, Windows smartphones, and BlackBerry devices.

The services category includes websites or companies that provide a service—either one-time, ongoing, or as needed. You can also refer to Appendix B for a list of every product, service, and website referenced in this book.

## YOUR PORTABLE PIM

I often hear people say that they don't want an iPhone or a "CrackBerry" because they don't want to be *that* connected. They say, "People already have too many ways to reach me. I don't want to have to be available 24/7." My response is always the same: You don't have to be. Just because you have a phone, you don't have to turn it on. Just because it's on, you don't have to answer it when it rings. The same advice applies to email on your phone. In fact, you can have all the advantages of a smartphone without email if you choose.

As this book has stressed throughout the chapters, as long as you remain in control of your technology, the advantages far outweigh the disadvantages. Sometimes it's handy to be able to retrieve email on your device (especially if you follow the "Review, Process, Do" advice from Chapter 11). It can free you from having to be in the office, or even at a computer. In addition, having a smartphone that you sync with your computer gives you access to all your PIM data when you are on the go. You might run into some technicalities getting your tasks on your device, depending on what tools you're using. For example, on an iPhone, your task list from iCal or Outlook shows up in an app called Reminders. As of this writing, it's not particularly robust, but it fills the need to scan your list when you're away from your computer.

Having your task list with you can eliminate the anxiety caused by something you might be forgetting to do. In addition, having your PIM data always with you allows you to consult your calendar, retrieve an address from your contacts, quiet nagging thoughts by reviewing your task list, or capture an idea in a note, for example. If you decide to use Evernote, recommended in Chapter 13, then be sure to download the Evernote app to your smartphone as well.

If you use Google, recall the disadvantages I outlined in Chapter 7. A few of these issues in your task list can be mitigated by using a plug-in to your Google apps called Remember the Milk (RTM). Unlike Google Tasks, RTM enables you to search tasks, associate tasks with projects or other tasks, and set reminders. To use it, you need to create an RTM account, which is free, and then you can manage your tasks from your Google calendar, or from www.rememberthemilk.com, in a different browser window. If you choose to use this, download the RTM app to your smartphone, as this enables you to access your tasks while away from your computer. RTM is a good solution to the limitations of Google Tasks listed in Chapter 7.

▶ All software and apps recommended in this chapter are listed with their website addresses in Appendix B.

# LIFESTYLE, SHOPPING, AND HEALTH

In addition to your PIM data, it's also very handy to have other features available on a smartphone, such as the apps, voice recorder, camera and mp3 player, for example. Many apps are available on multiple devices; and if you can't find the exact app I mention, it's quite likely something very similar is available for your device. Regardless of what you choose, just remember that with so many ways to use a smartphone in a typical day, your goal is to take advantage of the conveniences it offers for yourself, not other people. Also note that in most cases, apps that are available for a smartphone are also available for a tablet running the same operating system.

> **NOTE** As I mentioned earlier in this chapter, the list of available apps is enormous and it changes daily. If an app that I mention in this chapter is no longer available, do an Internet search for the type of app and you'll easily find alternatives for your device.

## Reading

Smartphones are now built with larger screens designed to make them easier to view, which makes reading on a smartphone much better than it used to be, although it's admittedly not ideal. If reading on a smartphone doesn't bother you, you can download books, magazines, and newspapers, in addition to articles and blogs on websites, so reading material is always handy. Many major newspapers and magazines have free apps, and you can buy a subscription to read issues on your smartphone. The Kindle, Nook, and iBook apps provide the capability to store and read virtually any book published in this format (perhaps you're even reading this book on your device!). Also, an RSS reader app can deliver blogs and pages your're subscribed to directly to your phone.

▶ Don't forget to add www.regainyourtime.com/blog to your reader.

## Listening

▶ Regarding your data usage, most wireless carriers offer an app that enables you to check your minutes, text, data usage, and other pertinent account information from your device.

If you prefer not to read on the relatively small screen of a smartphone, note that most smartphones have music players built in, which provide not only music but also audiobooks, radio, and podcasts. Many radio and television news shows provide podcasts of their content, which enables you to catch up on, for example, the news any time, at your convenience. Of course, you can also load your digital music collection onto your device. If your own collection is lacking, or not in digital format, check out Pandora or Slacker, which enable you to choose a "station" by selecting a song, album, or artist that you enjoy, and the app will serve up a selection of similar music. Note that the content streams live from the Internet, so unless you have an unlimited data plan, it might be best to only use this on your smartphone when you have access to a wireless network. Both Pandora and Slacker also have a website, so you can use them from your computer if you prefer.

In addition to podcasts and music, a fee-based subscription service called Audible offers books in audio format, often read by the author, for download onto your smartphone. This provides you with the opportunity to consume a book at times when it used to be impossible—such as when you're getting ready for your day, making dinner, or doing routine chores. Having the ability to listen to a book from your smartphone enables you to turn mundane tasks, such as waiting in line or making your daily commute, into learning or entertainment opportunities.

All smartphones have speakers, but the quality isn't great for listening to music or podcasts, so you might prefer to use headphones or a speaker that you plug into the device. I purchased an affordable portable speaker that provides high-quality, magnified sound anywhere I want to listen to my books, podcasts, and music. A visit to your local or online electronics store will provide many options. I suggest avoiding the very low-end versions, but the prices are reasonable and coming down.

If you're shopping for a car, you might put an auxiliary outlet on your desired features list. By plugging an auxiliary cable into your car outlet and your smartphone, you can listen to those audio books, podcasts, or your favorite music through your car's stereo.

## Eating and Exercising

There are also hundreds of apps that make routine tasks like grocery shopping, planning and cooking meals, and exercising much faster and easier. Some suggestions include GroceryIQ, which sorts your list by store and aisle and enables you to share your list with other members of your household. A useful app that helps you make healthier choices at the grocery store is Fooducate, which deciphers ingredient labels into an easy rating system. Meal planning and cooking are made easier with apps like Dinner Spinner or BigOven. For exercising, look at Fitness Buddy or RunKeeper, which provide workout ideas and help you reach your exercise goals. There are also hundreds of activity-specific apps, so whether yoga, cycling, or weightlifting is your thing, a quick search can provide you with helpful options. Many of these apps social features built in, which means you can connect with other people with similar goals for camaraderie and motivation.

## Entertaining and Being Entertained

Even tasks related to leisure activities, like selecting a bottle of wine or choosing which movie to see, can be made easier with an app. Snooth can help you select a good bottle of wine in your price range that will complement your meal or occasion. Beer Brands offers the same service for beer; and if you prefer mixed drinks, there are several mixology apps that can have you emulating your favorite bartender in no time. Most experts agree that the average person doesn't drink enough water for optimal health. To remedy this, try Waterlogged, which reminds you to drink more water, and helps you track your water intake.

Flixster is my favorite app for movies because it tells you what's playing at your local cinemas, gives you ratings from both critics and viewers, and even offers the same for movies that are available on DVD. If you're not put off by the small screen size, with the purchase of a Netflix or Hulu Plus subscription you can watch television shows and movies from your device with their respective apps. Again, these are streaming services and data rates apply, so Wi-Fi is a good option for these apps.

If you live in or near a major metropolitan area, search your app store for "things to do *your city*," which is also helpful when you're traveling. Yelp is a must-have app that I use most often for restaurants, but it has user reviews for all kinds of services, such as salons, retail stores, and mechanics. It's indispensable when traveling but definitely will come in handy in your hometown too. Similar but slightly different is AroundMe, which helps you find the closest sandwich shop, gas station, or other retail location. You can also use the search feature to find out how close you are to the nearest branch of your favorite national retailer, or to find a locally owned option for the category you're looking for.

▶ Many of the apps listed in this chapter, such as Woot, Groupon, and Yelp, provide the same service via their website. However, because it's not always convenient to be at your computer, apps empower you with information when you are on the go.

▶ Don't forget the handy uses of the audio recording apps discussed in the "Capturing Thoughts" section of Chapter 6.

## Shopping

Using apps for shopping can save you time and money. Price-comparison apps, such as Snap Tell, enable you to scan a barcode to find the least expensive source for a particular item. Try SnapTell. Daily deal services provide opportunities to save money on big-ticket items like TVs (check out Woot) but also meals, personal care items, and consumer services. (Groupon is my favorite app for this.)

I never realized how handy the camera and video recorder on my smartphone would be, especially when combined with the capability to text images and video. I typically use this combination to solicit an opinion when someone isn't with me. Snap a picture and send it via text with the question, "What do you think?" Taking a quick photo is also useful for many types of errands. For example, if you need parts or supplies at the hardware store, snap a picture of what you're replacing (perhaps even with a ruler in front of it) before you head out. This alone can save you several trips! Emailing images and videos is also handy for sharing experiences with friends and family, or to report vandalism or other damage in your neighborhood to the police or homeowners' association, for example. The camera on the iPhone 4 and later is so good that it practically eliminates the need for a scanner for all but very large documents or pictures. For example, snap a picture of a business card poster, or other contact information for reference later.

## Sleeping and Relaxing

I've read that exposing yourself to the light of your device before you go to bed at night can disturb your sleep, but your smartphone can actually help you sleep. You can find apps that provide soothing sounds, meditation assistance, and even alarm clock apps that monitor your sleep cycles and wake you when you'll feel most rested! Some suggestions include White Noise, SleepStream 2 Pro, and Sleep Cycle Alarm Clock. If you're going to make use of your smartphone during sleep time or other times you don't want to be disturbed, take advantage of *flight mode*, which disconnects cell and Internet signals but still offers use of the other features. Your emails, texts, and voicemail messages will be waiting for you in the morning when you turn off flight mode, but in the meantime you'll be undisturbed.

## Planning Your Day

In the morning, your device can help you plan your day—consult your calendar and check whatever is relevant to you: weather, traffic, allergy or UV reports, and so on. The Weather Channel offers a great weather app, and Pollen.com offers an Allergy

Alert app that provides ratings on air quality for asthmatics in addition to providing allergy and UV reports. For traffic, check out Waze GPS & Traffic, or use the search feature in your app store with the terms *"your city"* plus the word "traffic."

Early morning can be a good time to review your email to see if anything there will affect your plans for the day, and also check social media if that is an important communication channel for you. All the major social networks have their own apps, but several also enable you to check them all from one place, such as HootSuite, TweetDeck, and Seesmic. If you see something there that requires more time, you can use the handy "mail link to this page" feature of most smartphones to email it to yourself for processing later.

This is just a small sample of the ways your smartphone can be useful for everyday experiences in your life. The next section illustrates ways to use it for increased productivity and efficiency when conducting business and traveling.

▶ Regarding checking email first thing in the morning, don't forget the rules from the "Developing a Better Way to Process" section in Chapter 11.

# BUSINESS AND TRAVEL

Business settings frequently require the easy and convenient exchange of contact information. An alternative to business card exchange is an app called Bump, which enables you to quickly and easily share contact information and other data on your device with other Bump users, by simply "bumping" your phones together. There are many more business uses for apps as well. Here's another example: You can use your smartphone to control your computer (such as to advance a slide show or presentation) with an app such as Mobile Mouse.

In meetings, take notes in your own handwriting (or draw pictures!) with your finger or a stylus using an app such as PenUltimate. If you need your notes translated to text, try WritePad, which uses Optical Character Recognition (OCR) to translate your handwriting into computer text. Your success will vary depending on your handwriting, so try this out first before assuming it will work flawlessly in an important situation.

If you use Google Voice as I recommend in Chapter 12, you'll definitely want the Google Voice app for your smartphone, which you can use to make calls from your phone but have your Google Voice number show up in the caller ID instead of your cell phone number. You can also retrieve your Google Voice messages from the app.

Another great business app is Expensify, which is the fastest and easiest way I've found to keep track of expenses related to a specific client trip or project, and the app will automatically create your expense report for you. You could also use this for

▶ Before embracing Bump in all situations, review the drawbacks of electronic business card exchange from Chapter 9.

▶ Some apps, such as those for reading, watching video, and taking notes, are better on a larger tablet screen than on your smartphone. Remember that most iPhone apps are also available for the iPad, and the same is true for Android smartphones and tablets.

personal expenses that have a budget, such as a remodel or for event planning. If you need to track your mileage for business or tax purposes, try MileBug. It creates mileage reports for you with the push of a button. To track financial data, if you are a Mac user, try iBank on your computer, combined with the iBank app on your device. These make keeping track of expenses fast and portable.

Smartphones make travel much more convenient. My favorite app/service is TripIt, which enables you to forward all your email confirmations regarding your trips—such as from airlines, hotels, and rental car companies—to TripIt, which organizes all the information into one window that is easily viewable from the app. You can also check the status of your flight from within the app. To check the status of someone else's flight, it's also handy to have as app such as Flightview; and if you fly with a particular airline, you'll probably benefit from having the airline's app as well.

If, like me, you hate to pack, an app called Packing takes some of the sting out the process. You can store your own customized packing lists in it. Google Maps is a common GPS app, but personally I prefer Mapquest 4 because it speaks to you like an actual GPS system, which is safer than having to read the directions in Google Maps.

▶ As of this writing, Siri recently debuted on the iPhone 4S, and voice recognition is adding even more convenience to smartphone use.

## MISCELLANEOUS

The following are a few more of my favorite apps, which don't fit well into any of the categories already mentioned:

- ▶ **AppBox Pro:** This overall utility app contains conversion information (measurement and money), a date calculator, a countdown clock, a language translator, a flashlight (MyLite is good as well), and a level, among many other things.

- ▶ **Advanced English Dictionary (AED)**, **Constitution** (including the Bill of Rights), and **Declaration** (of Independence): These reference apps are handy to have when you need to look up a word, or some information from these important documents, respectively.

- ▶ **Flickr** or **MyPics** (for **Picasa**): These apps are mobile gateways to Flickr and Picasa that are helpful if you store your pictures online in one of those services. They enable you to view and share your photos via email, among other handy features.

- ▶ **Emoji Free:** This app puts images into your text messages (the "thumbs up" image comes in handy as a quick response). Only people using an iPhone or Android device can see the images, however. They will appear as a text character to other recipients.

The following tools are websites instead of apps, but I use them frequently and find them handy, so I thought I'd share them here:

▶ **When Is Good:** If you're trying to find a convenient time to do something with other people whose calendars you don't share, try this website.

▶ **Google Forms:** Use this Google app to create a questionnaire for collecting input. The results are dropped into a spreadsheet in Google Docs for you, which you can then share or download if necessary.

▶ **Survey Monkey:** This website is another survey tool, which has a free option and a paid subscription.

▶ **FillAnyPDF.com:** This website is helpful if you don't have a scanner and a fax machine or PDF-creation software, but you need to fill out and/or sign a document that has been emailed to you. You can upload the document and the site allows you to make edits to the document online. You can enter your information by typing or "writing" with your mouse, and then save the form back to your computer.

▶ **Dropbox:** This is probably the most popular service for online document storage. Use it to keep documents online instead of only on your local computer so that you can access them from other places or easily share them. There are both free and paid versions, and versions for all the common devices.

▶ **Buffer:** If you use social media, you'll love Buffer. It's a service (with free and paid versions) that enables you to create a daily and weekly posting schedule to Twitter, LinkedIn, and Facebook (posts can be different for each) and then create a "queue" of your updates. Instead of your updates going simultaneously to all of your social media channels, with Buffer you can stagger the same update at different times, and create days' or weeks' worth of updates in one sitting. You can always post immediately from Buffer, or you can add to your queue.

## SUMMARY

All the apps and scenarios described in this chapter have one thing in common: They enable conveniences for you, not others. You can manage all the features so that *you* are in control of your time, and prevent distractions and interruptions when you need to make progress on other things. It can be a little overwhelming and time consuming to embrace all of this new technology, but honestly I think you will be amazed often, as I am, at how much easier and more convenient they can make your life.

# QUICK TIPS

The following are some important points from this chapter (also suitable for tweeting). For more information on Twitter, including relevant usernames and hashtags, please refer to the "Read This First" chapter.

- ▶ Your smartphone can free you from the office by allowing you to access your PIM data remotely and work where you like.

- ▶ Using a capture tool app lets you quiet nagging thoughts by emptying your mind into your task list.

- ▶ Catch up with the news on your own time with podcasts from most major broadcasters.

- ▶ Waiting in line or making your daily commute becomes a chance to catch up on "reading" using podcasts and audiobooks.

- ▶ Use GroceryIQ to share your grocery list and sort by store and aisle to make errands more productive.

- ▶ Many of your favorite deal websites (such as Groupon) have apps to help you save on the go.

- ▶ Get the best deal using barcode scanning apps to compare prices on a particular item.

- ▶ Use your smartphone camera to snap a picture before you head to the hardware store to make it easier to find an exact match.

- ▶ Try an app like Bump instead of exchanging business cards to save on data entry.

- ▶ Apps for tracking expenses, like Expensify or iBank, make the task fast and portable.

- ▶ Use a trip planning app like TripIt or Flightview to coordinate all your itineraries and check flight status.

- ▶ Scheduling sites like When Is Good help coordinate meetings with fewer emails.

- ▶ Use online document storage apps like Dropbox to back up your files, share, and access them on the go.

# PART IV

# APPENDICES

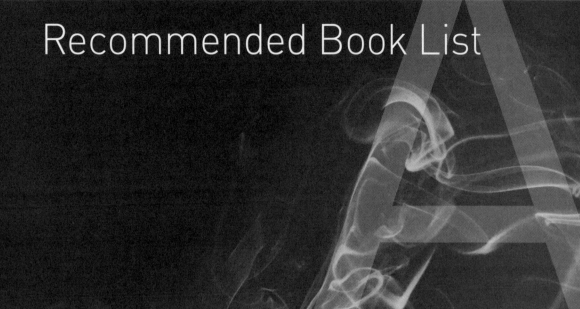

# Recommended Book List

If you are interested in further reading on the topic of this book and similar topics, following is the list of books I've learned from and referenced in the preceding pages. I think each one is worth reading. In addition to the books listed here by the chapter to which they relate, I also suggest you check out the articles referenced in the endnotes of every chapter, and the following:

- ▶ The Research and Resources page of my website at http://RegainYourTime.com/attention-management/research-resources/

- ▶ *The Way We're Working Isn't Working: The Four Forgotten Needs That Energize Great Performance*, Tony Schwartz, Jean Gomes, and Catherine McCarthy, Free Press, 2010

- ▶ Matt Richtel's awesome body of work in *The New York Times*, which you can find on the Web at http://topics.nytimes.com/topics/reference/timestopics/people/r/matt_richtel/index.html

You'll find an online link to everything in this appendix on the book website at www.Personal-Productivity-Secrets.com.

## CHAPTER 1

- ▸ *The Assault on Reason*, Al Gore, Penguin, 2008
- ▸ *Alone Together: Why We Expect More from Technology and Less from Each Other*, Sherry Turkle, Basic Books, 2011
- ▸ *Distracted: The Erosion of Attention and the Coming Dark Age*, Maggie Jackson, Prometheus Books, 2009
- ▸ *The Attention Economy: Understanding the New Currency of Business,* Thomas H. Davenport and John C. Beck, Harvard Business Review Press, 2002
- ▸ *Rapt: Attention and the Focused Life,* Winifred Gallagher, Penguin (Non-Classics), 2010

## CHAPTER 2

- ▸ *Nudge,* Richard Thaler and Cass Sunstein, Penguin (Non-Classics), 2009
- ▸ *The Secret Thoughts of Successful Women: Why Capable People Suffer from the Impostor Syndrome and How to Thrive in Spite of It,* Dr. Valerie Young, Crown Business, 2011

## CHAPTER 3

- ▸ *The 21 Indispensable Qualities of a Leader*, Dr. John Maxwell and Thomas Nelson, 1999
- ▸ *Seven Habits of Highly Effective People*, Steven Covey, Free Press, 2004
- ▸ *The 4-Hour Workweek*, Tim Ferriss, Crown Archetype, 2009

# CHAPTER 4

▶  *Information Anxiety,* Richard Wurman, Que, 1989

# CHAPTER 5

▶  *The Power of Full Engagement: Managing Energy, Not Time Is the Key to High Performance and Personal Renewal,* Jim Loehr and Tony Schwartz, Free Press, 2004

# Resources

This appendix contains further information on every resource mentioned in the book, except for other books and articles, which are addressed in Appendix A. You can also find all of these resources as hyperlinks on the book website at www.personal-productivity-secrets.com. If you find that any of these apps are no longer available, a search in your appropriate app store for the relevant subject will provide a list of similar alternatives.

# READ THIS FIRST

- www.personal-productivity-secrets.com
- www.regainyourtime.com

# CHAPTER 3

- Angie's List, www.angieslist.com
- Craigslist, www.craigslist.org
- Elance, www.elance.com
- Task Rabbit, www.taskrabbit.com

# CHAPTER 5

- Apple Mail, iCal, Address Book (part of the Mac Operating System), www.apple.com/macosx/apps/
- Gmail, http://mail.google.com
- Google Calendar, www.google.com/calendar
- Google Contacts, www.google.com/contacts
- Google Tasks, www.mail.google.com/tasks
- Mailtags, www.indev.ca/MailTags.html (this website address is case-sensitive)
- Microsoft Outlook, www.office.microsoft.com/en-us/outlook
- Time/system, www.timesystem.com

# CHAPTER 7

- Apple Reminders, www.apple.com/ios/features.html

## CHAPTER 9

▶ Ambient Devices, www.ambientdevices.com

▶ Mac Operating System, www.apple.com/macosx

## CHAPTER 11

▶ 43 Folders, www.43folders.com

▶ Inbox Zero, www.inboxzero.com

## CHAPTER 12

▶ Gmail Priority Inbox, mail.google.com/mail/help/intl/en/priority-inbox.html

▶ Google Voice, www.google.com/voice

▶ Otherinbox, www.otherinbox.com

▶ SpamArrest, www.spamarrest.com

## CHAPTER 13

▶ Apple Time Machine, www.apple.com/findouthow/mac/#timemachinebasics

▶ Evernote, www.evernote.com

## CHAPTER 16

▶ Advanced English Dictionary, http://jdictionary-mobile.com/index.php

▶ AppBox Pro, http://allaboutapps.info/wordpress/appbox-pro

- ▶ AroundMe, `www.tweakersoft.com/aroundme.html`
- ▶ Audible, `www.audible.com/wireless`
- ▶ Beer Brands (Android), `https://market.android.com/details?id=com.webworks.beerbrands&hl=en`
- ▶ Beer Brands (iPhone), `http://itunes.apple.com/us/app/7-800-beer-brands-free/id299434331?mt=8`
- ▶ Big Oven, `www.bigoven.com/software`
- ▶ Buffer, `www.bufferapp.com`
- ▶ Bump, `http://bu.mp/`
- ▶ Constitution (Android), `https://market.android.com/search?q=constitution&c=apps`
- ▶ Constitution (iPhone), `http://itunes.apple.com/us/app/constitution-for-iphone-ipod/id288657710?mt=8`
- ▶ Declaration (iPhone), `http://itunes.apple.com/us/app/declaration-for-iphone-ipod/id289320718?mt=8`
- ▶ Declaration (Android), try searching "US Constitution plus more" at `www.market.android.com/`
- ▶ Dinner Spinner, `http://allrecipes.com/features/applications/dinner-spinner/`
- ▶ Emoji Free (Android), `https://market.android.com/search?q=emoji&c=apps`
- ▶ Emoji Free (iPhone), `http://itunes.apple.com/us/app/emoji-free!/id332509635?mt=8`
- ▶ Expensify, `www.expensify.com/mobile`
- ▶ Fill Any PDF, `www.fillanypdf.com`
- ▶ Fitness Buddy (Android), `www.androidzoom.com/android_applications/sports/fitness-buddy_bxpod.html`
- ▶ Fitness Buddy (iPhone), `www.fitnessbuddyapp.com/`
- ▶ Flickr, `www.flickr.com/mobile`
- ▶ Flightview, `www.flightview.com/corporate/products/flightview-mobile-apps.aspx`
- ▶ Flixster, `http://community.flixster.com/wap/apps`
- ▶ Fooducate, `www.fooducate.com/`

- GoogleVoice, www.google.com/mobile/voice/

- GroceryIQ, www.groceryiq.com

- Groupon, www.groupon.com/mobile

- Hulu Plus, www.hulu.com/plus/devices?src=sem-plus-google

- iBank, www.iggsoftware.com/ibank, for apps go to www.iggsoftware.com/ibankmobile

- MapQuest 4, http://wireless.mapquest.com/

- MileBug, http://milebug.blog.blogspot.com/p/home.html

- Mobile Mouse, http://mobilemouse.com/

- MyPics, www.uvento.com/mypics

- Netflix, www.netflix.com

- Packing Pro (Android), search for "Packing List" at market.android.com

- Packing Pro (iPhone), www.quinnscape.com/PackingPro.asp

- Pandora, www.pandora.com/#!/go/mobile

- PenUltimate, www.cocoabox.com/

- Pollen.com, www.pollen.com/allergy-tools.asp

- Remember the Milk, www.rememberthemilk.com

- Run Keeper, http://runkeeper.com

- Slacker, www.slacker.com/everywhere/

- Sleep Cycle Alarm Clock, www.sleepcycle.com/

- SleepStream 2 Pro, http://sleepstream.explosiveapps.com/

- SnapTell, www.snaptell.com/apps/

- Snooth (iPhone), www.snooth.com/iphone-app/

- Survey Monkey, www.surveymonkey.com

- TripIt, www.tripit.com/uhp/mobile

- Waterlogged (Android), https://market.android.com/search?q=waterlogged

- Waterlogged (iPhone), http://shadelsoftware.com/waterlogged/

- Waze GPS & Traffic, www.waze.com/download/

- Weather Channel, www.weather.com/services/mobilesplash.html

- When Is Good, www.whenisgood.net

- White Noise, www.tmsoft.com/
- Woot, www.woot.com, for apps visit https://woot.wikia.com/wiki/Woot-Off_Checkers (scroll down to "Woot Apps")
- WritePad, www.phatware.com/index.php?q=product/details/writepad
- Yelp, www.yelp.com/yelpmobile

# Glossary

Many common words and phrases have a specific meaning in the context of the Empowered Productivity™ System and this book. This glossary includes these contextual definitions plus the definitions of general terminology. If you want to find the place in the book where the word or phrase is used in context, refer to the index.

**60-Second Rule**—An email-processing technique designed to prevent you from prematurely skipping a message when you might be able to quickly address the item and dispatch it. This helps you avoid leaving messages in your inbox to be dealt with later, which is inefficient and creates clutter.

**Action Files**—Files holding those items you are actively working on. These files should mirror your Task categories, including Next Actions, Projects, and Waiting For, and you should store them within easy reach of your workspace.

**actionable verb**—A verb whose action is clear, such as *call*, *write*, or *email*. (*See also* vague verb.)

**ADD**—Attention Deficit Disorder, a biological condition of the brain that causes a person—child or adult—to have poor attention and focusing skills. It is also often characterized by distractibility.

**ADT**—Attention Deficit Trait, a term coined by psychologist Dr. Edward Hallowell that refers to an acquired and situational form of ADD whereby people who are accustomed to a constant stream of digital stimulation feel bored when it is absent.

**ambient information**—Information in the environment that is readily available. We react to ambient information without thinking and it does not require conscious interaction. It includes information taken in via the senses in a peripheral way as well as some forms of subtle advertising.

**ambient information technology**—Devices that allow information to be consumed in the background, sometimes without the conscious knowledge of the recipient.

**apps**—Usually refers to mobile device software or web-based software.

**arbitrary (due dates)**—Refers to a due date that is assigned to a task for no particular reason except for its relative importance to the other items on the list.

**Archive Files**—Files for documents that you will rarely, or never, need to access. These files are for items you can't discard for legal or historical reasons or that you don't want to discard for sentimental reasons. You should store them somewhere other than your immediate workspace, such as in an attic, a garage, or a storage room.

**ASCII sort**—A way to organize information using the specific way a computer allocates symbols.

**Attention Age**—The view of industry that suggests that because information is so abundant, its value has decreased, and what is therefore gaining value is the commodity that information consumes: attention.

**attention management**—A method of choosing whether to maintain focus on a specific task without acknowledging unwanted interruptions. It is the practice of controlling where your attention is directed rather than succumbing to the constant demands of your surroundings from technology, media, and other people.

**balance**—1. Ensuring that a particular area of your life does not eclipse all others. 2. The ability to allocate your full attention to the current moment and experience.

**brain dump**—A process by which you capture your free-flowing thoughts, using a computer or writing utensil and paper, listing one item per line, as a way of freeing your mind of commitments, "to-do" items, and other details you need to remember. A brain dump should be done without initially censoring or organizing thoughts.

**calendar items**—Activities that must happen on a certain day, or on a certain day and at a certain time. Otherwise some renegotiation is required or negative consequences will result. (*See also* strong relationship to time.)

**cloud**—The storage of information online rather than locally on a personal computer.

**cognitive switching**—Often confused with multitasking. The process of switching back and forth between thoughts or tasks, often so rapidly that it appears that they are being considered simultaneously. This process is actually linear rather than simultaneous, making "multitasking" less effective than most people suppose. (*See also* mental flexibility *and* multitasking.).

**commitments, communication, and information**—Collectively, all of the relevant details necessary to manage in the service of a busy life.

**crises**—Minor or major unforeseen events that disrupt your plans and expectations for a given time period. (*See also* Eisenhower Matrix.)

**CRM**—Customer Relationship Manager, software that tracks information and business processes by their relationship to contact details. Examples include Act, Salesforce, and Sugar.

**digital convergence**—The phenomenon where one device can deliver all of the same information and experiences that once were distinct and had to be experienced separately.

**discretionary time**—Time that can be spent choosing the order and priority of actions; not dictated by a specific schedule or assignment from someone else. For example, a doctor with a full schedule of patients to see at specific times has less discretionary time than a computer programmer who is mostly left alone to do her work.

**downtime**—Leisure time. May or may not be spent away from technology and the Internet. (*See also* unplugged.)

**early adopters**—Those who relish new technology and are typically among the first to purchase and use it.

**Eisenhower Matrix**—A type of task organization developed by President Dwight Eisenhower that uses four quadrants to prioritize issues and tasks. The quadrants are Low Importance, Low Urgency (*see* shoulds); High Importance, High Urgency (*see* crises); Low Importance, High Urgency (items clamoring for your attention that can usually be delayed); and High Importance, Low Urgency (tasks that lead to achievement of your significant results).

**electronic paper**—An electronic device that provides the ability to create an electronic document without a keyboard by writing using a finger or special implement. (*See also* stylus.)

**Empowered Productivity System**—A personal and professional workflow methodology for managing and controlling commitments, communication, information, and all manner of details necessary in the service of your life. Developed by RegainYourTime.com.

**external distractions**—Interruptions caused by other people or technology. (*See also* internal distractions.)

**flow**—Total and energized immersion in the task or activity at hand; a state of maximized achievement.

**Future**—A category of tasks for goals and activities that are planned to be done but will not be done immediately. Maintaining a Future list is an effective way to avoid forgetting items while still maintaining focus in the present.

**Handy Reference Files**—Files for items that do not require action but that you might need to access easily. Examples include insurance policies, medical records, product manuals, and warranties. You should store them within easy reach of your workspace.

**Handy Reference: Financial**—A subset of your Handy Reference Files that you might need to access easily. These files include items related to financial issues, such as paid bills, bank and credit card statements, and investment information.

**hashtag**—A word or phrase preceded by the pound sign (#), used in Twitter to highlight a keyword or topic and to categorize tweets.

**Information Age**—The idea that the late twentieth century and beyond has brought a change in traditional industry to an economy that is primarily based on the exchange and manipulation of data rather than the production and exchange of goods.

**information management**—Using a system, digital or otherwise, to control and organize information.

**intermittent reinforcement**—A psychological term whereby information given to us at random times conditions us to look for that information all the time, thereby interrupting our ability to focus on the task at hand.

**internal distractions**—Interrupting thoughts that come unbidden to our minds. They're unrelated to and distracting from the task at hand. (*See also* external distractions.)

**iOS**—The operating system for Apple mobile devices.

**jump the thread**—An inefficient habit that refers to changing topics during an email exchange without changing the corresponding subject line.

**knowledge workers**—Professionals who use their knowledge about a particular field (rather than physical skill or manpower) to advance a common goal (for example, growth and profitability of their company).

**Lion Syndrome**—A feeling of being overwhelmed when considering all the possible things that could be done, while simultaneously feeling a loss of control over how these tasks are accomplished. Derived from an anecdote of an animal tamer's method of subduing a lion by presenting multiple "threats" (four legs of a stool) simultaneously.

**live-sharing**—Broadcasting experiences live and in real time.

**Location**—A group of categories for items on a task list used for tasks or activities that can only be accomplished in a specific physical location; for example, you would assign a category of Home to tasks that you can only complete when you are physically at your home.

**mental clutter**—The constant and distracting internal chatter about the tasks and activities necessary to keep your life running smoothly.

**mental flexibility**—The ability to switch between tasks easily, an ability which generally peaks around age 20 and then decreases with age. (*See also* cognitive switching.)

**multitasking**—1. The act of physically doing two or more things at the same time; 2. Switching your attention back and forth rapidly between tasks and/or ideas. (*See also* cognitive switching.)

**natural energy patterns**—A reference to circadian rhythms, the "body clock" that determines peaks and valleys in energy levels.

**Next Actions**—A category of items on a task list assigned to single-step activities for which all the information needed to complete them is available and at hand. Next Actions include tasks and activities that can be completed in one sitting. Each task categorized as a Next Action should start with a verb that is specific and immediately actionable, rather than a verb that is vague and unclear. (*See also* actionable verb *and* vague verb.)

**Notes**—A storage place for reference information that does not require action.

**OCR**—Optical character recognition, the conversion of scanned documents into actual text that can be edited on a computer.

**One More Thing Syndrome**—Experienced by people who, when confronted with new technology or a new communication channel such as Twitter, react negatively due to the belief that they can't handle, or aren't interested in, "one more thing." (*See also* early adopters.)

**OS**—Operating system, a computing platform.

**OS X**—Refers to the Mac operating system by Apple. (*See also* iOS.)

**PIM**—Personal information manager, an electronic tool (platform, software, or apps), such as Microsoft Outlook, or collection of tools that stores and organizes personal information. In the context of the Empowered Productivity System, a good PIM should incorporate email, tasks, calendar information, contacts, and notes.

**platform-neutral tools**—Tools that can be used on any operating system. Usually refers to Internet-based tools that can be accessed through any web browser.

**preactive**—The act of planning and strategizing; the prelude to "proactive."

**prioritizing by due date**—The act of organizing tasks on a task list by assigning a specific due date to each task, within the context of the rest of the list, in order to offer a realistic assessment of one's daily and ongoing workload.

**proactive**—The act of choosing what to allocate one's time and attention to. (*See also* reactive.)

**process/processing**—A verb that refers to the act of assessing your commitments, communications, and information to determine what (if any) action or sequence of actions is required, when it's required, and whether the item requires storage or discarding.

**productive**—Achieving or making progress on significant results. (*See also* significant result.)

**productive time**—The period of time between the unofficial start of your day (awake and preparing for the day) and the completion of the last piece of personal or professional business for the day.

**productivity**—The extent to which you make progress on your significant results.

**productivity methodology**—A set of behaviors, techniques, and habits that form an effective process for managing personal and professional workflow.

**Projects**—A category of tasks and activities on a task list for items that can only happen in multiple steps over multiple time periods; items categorized as Projects must have a definable beginning and end.

**reactive**—Inadvertently relinquishing control over your attention by automatically attending to whatever happens to demand it without exercising conscious thought over whether the interruption should be allowed. (*See also* proactive.)

**reference information**—Information that does not require action in and of itself. You keep it because you might need it later.

**reminders**—A feature of electronic tools that provides a visual and audible message at a particular time set by the user.

**Reminders**—Refers to both a component of Apple iCal software and an iPhone app in which tasks are stored.

**responsive**—The thoughtful and considered decision to attend to the demands of others rather than reflexively and automatically surrendering to others' needs without considering those needs in the context of your own priorities. (*See also* reactive.)

**sabotaging (one's productivity and attention)**—Engaging in habits that lead to distraction and fractured attention, impeding progress on significant results.

**significant results**—Goals that are personally lofty or important, in the context of an hour, a day, or a lifetime. (*See also* productive *and* productivity.)

**Screen Invasion**—A term coined by Matt Richtel referring to the constant presence of a screen (computer, phone, television, movie, and so on) experienced by users of modern technology.

**shoulds**—Nagging and undesirable tasks that typically have little effect on significant results that you attend to out of a sense of guilt. (*See also* Eisenhower Matrix.)

**smartphone**—A web-enabled mobile device that makes calls and also has advanced computing capabilities, including the ability to sync with a personal computer or the Internet and host apps, such as those for storing PIM data.

**social media**—Also known as social networks or social networking. Any web-enabled platform that allows one-to-many or many-to-many two-way communication that is generally somewhat public, although it might offer some privacy restrictions. Examples include Facebook, Twitter, and blogs.

**Someday/Maybe**—A category of items on a task list that seem like a good idea at the moment. These items may or may not be acted on in the future, but they definitely will not be acted on in the near future. This category is useful to assign to dreams, ambitions, and interesting ideas so they are not forgotten.

**speed bumps**—Habits that interfere with productivity by preventing the continual progression of tasks and activities; habits that sabotage rather than support the achievement of significant results.

**Stage 1 Productivity**—Primarily reacting; continuously and reflexively attending to the demands of others.

**Stage 2 Productivity**—A blend of proactive and reactive behavior.

**Stage 3 Productivity**—Consistently making progress toward significant results and also incorporating time for planning, strategizing, and reflecting.

**strong relationship to time**—A task or activity has a strong relationship to time if failing to complete the task or activity on a specific day or on a specific day *and* at a specific time would have negative consequences usually related to other people. (*See also* calendar items *and* weak relationship to time.)

**stylus**—A type of instrument that provides the ability to write on an electronic device made for this purpose. (*See also* electronic paper.)

**supporting (your productivity and attention)**—Adopting habits that facilitate control over attention and focus, leading to progress on significant results. (*See also* sabotaging.)

**System**—The combination of the Empowered Productivity System methodology plus the prescribed use of integrated PIM support tools.

**Talk To**—A category for information that you need to share with other people at some point but not necessarily immediately; items on a Talk To list contain the names of people communicated with frequently and topics requiring discussion during the next encounter with that person. Add items to this list to ensure all necessary information is covered during that encounter.

**task list**—A place to store tasks and activities to be completed at no particular time (*see also* weak relationship to time); interchangeable with to-do list except when referring to the components of Microsoft Outlook, which has two distinct features, one called a Task List and one called a To-Do List.

**Task List**—A component of Microsoft Outlook where tasks are stored, organized, and tracked for completion.

**T.E.S.S.T.™**—A decision process that helps the user keep paper and email from creating clutter. It's an acronym for

- ► Take immediate action
- ► Empower yourself and others
- ► Suspend it to your Next Actions
- ► Store it for future reference
- ► Trash or recycle it

**time-blocking**—Making an appointment with yourself, which you schedule on your calendar, to devote time to a particular task or to be proactive in general.

**time management**—An outdated term to describe the act of taking conscious control of the amount of time spent on specific tasks or activities. This term is outdated because how you spend your time is now only relevant to the extent that you also devote your attention to something. (*See also* attention management.).

**to do list**—Also seen as "to-do list." A place to store tasks and activities to be completed at no specific time (*see also* weak relationship to time); interchangeable with task list except when referring to the components of Microsoft Outlook, which has two distinct features, one called a Task List and one called a To-Do List.

**To-Do List**—a component of Microsoft Outlook that incorporates both tasks entered in the Task List, and also any item within Outlook that has been marked with the "flag" feature.

**tools**—A catch-all word for software, hardware, devices, apps (electronic tools), or paper products (paper tools) that can be used for a specific purpose related to productivity or organization.

**Two-Minute Rule**—A component of the T.E.S.S.T. decision process that states that during processing time, if an action is encountered that will take approximately two minutes or less to be completed, it should be done when you encounter it. However, you should avoid implementing the Two-Minute Rule outside of processing time because it creates the opportunity for random thoughts to distract you from the task at hand.

**unplugged**—The situation of spending time away from technology and the Internet.

**vague verb**—A verb whose specific action is unclear, such as *plan*, *develop*, or *implement*. (*See also* actionable verb.)

**Waiting For**—A category of items on a task list that are your responsibility, but that you can't currently act upon because they require action by another person before you can complete the task or activity; your responsibility for items with a Waiting For category is to ensure that they are not forgotten and that you complete them after the information that is "waiting for" is provided.

**weak relationship to time**—A task or activity has a weak relationship to time if it could be accomplished at any time within a particular date range without directly affecting other activities or causing other notable consequences. (*See also* task list, to do list, and strong relationship to time.)

**Weekly Update**—A set of behaviors intended to be performed at least weekly that serves to create a habit of the effective behaviors of the Empowered Productivity System.

# Index

# Save *20%* at

RegainYourTime.com

**TURNING CHAOS INTO CONTROL** ⟶

Visit RegainYourTime.com for a wealth of information including:

- Additional tips and articles on productivity
- Recommendations on the latest apps & software
- Best practices & technology how-to's
- Training products, classes, and *more*!

Use the code ***secretsbook*** to save 20%
on any product purchase!